POLICE PROMOTION HANDBOOKS

No. 2 CRIMINAL EVIDENCE AND PROCEDURE

BAKER AND WILKIE'S

POLICE PROMOTION HANDBOOKS

No. 1 CRIMINAL LAW

No. 2 CRIMINAL EVIDENCE AND PROCEDURE

No. 3 GENERAL POLICE DUTIES

No. 5 ROAD TRAFFIC

POLICE PROMOTION HANDBOOKS

No. 2 CRIMINAL EVIDENCE AND PROCEDURE

FIFTH EDITION

By

E. R. BAKER, O.B.E., Q.P.M., LL.B.
Formerly Deputy Chief Constable, South Wales Constabulary

and

F. B. DODGE
Chief Inspector, South Wales Constabulary

LONDON
BUTTERWORTHS
1976

ENGLAND:	BUTTERWORTH & CO. (PUBLISHERS) LTD. LONDON: 88 Kingsway, WC2B 6AB
AUSTRALIA:	BUTTERWORTHS PTY. LTD. SYDNEY: 586 Pacific Highway, Chatswood, NSW 2067 Also at Melbourne, Brisbane Adelaide and Perth
CANADA:	BUTTERWORTH & CO. (CANADA) LTD. TORONTO: 2265 Midland Avenue, Scarborough M1P 4S1
NEW ZEALAND:	BUTTERWORTHS OF NEW ZEALAND LTD. WELLINGTON: 26/28 Waring Taylor Street, 1
SOUTH AFRICA:	BUTTERWORTH & CO. (SOUTH AFRICA) (PTY.) LTD. DURBAN: 152–154 Gale Street
U.S.A.:	BUTTERWORTH (PUBLISHERS) INC. BOSTON: 19 Cummings Park, Woburn, Mass. 01801

Reprinted 1977

ISBN: 0 406 84129 2

PREFACE

This book, which is No. 2 in the series of *Police Promotion Handbooks,* is designed to cover the syllabus relating to Evidence and Procedure for the police promotion examinations. Its preparation has been based on principles designed to achieve the same purposes as the other books in the series, namely, to enable a student to acquire both the fundamental knowledge and the technique of answering questions necessary to pass the examinations, and at the same time to provide a solid basis for the more ambitious student who seeks to acquire a wider range of knowledge.

Since the fourth edition was published there have been many changes in the law relating to criminal evidence and procedure, the most important of which are those brought about by recently introduced sections of the criminal Justice Act 1972 and by the Powers of Criminal Courts Act 1973, the Juries Act 1974, the Rehabilitation of Offenders Act 1974, as well as the Police (Disposal of Property) Regulations 1975, all of which, in so far as they affect the examination syllabus, have been incorporated in this new edition, as well as recent cases which have reflected changes in law and practice.

The position with regard to evidence of identification has recently been clarified by the Court of Appeal (in *R.* v. *Turnbull and others* (1976)), and the Attorney-General has given guidelines for prosecutors on the matter. This important topic is dealt with in Appendix 7 of this edition.

E. R. Baker
F. B. Dodge

September, 1976

CONTENTS

APPENDICES

CHAPTER I

EVIDENCE

INTRODUCTION

Criminal Law falls into two parts, *viz:*

(1) *Substantive Law*—that part of the Criminal Law which creates and defines crimes and provides penalties.

(2) *Adjective Law*—that which provides and specifies the legal means by which the substantive law may be enforced, i.e. *Proof and Procedure.*

It is with Adjective Criminal Law that this handbook is concerned.

Proof

In law, the means by which proof can be effected are threefold, *viz:*

(1) *Judicial Notice*

(2) *Presumptions*

(3) *Evidence*

JUDICIAL NOTICE

Definition—certain matters are so universally known or clearly established as matters of common everyday knowledge that their existence can be accepted by the Courts without evidence of them.

The Court is said to take "Judicial Notice" of these matters. They relate to:

(i) *Undoubted Facts*, e.g. that the earth moves around the sun, 2 and 2 are 4, there are 366 days in a leap year, etc.

(ii) *Law, Procedure & Custom*, e.g. That statutes are either public or private statutes, and whereas no proof is required of a law regarding offences applicable to everybody (re. Public Acts of Parliament), there must be a proof by a printer's copy of any Private Company's Law.

(iii) *Constitutional and Political Matters*, e.g. that Mr. A. is the Prime Minister, or Mr. B. the leader of the opposition.

(iv) *Official Seals & Signatures of Certain Kinds*, e.g. The Fiat of the Attorney General.

(v) *Territorial & Geographical Matters and Divisions.*

(vi) *The Official Gazettes.*

R. v. *Luffe* (1807)

The Court in effect says: "We know that without being told". The large variety of facts within this category include:—all statute and common law, orders and regulations, court procedure, judicial seals, Judges' signatures and titles, the ordinary meaning of words, the ordinary course of nature, ordinary measures of time, weights and measures, etc.

LEGAL PRESUMPTIONS

Definition—are the conclusions which, by law, must or may be drawn by the Court upon proof of certain facts.

A legal presumption may be either:

(a) **Irrebuttable (or Conclusive)** i.e. is bound to be accepted, no evidence to the contrary being admissible. It is an inference the Court *must draw.*

Examples:

Upon proof of:	*Presumption*
Age under 10 yrs:	Not capable of committing crime.
Age under 14 yrs:	Incapable of sexual intercourse.

R. v. *Waite* (1892)

Held that a boy under 14 is incapable of sexual intercourse. No evidence is admissible to show he had in fact arrived at the full state of puberty, and could commit the crimes.

(b) **Rebuttable (or Inconclusive)**—conclusion to be drawn in the absence of proof to the contrary. Evidence is admissible to rebut the presumption, e.g.:

(i) Every person is presumed sane *until the contrary is shown.*

(ii) Every man is presumed innocent *until proved guilty.*

(iii) A child over 10 years and under 14 years cannot commit crime *unless proved to know right from wrong, or of mischievous nature.*

(iv) A person not heard of for 7 years by those who would normally be expected to hear of him, is presumed dead, *in absence of evidence to contrary.*

NOTE: Until it was abolished by the C.J. Act 1967, s. 8, it was a rebuttable legal presumption that every sane person intended the natural and probable consequences of his actions. Section 8 provides that this presumption is not now legally binding, and the court (or jury) should decide instead whether the consequences were intended or foreseen by reference to all the evidence, drawing such inferences from the evidence as appear proper in the circumstances.

Presumptions of Fact—are merely conclusions which may be logically inferred from given or proved facts. *Always rebuttable* of course. It is the purpose of circumstantial evidence to raise a presumption of fact, i.e. of guilt or innocence of accused.

Summary. Evidence is not required to prove facts which Courts must know (by Judicial Notice) or must take for granted (by presumptions), but otherwise all proof is effected by evidence.

KINDS OF EVIDENCE

Definition—evidence includes all the legal means, exclusive of mere argument, which tend to prove or disprove the facts under judicial enquiry (i.e. in issue).

Evidence is classified according to:

(i) The manner of its presentation to the Court (oral, documentary and real).
(ii) The nature of the evidence (direct and circumstantial).
(iii) The application of the "Best Evidence" rule (Primary and Secondary), and
(iv) The source from which it is derived (direct and hearsay).

(1) According to the manner of its presentation

This may be:

(a) *Oral* (*or Parol*) *Evidence*—by word of mouth.

(b) *Documentary Evidence*—by the contents of any printed or written document.

(c) *Real Evidence*—by the production of any article or thing.

(b) and (c) can take the form of "exhibits".

Oral evidence always accompanies documentary or real evidence to explain them, e.g.—to read contents or explain its connection with the case. Consider a "street betting" case as illustrative of "oral", "documentary" (betting slips), and "real" (betting clock) evidence.

R. v. *Francis* (1874)
Witnesses can testify as to the state of material objects without their production as exhibits, but they should be produced whenever conveniently possible.

R. v. *Nowaz* (1976)
Police officer allowed to give oral evidence of a forged document he had seen, where production of that document was not possible because its holder claimed diplomatic immunity.

(2) According to its nature, as Direct or Indirect

(a) *Direct Evidence*—evidence of the facts in issue (or, in other words, of the facts which constitute the crime). The evidence of an eye-witness.

(b) *Indirect or Circumstantial Evidence*—evidence not of the facts in issue, but of other facts from which the existence or otherwise of the facts in issue may be logically inferred.

example:

evidence: "A" found in possession of jemmy.

nature: "Direct if charge is"going equipped".
"Indirect" (or "circumstantial") if charge is burglary.

(3) Based on the Best Evidence Rule—Primary and Secondary Evidence

Documents

The Best Evidence Rule, at one time widely applied, but now limited in the main to proving the contents of documents, is that the *best evidence* (or that which affords the least doubt, e.g. the document itself) is required and that evidence inferior to this (e.g. a copy) is inadmissible except in special circumstances. The rule indicates the division of evidence (as to documents) into:

(1) *Primary Evidence*, the best, or affording the greatest certainty e.g. the original, and

(2) *Secondary Evidence* i.e. inferior, substituted, or such as itself indicates a more original source of information, as a copy would the original.

The present rule is, therefore, that *to prove a document or its contents Secondary Evidence will not be admitted except on proof of good reason for the absence of Primary Evidence.*

Secondary evidence (documentary) may be admitted if it is proved that primary evidence cannot be adduced because:

(a) It is in the possession of the other party, who has failed to comply with a notice to produce, or

(b) It is in possession of a stranger not bound to produce, after notice to produce and failure to comply, or

(c) It has been destroyed, or

(d) It has been lost and not found after rigorous search or

(e) Its production is impracticable, e.g. would disintegrate on careless handling.

R. v. *Morton* (1815)

When the original is lost or has been destroyed, and proper search has been made for it, it is necessary to satisfy the court either as to the destruction of the original, or that a sufficiently thorough search has been made and that the paper really is lost.

The Queen's Case (1820)

The law requires that the best evidence must be given of which the nature of the case is capable. The best evidence of the contents of a document is the document itself, and therefore, as a general rule, the contents of a document which is capable of being produced must be proved by the production of the document itself and not by oral evidence.

Doe d. Gilbert v. *Ross* (1840)

Whenever a copy of a document may be used, parol evidence of it may be given. Either is called "Secondary evidence".

Tracy Peerage (1843)

Where the original is a fixed inscription of a tombstone secondary evidence has been held admissible—as also a placard posted on a wall, *Bruce* v. *Nicolopule* (1855).

Williams v. *Russell* (1933)

A Constable may testify to the contents of the defendant's licence and certificate of insurance which he has read (no notice having been given).

R. v. *Nowaz* (1976)—see p. 3

Tape Recordings

R. v. *Ali aud Hussain* (1966)

With regard to admissibility in evidence there is no difference between a tape recording and a photograph. It is for the judge to consider its accuracy and admissibility, and for the jury, as a matter of fact, whether to treat it as such. The best evidence rule applies provided that (a) the accuracy of the recording can be proved; (b) the voices recorded are properly identified, and (c) the subject matter is relevant and otherwise admissible. If the original is lost, the copy has to be proved to be a true copy.

R v. *Stevenson, Hulse & Whitney* (1970)

Original tapes, like photograph negatives, have to be retained in strict custody. A tape recording is to be treated with care and circumspection by those who obtained it in the first place. If impugned and it appears likely that the evidence offered was not the original, the court has no alternative but to reject.

R. v. *Robson and R.* v. *Harris* (1972)

The court has to be satisfied that a tape recording is authentic. It was argued that the best evidence rule applied and that tapes should be excluded unless shown to be originals or true copies of the originals in cases where the absence of the original could be satisfactorily explained. A further objection was that transcripts from the tape should not be furnished to the jury because some words on the tape were not identifiable by ear. *Held:*—The judge is required to do no more than to satisfy himself that a prima facie case of originality has been made out for the prosecution by evidence defining and describing the origin and history of the recording up to the moment of production. If this evidence is unshaken by cross examination it is not incumbent to hear and weigh other evidence. The tapes remain subject to the more stringent test that the jury must be satisfied of authenticity before taking account of contents. With regard to the transcripts these should be supplied with a warning as to doubtful passages and that doubtful passages should be resolved in favour of the defence.

NOTE: For DOCUMENTARY EVIDENCE see also Chapter XI.

(4) Based on "Hearsay" Rule, as "Direct" and "Hearsay" The "Hearsay rule".

To prove the truth of what was said or written:

(a) No witness can testify as to what he heard someone else say, and

(b) No document can be used in evidence except by the person who made it.

Such is "Hearsay" Evidence.

Ratten v. *The Queen* (1971)

The defence to a charge of murder of a woman was that the gun accidentally "went off" while being cleaned. In rebuttal the prosecution called evidence of a telephone operator that shortly before the time of the shooting she had received a call from the address concerned and a woman had hysterically said "Call the police, please" and hung up. Objection was made on the ground that this evidence was hearsay. *Held*:—This evidence is not hearsay. Words spoken are just as much facts as any other actions. The question of hearsay arises only when the words are relied on to establish some fact narrated by the words. Even if hearsay the words in this case could have been admissible as part of the "*res gestae*" as there was a close connection between the statement ascribed to the deceased and the shooting which occurred very shortly afterwards.

In contrast to "Hearsay": *Direct Evidence* is evidence by a witness of what he himself has perceived by his own senses.

N.B.—Evidence of what someone else said is "Direct" and not "Hearsay" when it is tendered not to prove the truth of the statement but that it was in fact made.

Exclusion of Hearsay—Reasons:

(a) Statement not made on oath and no adequate guarantee of truth.

(b) Statements tend to lose truth by repetition.

(c) Would tend to encourage use of weaker means of proof.

(d) Defendant, not present, had no opportunity to deny or to question its truth.

(e) Would prolong proceedings and provide scope for fraudulent practice.

Exceptions to rule as to inadmissibility of "Hearsay":

These are many. All of them become admissible as exceptions because the full range of objections (above) do not apply. Try to justify each exception by applying (a) to (e) above to it.

Learn the headings of the exceptions as follows:

1. Statements by the accused.
2. Statements in presence and hearing of accused.
3. "Dying Declarations".
4. "Recent (or early) Complaints".
5. Res Gestae.
6. Depositions.
7. Statements contained in trade or business records.
8. Statements made by deceased persons in certain cases.
9. Entries in certain public documents.
10. Evidence by certificate, or statutory declaration.
11. Written statements admissible in evidence by virtue of C.J.A. 1967.

1. **Statements by Accused**—Any relevant statement made by the accused is admissible, subject to the conditions relating to *Admissions* and *Confessions* (considered later on p. 49).

2. **Statements made in presence and hearing of Accused**—Note—"presence *and* hearing". Care must be taken to give evidence not only of the statement but of the reaction to it of the accused whether by words or demeanour.

Important—a statement made in the presence and hearing is evidence against the accused only in so far as he, by words or conduct, appeared to accept it as true. If nothing that he did or said can be construed as his acceptance of it, then the jury will be directed to ignore it.

3. **"Dying Declarations"**—If a person is dying from injuries sustained and knows he is dying, then any statement he makes concerning the circumstances in which his injuries were caused may become admissible as a "Dying Declaration" on charges arising out of the death (see p. 51).

4. **Recent Complaint (Early Complaint)**—The statement of complaint made by the victim of a sexual offence *provided* it was made as soon as reasonably practicable after the occurrence to someone to whom the complaint could be expected to have been made. It is admitted, not as corroboration, but as evidence

from which the consistency of the "story" of the victim can be judged, and as tending to negative consent. If the complaint is so closely associated with the offence that it is part of it, then it may be admitted as "res gestae" (see below).

R. v. *Lillyman* (1896)

R. v. *Coulthread* (1933)
An early complaint is admissible as evidence of the consistency of the conduct of the complainant and to negative consent, but not as proof of the truth of the contents—nor as corroboration of his or her evidence.

R. v. *Osborne* (1905)
A complaint made in answer to questions of a suggestive character should not be admitted, but a complaint made as the result of questions not of a "leading" character is admissible.

R. v. *Norcott* (1916)
Questions not of a leading or suggestive character but applying some pressure to explain visible mental disturbance are not an inducement which will invalidate a complaint.

R. v. *Evans* (1924)
One cannot corroborate oneself. Therefore "early complaint" is not corroboration.

R. v. *Cummings* (1948)
"The fact that the prosecutrix in a case of rape had made an early complaint has always been regarded as one of the most important matters in a case of this description. It supports her case because it shows consistency of conduct on her part. Who is to decide whether the complaint is made as speedily as could reasonably be expected? Surely it must be for the Judge who tries the case." Evidence may be given that the victim (even though she consented, where consent is no defence) made spontaneous complaint on the first opportunity which reasonably offered itself after the offence. This need not be to the first person she saw.

R. v. *Strachan* (1954)
Once the Judge has decided that the complaint was made as early as could reasonably be expected, its weight is a matter for the jury and any delay may detract from its value.

5. **Res Gestae**—Sometimes the nature of an act cannot be understood except by reference to statements or words accompanying it. Such words form part of the act (res gestae) and are admitted for that reason, i.e. to explain the nature of the act with which the statement was associated. For example the "V" sign with the fingers has a variety of meanings, and accompanying words might well provide the only means of accurate interpre-

tation. Again, in the case of an accused who is deaf charged with being one of an unlawful assembly, exception 2 p. 7 could not apply, but words used by others could be admissible under this heading as indicating the purpose of the meeting.

> *R.* v. *Dammaree* (1710)
> In "Riot" trials, the cries of the mob were admitted.
>
> *R.* v. *Hunt* (1820)
> As to whether the meeting was seditious, the following was held to be admissible—(1) Circumstances of the mob at the meeting (2) Contents of seditious banners, placards, etc., not produced at trial.
>
> *R.* v. *Foster* (1834)
> On an indictment for manslaughter, a statement made by the deceased immediately after he had been run over, as to how the accident happened, was held admissible (not as a dying declaration), but as res gestae.
>
> *R.* v. *Fowkes* (1856)
> Witness was in a room with the victim when he saw, outside the closed window, a man with a gun who shot the victim. At that moment the witness shouted "There's Butcher" (the accused). This cry was admitted and helped to identify the murderer.
>
> *McLaren* v. *Macleod* (1913)
> On a charge of keeping a brothel, evidence of conversations tending to criminate the defendant, which police officers stationed outside had overheard passing between inmates of the house in the absence of the defendant, was held admissible to explain the character of the house.

See also *Ratten* v. *The Queen* (1971), p. 6.

6. **Depositions, etc.**—i.e. records which can be taken of the evidence of a witness and used in the absence of the witness in certain cases. See "Recording of Evidence", p. 48.

7. **Trade or business records**—By the Criminal Evidence Act 1965 statements are admissible when contained in *a document* forming part of trade or business records compiled in the course of that trade or business from information supplied by persons who may reasonably be supposed to have personal knowledge of the matters with which that information deals. This exception to the hearsay rule applies not only when such a person is dead (see exception 8 (a) below) but also when he is beyond the seas, or is too unfit to attend as a witness, or cannot be identified or found, or in the circumstances cannot be expected to have any recollection of the matters dealt with in the information he supplied.

Evidence from bankers' books is governed by a special statute. *Bankers' Books Evidence Act* 1879.

The conditions applying to the admissibility of a copy of an entry in a banker's book are as follows:

(a) Proof that the book was at the time one of the ordinary books of the bank.

(b) Evidence that the entry was made in the ordinary course of business.

(c) Evidence that the book is in the custody or control of the bank.

(d) Proof that the copy has been examined with the original entry and is correct, by the person who made the examination.

The above evidence may be given orally or by affidavit by a partner or officer of the bank or, in the case of (d) by the examiner of the entry. A banker is not compelled to produce such books except by a special order of a judge of the High Court. Inspection of bank books may be ordered by the Court before whom a legal proceeding is held.

8. **Statements made by deceased person in certain circumstances**—These are:

(a) In accordance with Legal Duty, or regular *Course of Business*, e.g. police records, notebooks, official receipts.

Price v. *Torrington* (1703)

Deceased drayman had made a routine entry of the delivery of bottles of beer, legal duty—admitted.

Sturla v. *Freccia* (1879)

A declaration of deceased made in the course of (business or professional) duty to an employer is admissible if (a) it concerns a transaction in which the deceased has taken part, (b) the declaration is made at or near the time of the transaction, (c) it is made in the usual routine of business, (d) the declarant had no reason to misrepresent it.

Rowlands v. *De Becchi* (1882)

The question being whether 'A' murdered 'B' a policeman, at a certain time and place—an oral report by 'B' in the course of his duty to his Inspector, that he was about to go to that place at that time in order to watch 'A's movements was held admissible.

R. v. *Hall* (1973)

Where, at a retrial, a witness at the first trial had died, it was held that the record of the evidence he had then given was admissible.

(b) As to bodily or mental feelings, in cases where these are material, e.g. murder by poisoning.

R. v. *Closter* (1888)

Statements, in absence of prisoner, as to pain, discomfort, bodily feelings then felt by the deceased are admissible, but not as to their cause.

(c) About a fact, peculiarly within knowledge of deceased, which:

(i) He had no reason to misrepresent, and

(ii) was against his pecuniary or proprietary interest, which he must have known.

Higham v. *Ridgway* (1808)

In this leading case a man-midwife entered his receipt for payment for attending a birth on a certain day. As the entry admitted payment, it was against his interest and the whole entry was used to prove the age of the child.

Doe, d. Sturt v. *Mobbs* (1841)

The entry need not be written by the hand of the deceased, if he signed or authorised it.

Doe, d. Ashburnham (*Earl*) v. *Michael* (1951)

The account books of a deceased person are admissible as declarations against interest, if the entries have been made by such person, or by someone acting on his instructions, or have been in any way adopted by him.

9. **Entries in certain Public Documents** *made by Officer performing a Public Duty*—This is a broad exception which ranges over all kinds of public records, e.g. of births, deaths and marriages; of official surveys; parish registers; maps and charts, etc.

Sturla v. *Freccia* (1879)

Parish registers are public documents, therefore entries in them relating to birth, death, or marriages may be proved by the production of an examined copy.

Irish Society v. *Bishop of Derry* (1846)

In public documents made for the information of the Crown, or all the Queen's subjects who may require the information they contain, the entry of a public officer is presumed to be true when it is made, and is for that reason receivable in all cases.

Note—Methods of proof of entries in public documents. In the absence of the original, a copy of any public document is admissible, if properly prepared, *viz*:

(a) A Government Printers' copy (i.e. published by H.M. Stationery Office) of Statutes, Orders, Regulations, Proclamations, etc.

(b) An examined copy produced by the witness who swears on oath that he had compared it word by word with the original.

(c) Judicial Records set out under a seal of the Court or made by the custodian officer of the Court (e.g. certified certificates of previous convictions, etc.).

(d) A certified copy authenticated by a signature of the proper custodian officer, e.g. births, marriage, death certificates.

10. **Evidence by Certificate and Statutory Declaration, etc.**—As to:—

Declarations and certificates of service see p. 70.

Statements of fact and forms for guilty pleas and mitigating circumstances—see p. 141.

Other forms of certificates—see "Documentary Evidence" on p. 203.

11. **Statements of evidence, including formal admissions,** admissible by virtue of the C.J.A. 1967 *are dealt with:*

as regards committal proceedings on p. 56,

and other criminal proceedings, on pp. 52, 54.

Summary Chart

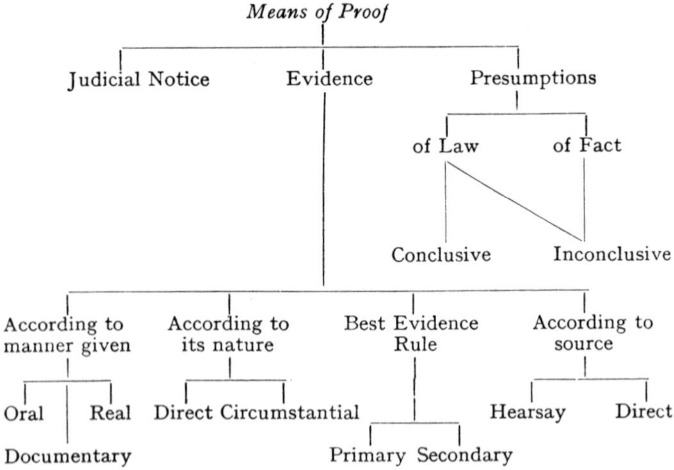

Types of Evidence—Note—It is important to bear in mind that each of the above classifications covers the whole field of evidence and bears no relationship to the others. Oral evidence, for example, cannot be contrasted with circumstantial evidence (which comes under a different classification), but it can with Documentary and Real. This is particularly important to remember with regard to "Direct Evidence" which has different meanings according to the context in which the term is being used. In answering a question as to its definition the candidate should be careful to point out this dual meaning, and to say that when contrasted with circumstantial evidence it means "this" and when compared with "Hearsay" it means "that".

It is always a good thing, when asked to define a type of evidence, to introduce the classification on which it is based For example, if asked to define "Secondary Evidence", explain first that the term is used in contrast with "Primary Evidence" in the application of the "Best Evidence" rule. Explain the Best Evidence rule, which calls for "Primary Evidence", then define "Secondary".

Again, if question refers to "oral evidence" the answer is not complete unless, in addition to giving the definition, you explain that it is one of the three ways in which evidence can be presented to the court, the other two being "Documentary" and "Real", each explained shortly. If you have the subject at your finger-tips the enlarged answer makes no great demand on time and gathers those extra marks.

PROGRESS CHECK NO. 1

Before proceeding further with the study notes satisfy yourself that you have mastered everything up to this point.

The following questions are designed to test progress, but do not attempt them until you feel confident. If you have any doubt, go through the preceding pages before trying the test. The questions are in order and are intended for oral answer, so it would be best to ask someone to check your answers from the text as you go along.

Questions for Oral Answer

1. Define "Substantive Law".
2. Contrast "Substantive law" with "Adjective Law".
3. In what three ways can Proof be effected in law?
4. What is meant by "Judicial Notice"?
5. Specify 6 headings covered by "Judicial Notice".
6. Define "Presumption of Law"
7. Name the two classes of "Presumptions".
8. Give two examples in law in each of these two classes.
9. Define "Evidence".
10. Specify the four headings under which evidence is classified into various types.
11. Name the types of evidence under each of these headings, and define each one.
12. What is meant by "Direct Evidence"?
13. What is the "Best Evidence Rule"?
14. Why is "hearsay evidence" generally inadmissible?
15. By what titles are the exceptions to the "hearsay rule" known?
16. Define each of these exceptions.
17. What are the provisions of the Bankers' Books Evidence Act 1879?

18. What evidence is needed to support the admission in evidence of tape recordings?

WITNESSES

Competency of Witnesses—Who Can Give Evidence?

The general rule is that *anyone is competent to give evidence*, but there are *exceptions* with regard to :

1. Mentally disordered persons.
2. Children of tender years, and
3. Persons rendered unfit by drink, drug, etc.,

And *Special Rules* relate to:

4. Defendants.
5. The wife or husband of a defendant, and
6. Accomplices.

A. The Exceptions:

These are:

1. *Mentally Disordered Persons.*—Subject to the degree of derangement may be completely incompetent, or not competent on certain matters only.

> *R.* v. *Hill* (1851)
> If the Judge considers a very young person, a feeble minded person, an idiot or lunatic, not fit to give evidence, that person is not allowed to. In the case of a lunatic tendered as a witness during a lucid interval, it is for the Judge to ascertain whether he is of competent understanding to give rational evidence. If the Judge is satisfied on these points he should admit him as a witness and leave the jury to determine whether his evidence is affected by his insanity and what degree of weight is to be attached to it.

2. *Children of Tender Years.*—Always competent unless not mature enough to understand the duty of speaking the truth. If not of sufficient intelligence to understand the nature of the oath can give evidence unsworn, but in this case *the law* requires corroboration to secure conviction. In *practice* corroboration is required even when the child is sworn, but it cannot be provided by the *unsworn* evidence of another child.

> *R.* v. *Whitehead* (1866)
> The competency of a witness to give evidence is a question for the Court to decide, which may be done by a preliminary examination of the witness or by other evidence. Where a Judge has admitted a witness as competent, but in the course of the examination he discovers that she is incompetent, he is entitled to stop the examination, strike out the whole of her evidence and direct the jury to consider the case solely upon the evidence given by the other witnesses.

R. v. *Moscovitch* (1924)

A child is a competent witness, whether sworn or not. Power to exclude is limited to the usual inquiry about the child's understanding of an oath or the duty of telling the truth.

R. v. *Dunne* (1929)

The Judge (magistrate) must satisfy himself of the child's understanding by questioning the child, in court.

R. v. *Campbell* (1956)

The sworn evidence of a child of tender years does not as a matter of law need to be corroborated, but the jury should be warned of the danger of convicting on such evidence. A similar warning must be given when the unsworn evidence of a child is corroborated by the sworn evidence of another child.

R. v. *Wallwork* (1958)

It is most undesirable that a child as young as five should be called as a witness.

3. *Drunkenness, etc.*—No court will allow a witness to testify while under the influence of drink or drug.

Physical disabilities such as blindness, deafness, dumbness, do not affect their competency outside the limits of their incapacity.

R. v. *Ruston* (1786)

A deaf and dumb witness may give evidence if intelligence can be conveyed to and received from him by signs and tokens, but the Court must be satisfied that he understands the obligation of an oath.

Morrison v. *Lennard* (1827)

Where the deaf and dumb witness can write, he will be allowed to write down his answers to the questions put to him.

R. v. *Imrie* (1917)

The evidence of a deaf witness unable to express himself intelligently, which cannot be faithfully interpreted, must be excluded altogether.

B. The Special Rules

These apply to:

4. *The Defendant*—can give evidence in own defence, or defence of another jointly charged with him, but cannot be compelled to do so.

5. *The Husband or Wife of the Defendant.*—

General Rule (a) For *Prosecution*—not competent.

(b) For *Defence*—only on application of Defendant.

Exceptions:—Competent in following cases:

(a) *For Prosecution*

(i) Theft Act 1968, s. 30 (2).

In any proceedings brought by one spouse against the other, that spouse is a competent witness for the prosecution.

(ii) Charge of bigamy. (C.J.A. Act 1914)

(iii) Offences under Ministry of Social Security Act 1966.

(iv) Charge of nuisance to a public highway (compellable as well). (Evidence Act 1877)

(v) *Common Law* (compellable as well)

(a) In any proceedings against one spouse based on personal injury caused by that spouse on the other, and

(b) in any proceedings against one spouse for forcible abduction and marriage of the other,

the other spouse is competent *and* compellable.

(b) *For Defence*

(i) *Criminal Evidence Act 1898, s. 1.*

The spouse of an accused person is a competent witness for the defence, whether accused is charged solely or jointly with any other person.

NOTES: Failure to testify not to be commented on by prosecution. Cannot be compelled to disclose communications made to accused during marriage.

(ii) See (c) below.

(c) *For Prosecution or Defence*

(i) *Theft Act 1968 s. 30 (3)*

Where one spouse is charged, *in proceedings not brought by the other spouse*, with an offence connected with the person or property of the other spouse, the latter is a competent witness for the defence or prosecution whether accused is charged solely or jointly with another person—provided that

(a) that spouse (unless compellable at common law (see above)) shall not be compellable to give evidence or, in evidence, to disclose any communication made to him or her during marriage by the accused, and

(b) his or her failure to give evidence shall not be commented on by the prosecution.

R. v. *Noble* (1974)

A wife, charged with forgery of husband's signature, claimed she had her husband's authority for this. Evidence of the husband held admissible to rebut this claim.

(ii) *Criminal Evidence Act 1898, s. 4*

The husband or wife of the accused is a competent (but not compellable) witness for prosecution or defence with regard to offences specified in the Schedule to this Act.

The Schedule includes the following offences:

(1) Child Destruction

(2) Offences in 1st Schedule to Children & Young Persons Act 1933, i.e. the following offences in relation to Children & Young Person:

(a) Murder or manslaughter (or aid or abet, counsel or procure);
(b) Infanticide, abandoning child, causing bodily injury;
(c) Cruelty, allow to be in brothel, exposure to risk of burning, used for begging, dangerous performances;
(d) Offences under the Sexual Offences 1956—procurement by threats*, or by false pretences, or by drugs, intercourse with girls under 16* or a defective, incest*, buggery*, indecency between men, indecent assault, assault with intent to commit buggery, abduction of unmarried girl, causing prostitution*, procuration*, detention in brothel, permitting girl to use premises for prostitution, causing or encouraging offence of prostitution, intercourse with or indecent assault on girl.

* includes attempt to commit this crime.

(3) Neglect to maintain, or desertion of, wife or family.

(iii) *Criminal Justice Administration Act 1914, s. 28*—in a case of bigamy the spouse of the accused is a competent witness for prosecution or defence, without consent of the accused.

(iv) *Sexual Offences Act 1956*—makes spouse of accused a competent witness for defence or prosecution, for the offences under the Act of—rape, indecent assault, abduction, unlawful sexual intercourse, defilement of girls, procuration, incest, and trading in prostitution. (Note that this provision is not limited to offences against juveniles as that of the Children & Young Persons Act 1933 (above), Conditions (a) and (b) to Theft Act (above) apply).

N.B.—The spouse of the accused is a compellable witness only in prosecutions for offences to which the Common Law exceptions relate.

R. v. *Acaster* (1912)

Where a spouse is not a compellable witness the Court should enquire whether he or she objects to giving evidence.

6. *An Accomplice.*—

For Defence—competent, and compellable also in the case of a co-defendant who has been acquitted and discharged (*R. v. Conti* (1974)).

For Prosecution—"King's (Queen's) Evidence"—competent *only*:

(a) When case against him is concluded by pleas of guilty and sentence, acquittal, withdrawal of prosecution, or "nolle prosequi" entered.

(b) When not being tried with prisoner against whom he is to testify.

Witnesses—Compellability

Who can be compelled to testify?—The rule is that any person who is a competent witness and can give information relating to a case can be compelled by process of law to attend as a witness (e.g. by summons, subpoena, warrant) and to testify (refusal can be met by committal to prison for contempt).

Exceptions

The following persons cannot be compelled to testify:

1. *The Defendant*—though competent in own defence or of another jointly charged with him, he cannot be compelled to testify. If he does, "incriminating" questions may be put to him, but not relating to offences other than that with which charged (except in certain circumstances when his character is a fact in issue, see later). Prosecution must not comment on his failure to testify. Instead of giving evidence he may make an unsworn statement to the Court, on which he cannot be cross-examined.

2. *The Husband or Wife of the Defendant*—Of the cases in which the spouse is competent to give evidence (see under previous heading) he or she is compellable *only* in the two governed by the *Common Law*:

1. Personal injury by one on the other.
2. Abduction (forcible) followed by marriage;

and, by the Evidence Act 1877, in a charge of nuisance to a public highway.

R. v. *Lapworth* (1930)

On appeal it was contended that the wife should not have been called by the prosecution against her husband who was charged with her attempted murder by strangling and with doing her grievous bodily harm on the grounds that there was no direct authority that she was a compellable witness. Held that the wife was not only competent but had always been compellable at common law in respect of any charge which affects her person or liberty (e.g. bodily injury or violence), otherwise when an assault was committed in secret by one spouse upon the other, there would be no means of proving it.

3. *An Accomplice*—Though competent in some cases (see top of page) is *not* compellable except as in *R.* v. *Conti* (1974), above.

Witnesses—Privilege

Certain witnesses may be able to claim *privilege* on specified matters, in which case he or she cannot be compelled to answer questions relating to them.

1. *Incriminating Statements*—no witness can be compelled to answer any question or produce any document tending to incriminate himself.

Boyle v. *Wiseman* (1855)

A witness cannot refuse to be sworn and examined on the ground that the only answers he can give may tend to incriminate him. He must claim his privilege after he has been sworn or has affirmed, and when the particular questions are put to him.

R. v. *Sloggett* (1856)

If a witness answers without objection a question for which he might have claimed privilege his answer is admissible in evidence against him on a subsequent criminal charge as to the offence admitted.

R. v. *Coote* (1873)

The privilege of refusing to answer a question is for the witness alone to claim, and he may insist on it, or waive it, as he thinks fit, and he is presumed to know that the law entitled him to decline to answer incriminating questions. If the witness objects to answer a question as tending to incriminate him, there being good ground for the objection, and he is improperlv compelled to answer, the answer is not admissible against him on a subsequent proceeding.

2. *Against Public Policy*—the court will not compel a witness to answer a question if it considers this would be contrary to interests of public (e.g.—the name of an informant, or the contents of a confidential report). A constable who does not wish to disclose the names of persons on whose information he has acted in the investigation of crime, should ask the Court whether he is bound to do so. Usually, the Court will protect him unless the evidence is directly material or necessary in the interests of the prisoner.

R. v. *Richardson* (1863)

A police witness (attempted murder by poison) was held bound to disclose who gave the information which led him to find the bottle containing the poison in a place used by the accused, as being necessary in the interests of the prisoner.

Webb v. *Catchlove* (1886)

The police in a betting prosecution, had to disclose in whose houses they were hidden when they watched the commission of the alleged offences, on the ground that the information sought was directly material.

Marks v. *Beyfus* (1890)

A criminal prosecution instituted or carried on by the D.P.P. is a public prosecution, and he cannot be required to disclose the name of the person from whom he has received the information and the nature of the information received, unless upon the trial of a prisoner the Judge is of opinion that the disclosure of such information, is necessary or desirable in order to show the prisoner's innocence.

3. *Crown Privilege—Crown and Police Documents*—For many years the accepted legal principle was that the Government had a *total* discretion about producing official documents in court as evidence. This has been changed by the following decision of the House of Lords.

Conway v. *Rimmer* (1968)

C. was a probationer constable suspected of stealing a torch. His Superintendent advised him to resign on the grounds of adverse probationary reports. C. refused and was prosecuted. Q.S. stopped the case without hearing the defence. C. sued Superintendent for malicious prosecution and required production of Force probationary reports concerning himself, including the Training Centre report. The Home Office advised refusal on grounds of Crown privilege, and was upheld on appeal, which then went to the House of Lords, where it was declared that the Appeal Court was wrong, and that where a court finds that "disclosure would not be prejudicial to public interest, or that any possibility of such prejudice is insufficient to justify a document being withheld, disclosure will be ordered". With regard to police documents and privilege Lord Reid said: "The position of the police is peculiar. They are not servants of the Crown and do not take orders from the Government, but it has never been denied that they are entitled to Crown privilege with regard to documents. It is essential that they should have it. They carry on an unending war with often highly intelligent criminals, so it is essential that there shall be no disclosure of anything which give useful information to those who organise criminal activities . . . But, after a verdict has been given, or it has been decided to take no proceedings, there is not the same need for secrecy . . . I think it most improbable that any harm will be done by the disclosure of the probationary reports on Mr. Conway.

R. v. *Lewes JJ, ex p. Home Secretary* (1971)

Witness summonses were issued for a police officer and the secretary to the Gaming Board to give evidence and produce a letter written by the police to the Gaming Board in reply to a request for information. Claim of Crown privilege. *Held:*—that as it is necessary for the proper functioning of the Gaming Board that the police should give full and candid information the over-riding public interest was for non-disclosure. The witness summonses were set aside.

4. *Husband and Wife*—neither can be compelled to disclose any confidential statement made by one to the other during the marriage.

R. v. *Simons* (1834)
Although neither husband nor wife can be compelled to give evidence of conversations between themselves the evidence of a third person as to what he has heard during a conversation between them is admissible as evidence of a fact.

O'Connor v. *Marjoribanks* (1842)
The rule that communications between husband and wife need not be disclosed in court is not limited to communications of a confidential character.

5. *Lawyer & Client*—statements to lawyers in a professional capacity are privileged and only the client can consent to their disclosure.

N.B.—No similar legal privilege extends to communications made to a doctor, or to a priest in confession, but some degree of privilege is sometimes afforded in practice to the latter. This degree of privilege is not relevant where a doctor is required by statute to give information, such as in s. 168, Road Traffic Act 1972 (*Hunter* v. *Mann* (1974)).

R. v. *Kingston (Duchess)* (1776)
Medical men are obliged to disclose the information which they acquire by attending in their professional capacities, the law of privilege not extending to such cases.

R. v. *Cox & Railton* (1884)
Communications made in professional confidence to counsel, solicitors, their clerks or interpreters are privileged only if made in the legitimate course of professional employment. A request on how to commit a crime is not protected, as the furthering of a criminal object is no part of a solicitor's occupation, the communications are not made in the course of any professional employment, and if he was not aware, then there is no professional confidence.

Number of Witnesses

The general rule is that the evidence of *one witness* may be sufficient to convict an accused person, but at least *two witnesses* are required *by law* in a case of:

Personation at an Election.

Note. The above requirement is for more than corroboration.

CORROBORATIVE EVIDENCE

Corroboration—Meaning

This term means: *Evidence from some other independent source implicating the accused in a material particular and tending to support the truthfulness and accuracy of evidence already given* i.e. confirming in a material particular not only that the crime was committed but also that the accused committed it.

Circumstances in which Corroboration is required

In Personation corroboration of a material particular will not suffice—there must be at least two witnesses of the act complained of. *Corroborative* evidence is required in the following charges:

By Law:

(a) Procuration
(b) Perjury
(c) Unsworn evidence of child of tender years (see also "Competency")
(d) Opinion of witness as to rate of speed in speeding case.

R. v. *Manser* (1934)

When the unsworn evidence of a child is completely uncorroborated there is no evidence on which the jury can convict. Where there is some evidence which, in the opinion of the presiding Judge, could be treated as corroboration, then the question whether a child's evidence is corroborated or not is one for the jury to decide, assisted by a proper direction by the Judge. *Held* that the unsworn evidence of one child cannot be corroborated by the unsworn evidence of another child, but it can be corroborated by some other material evidence.

Brighty v. *Pearson* (1938)

A person cannot be convicted of speeding on the opinion of one witness. Where one saw defendant driving at one time and another saw him at a different time but not observed by the two witnesses at the same moment, it was held that the Statute requiring corroboration had not been complied with.

In Practice (though not required by law):

(a) Sworn evidence of child of tender years

D.P.P. v. *Hester* (1972)

The unsworn evidence of a child cannot corroborate the sworn evidence of a child in a cases where corroboration is required by law or practice, unless that unsworn evidence is itself corroborated by some other material evidence.

(b) In Sexual Cases (see *Police Promotion Handbook No.* 1; *Criminal Law*)

R. v. *Ross* (1924)

The evidence of the alleged victim of a sexual crime, whether he or she be adult or child, male or female, requires corroboration, and the jury should be warned that it is unsafe to convict on his or her evidence unless he or she is corroborated.

D.P.P. v. *Kilbourne* (1973)

Victims of sexual offences, though unknown to each other, can corroborate one another.

(c) Evidence of an Accomplice

R. v. *Pickford* (1914)

An accomplice is one who willingly takes part in a crime. One who does not consent, or is too young to consent, or who is an innocent tool, or a police spy is not an accomplice.

R. v. *Baskerville* (1916)

Corroboration is independent testimony which connects or tends to connect the prisoner with the crime, i.e. it must confirm some material particular not only that the crime has been committed but also that the prisoner committed it. The uncorroborated evidence of an accomplice is admissible in law but it is the duty of the Judge to warn the jury that it is always dangerous to convict a prisoner on the uncorroborated testimony of an accomplice or accomplices, and in his discretion to advise them not to convict but he should point out to them that it is within their legal province to convict upon such unconfirmed evidence.

R. v. *Jones* (1925)

The warning given to the Jury that it is unsafe to convict on the uncorroborated evidence of an accomplice or complainant should be followed by a direction that nevertheless, if after heeding that warning, they are satisfied that the witness concerned was speaking the truth they may still convict on such evidence.

The evidence of a co-defendant (i.e. not formally charged with the same offence) who implicates one of the other defendants when giving evidence to support his defence is distinguished from that of an accomplice. A conviction will be quashed if the trial Judge does not warn a jury of the danger of convicting without corroboration on the evidence of an accomplice, but although the evidence of a co-defendant might be coloured in such manner as to implicate one of his co-prisoners and absolve himself, there is nothing in law which requires the Judge to warn the jury even though it might be desirable.

R. v. *Barnes* (1940)

Where prisoners are tried jointly and one of them gives evidence *on his own behalf* incriminating a co-defendant, he is not in the position of an accomplice, nor does the rule with regard to the corroboration of an accomplice apply to his evidence unless the prosecution ask the jury to act on his evidence. The rule applies only to witnesses called by the prosecution.

Davies v. *D.P.P.* (1954)

A person who is called *as a witness for the prosecution* and who is a participant in committing the crime charged, whether as principal or accessory, is to be treated as an accomplice, as for example on a trial for theft, a person who has received stolen goods from the accused. If a co-accused pleads guilty and gives evidence for the prosecution, he is an accomplice, but a co-accused who has been acquitted of the offence charged, even on no evidence being offered, and who gives evidence for the prosecution is not an accomplice.

R. v. *Blank* (1971)

B was convicted of handling, mainly on the evidence of the thief. B did not give evidence and the judge directed the jury that this failure could be regarded as corroboration of the evidence of the thief (the accomplice). *Held*:—In no circumstances can the failure of a defendant to give evidence be regarded as corroboration.

BURDEN OF PROOF (OR "ONUS PROBANDI")

"Burden of Proof" has Two Meanings

(1) **The responsibility for proving guilt**—The rule of law is that it is for the prosecution to prove the accused guilty, and not for him to prove his innocence. "Onus Probandi" in this sense, therefore, is *always on the prosecution* and never shifts.

R. v. *Stoddart* (1909)

Where a case has been made out against the defendant and he calls evidence in reply to it, the court must consider the evidence on both sides, and if, after reviewing the whole of the evidence they are satisfied of the defendant's guilt, they may convict him, but if their minds are left in a state of doubt he must be discharged because the prosecution have not discharged the burden of proof which is still upon them.

R. v. *Schama & R.* v. *Abramovitch* (1914)

If the defendant gives an explanation which the jury think may reasonably be true, though they are not convinced that it is true, the defendant is entitled to an acquittal because the onus of satisfying the jury beyond reasonable doubt of the defendant's guilt is always on the prosecution.

Woolmington v. *D.P.P.* (1935) (House of Lords)

"Throughout the web of the English Criminal law one golden thread is always to be seen, that it is the duty of the prosecution to prove the prisoner's guilt, subject to the defence of insanity and subject also to any statutory exception—No matter what the charge or where the trial, the principle that the prosecution must prove the guilt of the prisoner is part of the common law of England and no attempt to whittle it down can be entertained".

(2) **The responsibility for adducing evidence.**—This is the sense in which the term is mostly used. This onus shifts. *It lies on the party who would fail if no evidence or no further evidence, were*

called at that point of the proceedings. In a criminal case, therefore, it always rests at the beginning with the prosecution and remains with the prosecution until a "prima facie" case has been made out.

A prima facie case is one to which the defence has to reply if conviction is to be avoided. When a prima facie case has been made out the "onus probandi" shifts to the defence. Thus when the defence claims that there is *no case to answer* it is equivalent to asserting that the prosecution has not succeeded in establishing a prima facie case for the defence to answer, and that the burden of proof is still with the prosecution and has not been discharged.

Establishing a prima facie case shifts the "onus probandi" to the defence, but it may be thrown back again to the prosecution by the defence, e.g.—by evidence of an alibi, which the prosecution will have to rebut or lose the case. Thus the onus can shift from one party to the other several times during a trial. *Read the definition again.*

> *Abrath* v. *N. E. Railway* (1883)
>
> The test is, which party will be successful if no evidence is given, or if no more evidence is given than has been given at a particular point of the case, for it is obvious that as the controversy involved in the litigation travels on, the parties from moment to moment may reach points at which the onus of proof shifts, and at which the tribunal will have to say that if the case stops there, it must be decided in a particular manner.
>
> *R.* v. *Carr–Briant* (1943)
>
> Whenever the burden of proof rests on the accused it may be discharged by satisfying the court of the probability of what he seeks to prove.

Important

On the question of adducing evidence certain legal provisions affect the establishment of a "prima facie" case, or, in other words, the point at which the onus probandi passes from the prosecution to the defence for the first time.

Normally in establishing a "prima facie" case the prosecution has to adduce evidence on each element of the charge, but the following legal provisions shift the onus on to the defence with respect to certain matters, viz:

1. **By Common Law.**—Any fact that is *peculiarly within the knowledge of the defendant* need not be proved by the prosecution. It is for the defendant to prove the contrary of what is alleged against him in such a case.

For example: It would generally be impossible to prove that a defendant has no driving licence, and this difficulty almost always applies when the negative is alleged. It is for the defendant to meet the charge by proving that he has a licence, if he can, after the need for his having a licence has been established.

R. v. *Turner* (1816)

'T' was convicted of possession of hares without legal authority. The Statute contained about 10 exceptions, each of which made the possession of hares legal. Held, that no burden lay on the Crown to prove that the accused could not avail himself of any exception. If a negative averment be made by one party which is peculiarly within the knowledge of the other party, the party within whose knowledge it lies and who asserts the affirmative is to prove it and not he who avers the negative.

R. v. *Burdett* (1820) & *R.* v. *Rutland* (1945)

When the burden of proving a negative averment lies on the Crown, as when the prosecution asserts that an accused person is not qualified, or authorised or licensed, on general principle some evidence in support of the assertion should be given otherwise the accused would have to prove his innocence. No burden lies on the Crown to show that every exception to the required qualification, authority or licence does not apply, the burden of proving such an exception or of the existence of a licence or authority lies on the accused.

Leathley v. *Drummond* (1972)

Onus of proof that a policy of insurance covers a particular vehicle is on the defendant.

2. **By Statute.**—Onus of proof normally on Prosecution is thrown on Defence in certain cases; e.g.

(a) On a charge of "going equipped", after proof of possession of an article made or adapted for committing burglary, theft or cheat, it is for accused to prove possession for some other purpose.

(b) Selling, making, possessing gold or silver counterfeit coins, *without lawful excuse*, proof of latter being on accused.

(c) Living with prostitute is deemed to be living on her earnings *unless accused proves the contrary*.

(d) In any case where the question arises whether a person is patrial or not then it is for that person to prove that he is patrial.

(e) To have in any public place any offensive weapon *without lawful authority or reasonable excuse*.

R. v. *Carr–Briant* (1943)

Where, either by statute or common law, some matter is presumed against an accused person—"Unless the contrary is proved"—the jury should be directed that the burden of proof on the accused is less than that required of the prosecution in proving the case beyond reasonable doubt, and that this burden may be discharged by evidence satisfying the jury of the probability of that which the accused is called upon to prove.

RELEVANCY (i.e. What facts can be proved?)

General Rules

The evidence of a witness must be confined to:

1. *Facts within his knowledge*, i.e., what he himself perceived by his senses, and not of opinions, inferences, thoughts, deductions, etc.:

   Exception. Opinions of experts in certain matters (see below).

2. *Not of any facts, but only those which are either:—*

   (a) *Facts in issue* (i.e. the facts alleged in the charge,) or

   (b) *Facts relevant to the facts in issue* (i.e. facts so closely related to the facts in issue that proof of them goes some way towards proving or disproving the existence or otherwise of the facts in issue).

   (c) *Facts which introduce or explain (a) or (b)*, e.g. identity of witness or things, relevancy of photographs, etc.

N.B.—In (a) above the evidence is *direct* and in (b) it is indirect or circumstantial.

Study Practice

Examiners often ask for examples. In the case of (a) and (c) above, this should present no problem. With regard to (b) consider the following headings:

1. *Introductory and explanatory facts* e.g. proving identity of things, photographs, etc.
2. *Opportunity* e.g.—in possession of suspect tools or weapons, or presence at or near the scene.
3. *Motive for the offence* e.g.—benefit accruing from death.
4. *Preparation to commit the crime* e.g.—buying poison.
5. *Conduct of accused after commission* e.g.—removing traces of crime, concealment.
6. *Conduct of victim after commission* e.g.—recent complaints.

The Main Exceptions to the General Rules

Opinion

Rule.—A witness may testify as to *facts* but *not his opinion.*

Exception—Persons with a *recognised special knowledge* of the subject concerned may be allowed to give their opinion.

(i) *On matters of Science, Art & Trade* e.g. doctor, lawyer, forensic science expert, fingerprint expert, etc.

> *Ramadge* v. *Ryan* (1832)
>
> The opinion of an expert witness is, in general, admissible in evidence when there is a question as to any point of science, art, medicine, foreign law, the genuineness of handwriting, or indeed any subject on which special

training or special experience is essential before a reliable opinion can be formed.

R. v. *Heseltine* (1873)

An expert witness may not only state his opinion, but he may state the grounds of his opinion and give evidence of experiments he has carried out, even in the absence of the defendant, to enable him to form the opinion.

(ii) *As to the Identity, Condition or Age of a particular person or thing.*

R. v. *Castleton* (1909)

A witness who has had special training and experience may give evidence of the resemblance between the fingerprints of an accused person, and fingerprints found on objects tending to implicate the accused and his opinion that the latter are the fingerprints of the accused and this may be the only evidence of identification.

(iii) *As to the appearance of Illness, Drunkenness, etc.*

(iv) *As to the character of the accused* i.e. general reputation (but see below).

(v) *As to general conduct of business or persons over a period of time.*

(vi) *Handwriting.*—The opinion of an expert is admissible after comparison of the disputed writing with a specimen of the accused's handwriting. Evidence of handwriting may *also* be given by the following:

(a) The writer himself.

(b) Any person who saw it written.

(c) A person acquainted with the person's handwriting.

(d) A person who has seen the accused write on other occasions.

(vii) *The speed of a vehicle.*—Evidence of opinion is admitted concerning speed of vehicles. When a witness says a vehicle was travelling at a very fast speed he is stating a fact, when he is asked to estimate the speed in m.p.h. he is being asked for an opinion (see also "Corroboration", p. 21).

CHARACTER

Rule.—Evidence of character or of criminal propensity cannot be given by the prosecution in order to establish the guilt of the person of the offence charged simply on the grounds that the character of the accused shows him to be the kind of man who would commit the crime.

Evidence of good character may be given by the defence but prosecution cannot give evidence of bad character, or of convictions (exceptions below).

Exceptions to the rule as to character

(1) To rebut defence of "Accident" or "Mistake"

Evidence may be given of the defendant having committed previous acts or offences similar to that charged against him:

(a) *Where the act charged is one of a series of similar acts by the Accused,* which are so closely connected that they form one transaction or a continuing offence, but only if these acts have common features which provide evidence of a connection between the acts or offences.

(b) *To prove Design, Criminal Intent, Guilty Knowledge etc.,* and at the same time rebut defence of no "mens rea" by proving a systematic course of conduct (usually in cases of fraud).

N.B.—It is for the court to decide whether evidence of such similar acts shall be admitted for the purposes mentioned, i.e. to prove mens rea or to rebut defence based on the absence of it. As to the effect of the Rehabilitation of Offenders Act 1974 on the use of previous convictions, see p. 242.

Makin v. *Att-Gen. for N.S.W.* (1894)
The body of the child in respect of whom they were charged with murder was found buried in the garden of the prisoners. In order to prove malice and rebut the defence of an accident, evidence was admitted to show that the bodies of other children taken in to nurse upon payment of a small sum had been found buried in the gardens of other houses occupied by the accused. It is not competent for the prosecution to call evidence tending to show that the accused had been guilty of criminal acts other than those charged for the purpose of leading to the conclusion that the accused is a person likely from his conduct or character to have committed the offence for which he is being tried. On the other hand, it is not rendered inadmissible because it tends to show that the accused committed other crimes if it is relevant to show that the crimes charged were either designed or accidental, or to rebut a defence otherwise open to the accused.

R. v. *Ollis* (1900)
On a charge of obtaining money by cashing a dishonoured cheque the defence was that the defendant expected to pay money into the Bank to meet the cheque. Evidence of three other similar cheques was admitted to prove the defendant knew the cheque would not be honoured.

R. v. *Bond* (1906)
A careful examination of the cases where evidence of this kind has been admitted, shows that they may be grouped under three heads:— (i) Where the prosecution seeks to prove a system or course of conduct. (ii) Where the prosecution seeks to rebut a suggestion on the part of

the prisoner of accident or mistake. (iii) Where the prosecution seeks to prove knowledge by the prisoner of some fact.

R. v. *Fisher* (1910)
On a charge of obtaining a pony and cart by false pretences, evidence that the prisoner obtained provender from other persons by false pretences different from those in the charge was held inadmissible as it did not tend to show a systematic course of conduct but merely that the prisoner was of a general fraudulent disposition. If all the cases had been frauds of a similar character, showing a systematic course of swindling by the same method, then the evidence would have been admissible.

R. v. *Porter* (1935)
In cases of fraud, where the accused has systematically defrauded various people by the same kind of false pretences, evidence of all the frauds may be given, whether they occurred before or after the one charged.

(2) When Defence puts "Character" in issue

If accused attacks character of *prosecutor*, or witnesses of prosecution, or seeks to establish his own *good* character by his own evidence, by evidence of witness, or by questioning prosecution witnesses on this point, he puts his "character" in issue, and he may be cross-examined as to previous convictions.* The question whether cross-examination of the defendant as to his character or previous convictions is allowed is a matter solely in the discretion of the Court. An allegation that a police officer planted or concocted evidence is an imputation against his character and the Court may permit cross-examination of the defendant as to his character.

* Criminal Evidence Act 1898, s. 1. The important case on this subject is *Selvey* v. *D.P.P.* (1968)—below. As to convictions for offences committed when under 17 see p. 190. As to the effect of the Rehabilitation of Offenders Act 1974 on use of previous convictions, see p. 242.

R. v. *Redd* (1923)
Where a witness suddenly and unasked praises the character of the prisoner, the latter is not to blame for it, and therefore this does not entitle the prosecution to call evidence of bad character.

R. v. *McLean* (1926)
Before cross examining prisoners as to character, the advocate should expressly ask leave of the court—and should refrain unless it appears a positive duty.

Stirland v. *D.P.P.* (1944)

A prisoner cannot put in issue part of his character only. Thus, a witness called to establish the prisoner's good character as to sexual morality may be examined with regard to the prisoner's previous convictions for offences involving dishonesty.

Selvey v. *D.P.P.* (1968)

The section covers not only an attack on prosecution witnesses to show their unreliability but also when casting of imputations on character is necessary to establish the defence, but an exception to this is a case of rape where an allegation of consent should not be regarded as an attack on the character of the female witness. If an imputation arises merely from an emphatic denial of the charge by the accused, this should not be regarded as being within the section. In all cases where the accused's conduct brings him within the section the court has a discretion whether to permit cross-examination as to character and this is an unfettered discretion. It is desirable that a warning should be given when it becomes apparent that the defence might expose defendant to such cross-examination.

(3) When "Character" is a "Fact in Issue"

i.e. When the charge itself alleges bad character or a previous conviction, e.g. on charges under special statutes:

(a) Common prostitute, importuning, etc., (Street Offences Act 1959) or behaving indecently in a public place (Vagrancy Act 1824, s.3.)—Proof that she is a common prostitute is required.

(b) *Suspected person or reputed thief* loitering with intent to commit an arrestable offence (Vagrancy Act 1824 s.4)—the accused may be convicted from, "the circumstances of the case and *his known character*".

(c) *Espionage*—Evidence of "known character" may be given to prove acts of accused to have been contrary to interests of State (Official Secrets Act 1911 and 1920, s.1.).

N.B.—The above cases, where character is a "fact in issue" must not be confused with those in which the penalty is increased for a repeated offence, and for which convictions and sentences must be proved *after* conviction and before sentence.

(4) To Prove "Scienter" in "Handling" Cases

On a charge of handling stolen goods* certain evidence can be given to prove that accused knew or believed the goods to be

* This provision applies only to a "handling" charge (s. 27 (3)). See *R.* v. *Davis*, below.

stolen goods, provided the following condition has been fulfilled i.e. that evidence has been given of the accused:

(a) having or arranging to have possession of the stolen goods, or

(b) undertaking or assisting in their retention, removal, disposal or realisation (or arranging to undertake or assist in this).

The evidence which may then be given at any stage of the proceedings is:

(a) that he had in his possession, or has undertaken or assisted in the retention, removal, disposal or realisation of stolen goods from any theft taking place not earlier than 12 months before the offence charged, and

(b) that he has within 5 years preceding the date of the offence charged been convicted of theft or handling stolen goods—provided, in this case, that 7 days notice in writing has been given him of the intention to prove the conviction. (Theft Act, 1968, s. 27 (3)).

R. v. *Powell* (1909)

Evidence of the thief that he had sold stolen property to the defendant at any previous time is admissible to prove guilty knowledge.

R. v. *Smith* (1918)

Evidence may be given as to what the prisoner said at the time in explanation of the property being so found in his possession, the circumstances in which the goods were found and all the facts which would be relevant if other property stolen were the subject matter of the charge.

R. v. *Davies* (1953)

Where the prosecution proceeds with alternative charges of theft and handling, evidence that would be admissible only by virtue of this section may not be adduced.

PROGRESS CHECK NO. 2

Questions for Oral Answer

1. Define Circumstantial Evidence.
2. Give a simple example of Direct Evidence in both meanings of the term.
3. Give 4 examples of "incompetent" witnesses.
4. When can "privilege" be claimed by a witness?
5. When is the spouse of the accused a "compellable witness" for the prosecution?
6. What is meant by "Compellability" of a witness?
7. When is an accomplice a competent witness for the prosecution?

8. What is the general rule regarding the number of witnesses required to prove a case?
9. Specify exceptions to this general rule.
10. Define "Corroborative" evidence.
11. Recite instances when corroboration is required (a) by law; (b) In practice.
12. What is the literal meaning of "Onus Probandi"?
13. What is meant by a "*prima facie*" case?
14. When is the "*onus probandi*" not on the prosecution?
15. What are "Facts in Issue"?
16. What is the general rule regarding "Evidence of opinion"?
17. When can evidence of opinion be given *other than by an expert*?
18. What persons may prove handwriting, other than an expert?
19. State 3 cases in each of which a previous conviction is a "Fact in Issue"

Answer the following questions in writing

1. (a) What is meant by the "Burden of Proof"?
   (b) Does this burden ever rest on the accused? Give examples to illustrate your answers.
2. A constable says to 'A' in custody for burglary "Tell me how you did it and I'll make no objection to your bail". 'A' replies "Fair enough, I took the stuff to Jones' Garage, it's there now". The constable goes to the garage and recovers most of the stolen property which was identified by the loser. How much of the above is admissible in evidence? Give reasons.
3. 'A' married 'B' in 1950. 'A' married 'C' four years later, 'B' being alive. Can 'B' & 'C' give evidence against 'A' on a charge of bigamy? Can either of them be compelled to give evidence?
4. 'A' is charged with burglary on the 6th. Comment on the admissibility or otherwise of the following statements by witnesses:—
   (a) "I loaned the screwdriver bearing my initials and now shown to me, to 'A' on the afternoon on the 6th".
   (b) "I saw 'A' waiting opposite the attacked premises at 8 p.m. on the 6th".
   (c) "Evans told me that 'A' had to get some money quickly before the 7th".
   (d) " 'A' asked me to say I played cards with him all night".
   (e) " 'A' paid a debt of £25 on the 7th instant".
   (f) " 'A' was concerned in a similar charge last year".

CHAPTER II

THE CRIMINAL COURTS

Abbreviations: L.C.J.—Lord Chief Justice.
C.A.—Court of Appeal.
Q.B.D.—Queen's Bench Division.
C.C.C.—Central Criminal Court.

1. The House of Lords—Appeals Only

This is the highest and final court of appeal.

Constitution.—It consists of the *Law Lords*: the Lord Chancellor (President); ex-Lord Chancellors; Lords of Appeal in Ordinary (i.e. life peers appointed for this purpose from among persons holding high judicial office or barristers); any other peers holding, or who have held, high judicial office.

Quorum—three

Function.—It hears criminal appeals from (and only from) C.A. or Q.B.D. on:

(a) questions of *law only* which are
(b) certified by the C.A. or Q.B.D. as being of *general public importance*, and where
(c) leave to appeal is given by the C.A. or Q.B.D. or by the House of Lords itself.

Special Note.—Each judge gives a separate judgment. In all other courts a single judgment is given by the presiding judge.

2. The Court of Appeal—Appeals Only (The Criminal Appeal Acts 1964, 1966 and 1968).

Constitution.—L.C.J., the Lords Justices of Appeal and judges of Q.B.D. comprising a civil and a criminal division. Judges are nominated by the Lord Chancellor (who is responsible for the administration of all courts except magistrates' courts), the L.C.J. and the Master of the Rolls to sit in the criminal division.

Quorum.—An uneven number not less than three. A single judgment is delivered by the court unless the presiding judge directs otherwise.

Function.—It hears appeals from Crown Courts by persons convicted on indictment—

(a) on a question of law alone;

(b) on a question of fact alone or mixed law and fact;
(c) against sentence* (except one fixed by law);
(d) on grounds that the jury's verdict was unsafe, unsatisfactory or that there was material irregularity in the trial.

* By the Criminal Appeal Act 1968, appeal now lies against sentence when an offender is dealt with by a Crown Court (otherwise than appeal from a magistrates' court) for an offence in respect of which he was *not* convicted on indictment. The subject of appeals is dealt with in greater detail later, see p. 219.

NOTES:

(i) An appeal in (b), (c) or (d) above requires leave of the C.A. or a certificate of the trial judge.

(ii) A judge may not sit as a member of the C.A. dealing with any conviction, sentence, judgment or order of a court in which he was concerned or in any of the preliminaries to that appeal.

3. The High Court of Justice

The Queen's Bench Division—Trial and Appeal

Constitution.—L.C.J. and High Court Judges ("puisne" Judges) attached to the Q.B.D.

Quorum: For a trial—one. For appeal—two.

Functions.—Trial: rare but includes exercise of the right to hear a trial through issuing orders of "habeas corpus" or "certiorari" e.g. in the case of the latter to direct that an indictment shall be removed to it from any lower court for some special reason, based on interests of justice.

Appeal: by way of "*case stated*" on question of *law* from

(a) a magistrates' court or
(b) from a Crown Court if arising from an appeal to that Court from a Magistrates' Court.

at the instance of any person aggrieved by the determination of the lower court on a point of law. See also p. 220.

Note.—The Q.B.D. is only one of the three divisions of the High Court. The two others are the Family Division and the Chancery Division.

4. Crown Courts

(1) *Introduction.* A Crown Court is a superior court of record established by the Courts Act 1971, to take over the criminal jurisdiction of Assizes and Quarter Sessions, which are abolished by the Act.

(2) *Administration.* The Lord Chancellor is responsible centrally for policy but for general administration purposes England and

Wales have been divided into six circuits, each of which is administered by a circuit administrator acting under the direction of the Presiding Judges for the circuit, of whom there are at least two. There is as well in each circuit court administrators whose main responsibility it is to ensure that arrangements for the functioning of all courts within the circuit are well maintained.

(3) *Judges.* The judges consist of High Court Judges, Circuit Judges and Recorders. A Recorder is a part time Judge who, to be appointed as such, must have had appropriate experience as a barrister or solicitor. Five years' service as a Recorder is a qualification for appointment as a Circuit Judge.

(4) *Jurisdiction.* A Crown Court has exclusive jurisdiction in trials on indictment for offences wherever committed. All proceedings in a Crown Court are to be conducted before a single judge, except in those cases (see para. (10) below) in which he is generally required to sit with justices.

(5) *Court Centres.* The Crown Court sits regularly at a number of different towns in each circuit specified by the Lord Chancellor, though a Court can sit at some other location from time to time if for any reason special circumstances make this desirable (e.g. a particular case involves an unusually large number of local witnesses). The town at which a Crown Court regularly sits is classed as court centre according to the authorised constitution and jurisdiction of its court, as follows:

(a) *A first-tier centre* is one at which the Court is served by High Court and Circuit Judges and deals with both *criminal and civil* matters.

(b) *A second-tier centre* houses a Court served by High Court and Circuit Judges, but deals with *criminal cases* only.

(c) *A third-tier centre* Court is served only by Circuit Judges and Recorders and deals with criminal cases only.

As to participation of magistrates see para. (10) below.

(6) *Classification of offences.* For the purposes of determining the Centre to which a particular case can be committed, offences have been classified as follows:

Class 1. The following offences are triable only by a High Court Judge:

(a) Any offence punishable by the death sentence.

(b) Misprision of treason and treason-felony.

(c) Murder.

(d) Genocide.

(e) Offences against Official Secrets Act 1911, s. 1.

(f) Incitement, attempt, conspiracy to commit any of the above.

Class 2. Triable only by a High Court Judge, unless a particular case is directed by the Circuit Presiding Judge to be tried by a Circuit Judge or Recorder:

(a) Manslaughter, Infanticide or a s. 58 Abortion.

(b) Rape or intercourse with a girl under 13.

(c) Sedition, mutiny or piracy.

(d) Offence against the Geneva Convention Act 1957, s. 1.

(e) Incitement, attempt, conspiracy to commit any of the above.

Class 3. All indictable offences other than those in Classes 1, 2 and 4. Class 3 cases are normally tried by a High Court Judge, but may be tried by a Circuit Judge or Recorder.

Class 4. Normally to be tried by a Circuit Judge or Recorder:

(a) All offences which may be tried either on indictment or summarily ("hybrid" offences).

(b) Conspiracy to commit any offence in (a).

(c) The following: cause death by dangerous driving; wounding or causing g.b.h. with intent; burglary in a dwelling (or part) if entry obtained by force, deception, tool, key or appliance, or if any person in the dwelling was subjected to (or threat of) violence.

(d) Any offence in class 3 if the Presiding Judge of the Circuit so directs in that particular case.

(7) *Committals for trial—to which Centre.*

Class 1, 2 *or* 3 *offence*—to most convenient* centre at which a High Court Judge regularly sits.

Class 4 *offence* —the most convenient* centre of a Crown Court†

* i.e. having regard to the convenience of the defence, prosecution and witnesses; to expediting trial; and to directions given as to which centre cases should normally be committed from that court.

† if justices consider a case should be tried by a High Court Judge they must indicate this, with reasons, in the papers sent to the Crown Court, and commit to the most convenient centre where a High Court Judge regularly sits. The following considerations have been specified as ones in respect of which justices should favour trial by a High Court Judge:

(a) case involving death or serious risk to life (but not by dangerous driving unaccompanied by aggravating features).

(b) case involving widespread public concern, or violence of a serious nature.

(c) dishonesty in respect of a substantial sum of money.

(d) accused holds public office or is a professional or other person owing a duty to the public.

(e) circumstances of unusual gravity, other than any of above.

(f) nature of prosecution is rare or novel, or a difficult or unusual issue of law is involved.

(8) *Committals for sentence or to be dealt with.* Normally to the most convenient location of the Crown Court included in the list of centres to which cases should normally be committed from that particular petty sessions area, but where the committal is in connection with a sentence previously imposed by a Crown Court (e.g. a probation order or a suspended sentence) the committal should be to that Court, unless this is inconvenient or impracticable.

(9) *Transfers of cases.* A Crown Court may transfer a trial from one centre to another. The defence or prosecution, if not satisfied with the place of trial fixed, can apply to the Crown Court for variation, and the application is heard by a High Court Judge in open court.

(10) *Justices of the Peace.*

(a) *Cases in which justices are required to sit.*

On any hearing by the Crown Court of:

(i) an appeal*, or

(ii) proceedings on committal to that court for sentence the Judge (or Recorder) has, normally, to sit with not less than two and not more than four justices, but the Judge (or Recorder) can continue with such a hearing if the requisite number of justices is not available through withdrawal or non-attendance. Justices need not be present in any hearing where a direction has been given that the above rule does not apply to it.

* special directions apply to the number and qualifications of justices to sit on appeals from licensing justices, or under the Betting, Gaming and Lotteries Act, 1963 or the Gaming Act, 1968, or from a juvenile court, and to certain committals from juvenile courts, as follows:

(a) *Licensing appeal.* Each justice must be a member of the Licensing committee appointed under the Licensing Act, 1964, and two (but not more than two) must be justices for the petty sessions area concerned.

(b) *Betting, etc.* Two (but not more than two) must be justices from the petty sessions area where the premises are situated.

(c) *Juvenile Courts.* In a hearing of an appeal from a juvenile court or a committal from such a court for sentence the number of justices shall be two, each of whom is a member of the juvenile court panel and who are chosen so that the Court shall include a man and a woman.

There can be dispensations from the above requirements for special circumstances or if the parties agree. A justice is disqualified if he was concerned as a justice in the court from which the appeal arises or the committal was made.

(b) *Cases in which justices are permitted to sit.*

Any jurisdiction or power of the Crown Court can be exercised by the Judge or Recorder sitting with not more than four justices. The classes of cases suitable for a court comprising justices are determined by directions from the Lord Chief Justice, with the concurrence of the Lord Chancellor. When a Judge or Recorder sits with justices the decision of the Court may be a majority decision. The Judge or Recorder, of course, presides and has the second or casting vote in case of an equal division.

5. Magistrates' Courts

Counties are divided into Petty Sessional Districts. In practice a J.P. for the county acts only within his Petty Sessional Area, but theoretically his jurisdiction extends over the whole of the county and the adjoining counties or boroughs. *Magistrates' Court* means any justice or justices of the peace acting under any enactment or by virtue of his or their commission or under the common law (Magistrates' Courts Act 1952, s. 124). There is no jury in a Magistrates' Court, which includes not only magistrates acting as "examining Justices" in committals but also the following:

(1) *A Petty Sessional Court*

Sittings.—These are held at the place at which magistrates regularly assemble at fixed times and dates. A sitting at any other time or date is known as a "*Special Sitting*" of the court.

Composition and Jurisdiction.—At least two Magistrates, but a single Justice may adjudicate on certain minor cases but only when expressly empowered by statute to do so, and in which case his power is limited to ordering payment of fine, costs, etc. not exceeding a total of one pound or 14 days imprisonment, e.g. simple drunkenness, idle and disorderly persons.

The maximum imprisonment the court can impose is:

(i) *Summary Offences.*—Generally not exceeding 6 months, but this may be exceeded if specially provided by the Statute which creates the offence (e.g. Assault Police: 9 months imprisonment; Customs and Excise offence; 12 months).

(ii) *Indictable Offences.*—(a) Single offence: 6 months.
(b) Two or more offences, sentences consecutive: 12 months.

A stipendiary magistrate is a legally qualified* paid justice who can do alone any act which by law requires two or more Justices.

* i.e. having at least seven years standing as a barrister, or as a solicitor.

Offences triable.—A Magistrates' Court may deal with:

(i) *Summary Offences*—petty offences, i.e. those which are triable summarily only, or in which the defendant has a right of trial by jury (generally in cases where the punishment may exceed 3 months imprisonment) but does not elect to go for trial.

(ii) *Certain Complaints*—e.g. dangerous dog, affiliation, etc.

(iii) *Indictable Offences triable summarily*—(i.e. where the defendant waives his right to trial by jury for the offences in the first schedule of the Magistrates' Courts Act 1952). If after hearing and conviction the court decides that a case demands greater punishment than it can inflict, the accused can be committed in custody to a Crown Court for sentence.

R. v. *Bodmin Justices* (1947)

Charges of gravity should not be reduced merely for the purpose of allowing jurisdiction in a magistrates' court.

(iv) "*Hybrid*" *Offence*:—i.e. an offence for which the statute provides punishment dependant on whether conviction is summary or on indictment.

A Magistrates' Court can:

(i) try summarily an indictable offence. (ii) hear a complaint.	ONLY when sitting in a petty sessional court-house.
and can	
(iii) try a summary offence (iv) conduct a means enquiry. (v) impose imprisonment.	ONLY when sitting in a petty sessional court-house or occasional court-house,

and must generally sit in "open court" (see p. 44).

(*N.B.*—juvenile courts and domestic courts are *not* open courts.)

A Magistrates' Court *may*, therefore, remand a person, act as examining justice(s), issue summons or warrant, remand a deserter or absentee in custody to await escort, etc., elsewhere than in a petty sessional or occasional court-house and need not sit in open court.

(2) *Occasional Court-House*

This is a place other than a petty sessional court-house which has been so appointed by *County* justices. If appointed after May 1953 it may not be used as such unless public notice of its appointment has been given. Borough justices are not empowered to appoint occasional court-houses. The maximum penalty which can be imposed by this court must not exceed that which can be imposed by a single magistrate (i.e. 14 days imprisonment, or an order to pay one pound).

(3) *A Domestic Proceedings Court*

This is not an open court and deals with matrimonial cases, etc. Often sits following the normal Petty Sessional Court.

(4) *Juvenile Courts*

Composition.—These consist of not less than two and not more than three magistrates, and must include one man and so far as practicable one woman on the bench. Special panels of suitably qualified Justices are appointed for a three year term by the Justices of each Petty Sessional Division. A stipendiary Magistrate may sit alone.

Sittings.—A juvenile court must not sit in a room within one hour (before or after) the sitting of a court other than a juvenile court. It can sit on any day to determine an indictable offence charge. It is not an open court and the persons who may be present are:

(a) members and officers of the court,
(b) parties to the case and other persons directly concerned,
(c) press representatives,
(d) persons specially authorised by the court.

Press, Radio and T.V. not to publish anything calculated to lead to the identification of *any* juvenile concerned in proceedings before *juvenile court*, though the court or Secretary of State may, in the interests of justice, dispense with this restriction. In the case of juveniles appearing before *any other court* (whether as accused, injured party or witness) *the court may* impose such restriction.

Jurisdiction—All charges against a child or young person (except homicide) and applications relating to children and young persons. A Juvenile Court *must* deal *summarily* with any indictable offence committed by a child or young person *unless* he is:

(i) charged with homicide;

(ii) over prosecutable age, is charged jointly with person of 17 or more, and court considers committal of both for trial necessary in the interests of justice.

(iii) aged 14–16 and is charged with an offence punishable by 14 years imprisonment or more, and the court considers that a "grave crime" penalty under C. & Y.P. Act 1933, s. 53 (see p. 190) might be imposed on conviction after committal. (C. & Y. P. Act 1933, s. 6).

An adult should never be deliberately brought before a Juvenile Court, but if a person is discovered during proceedings to be an adult, the Court may continue to hear and determine the case.

Magistrates' Courts (C. & Y.P.) Rules 1970

Note. In the following text "young person" includes a child defendant.

Trial for an offence

(a) Where a young person is not legally represented the court shall allow his parent or guardian to assist in conducting his defence, including cross-examination of witnesses.

(b) Where the parent or guardian cannot be found or cannot reasonably be required to attend the court may allow any other relative or responsible person to act as in (a).

(c) The charge is to be explained by the Court in simple language (suitable to age and understanding) and then the young person must be asked whether he admits the charge.

(d) Where the charge is not admitted prosecution witnesses are to be heard and can be cross-examined by or on behalf of the young person.

(e) Where not represented as in (a) or (b) above the young person can cross-examine. If, instead of questions, assertions are made, the Court can put the assertions to the witness in the form of questions.

(f) After a finding of guilt:

(i) the young person and parent or guardian (if present) is to be given opportunity to make a statement.

(ii) the Court must take into account such information as to general conduct, home surroundings, school record and medical history as may be necessary in the interests of the young person, particularly information provided by a local authority under the C. & Y.P. Act 1969, s. 9. If such information is not available consideration has to be given to the need for a remand to enable necessary enquiries to be made.

(iii) unless the Court is considering a hospital or guardianship order the written reports of a probation officer, local authority or doctor need not be read aloud.

(iv) if considered necessary in the interests of the young person, he (or his parent or guardian, if present) may be required to withdraw from the Court, but if this is done and reports are not read aloud:

(a) the young person must be given the substance of any information given as to character or conduct which the Court considers material to the manner in which the case is to be dealt with, *and*

(b) the parent or guardian (if present) shall be given this information, and, in addition, any information which may have been given as to character and conduct of home surroundings or health of the young person.

Hearing by magistrates sitting as examining justices.

Of the 1970 rules, only (a), (b) and (e) apply.

As to care proceedings, see p. 191.

Juveniles in "Adult" Courts

Circumstances in which juvenile chargeable.—A Juvenile "*must*" or "*may*" be charged and dealt with before an *Adult Court*, as follows:

Must—when charged *jointly* with an *adult* (C. & Y.P.A. 1933, s.46).

May—(i) when charged with *aiding abetting causing procuring allowing* or *permitting* an offence committed by an adult (C. & Y.P.A. 1963, s.18), and conversely when the juvenile is the principal offender (C. & Y.P.A. 1933, s.46).

(ii) When the offence (embracing an adult as well) arises out of the same circumstances (C. & Y.P.A. 1963, s.18) e.g., consuming an intoxicant on licensed premises under 18 years of age

(iii) When during the case it appears that the offender is a juvenile, the adult court may continue to deal with it if it thinks fit (C. & Y.P.A. 1933, s.46).

(iv) If on plea of guilty without appearance under M.C.A. 1957, s. 1 the Court has no reason to believe accused to be a juvenile, the accused shall be deemed to be adult for the purposes of s. 46. (Added by C. & Y.P. Act 1969).

N.B.—*Unless undesirable to do so*—a court (other than a Juvenile Court) must remit a juvenile found guilty of any offence (*except homicide*) to the appropriate juvenile court to be punished. (C. & Y.P. Act 1933, s. 56, as amended by 1963 Act). unless it is of opinion that the case can be properly dealt with by an absolute or conditional discharge (together with any such order than can be made with such a discharge), or by fine, or by an order requiring the parent or guardian to enter a recognizance to take proper care of him (C.J.A. 1972, Sch. 5).

Summary trial of a young person for an indictable offence (other than homicide).

Where a person under the age of 17 is before a magistrates' court charged with an I.O. other than homicide, he shall be tried summarily unless

(a) he is a young person who, under s. 33 of the C. & Y.P. Act, 1933, can be sentenced to detention because of the gravity of the crime and court considers he should be tried on indictment for that reason, or

(b) he is jointly charged with a person of or over 17 and the court considers it necessary in the interests of justice to commit both for trial,

and, in either of these cases, the court must commit for trial if the evidence is sufficient or the court can commit without hearing evidence under s. 1 of the C.J.A. 1967. (1969 Act, s. 6 as amended by C.J.A. 1972).

Open Court

The general rule is that all court proceedings are open to the public, but in some cases the public can be excluded for the whole or part of the proceedings (which are then said to be heard "*in camera*"), and in others (juvenile courts and domestic proceedings courts) the proceedings cannot by law be open to the public.

The law with regard to the exercise of the discretion of a court to hear all or part of the proceedings in camera can be briefly stated as follows:—

(a) *Generally*

Proceedings must be in open court unless the court directs otherwise on the grounds that justice would manifestly be defeated, or it would be contrary to public interest (e.g. in proceedings under the Official Secrets Acts).

(b) *C. & Y.P. Act* 1933

(a) *No child* (other than an infant in arms) shall be permitted to be in court except to give evidence or as otherwise required for the purposes of justice. Exempt are messengers, clerks and other persons required in court by virtue of their employment (s.36).

(b) Where in proceedings relating to offences or conduct contrary to decency or morality a child or young person is a witness, the court can direct that all persons except members or officers of the court, parties and solicitors and persons directly concerned with the case, be excluded while the evidence of that witness is being given (s.37).

NOTES:

(i) The unrestricted discretion of *examining justices* to sit in camera was abolished by the C.J. Act 1967, s. 6.

(ii) As to restrictions on press, radio and television reports on court proceedings see p. 140.

CHAPTER III

PROCEDURE BEFORE TRIAL

INTRODUCTION

Except for the rare occasions when a person is committed for trial direct from a Coroner's Court on a charge of homicide, all cases, whatever their nature have to be brought before a magistrate or magistrates, either for:

(a) *Hearing and determination*, in the case of a summary offence or one which can be dealt with summarily, though indictable, *or*,

(b) *Committal for trial* at a Crown Court.

In (a) the magistrates sit in open Court as a Magistrates' Court. In (b) the magistrate(s) form a court but function as "examining Justices" to prepare the evidence for the later trial and to decide whether or not the evidence is sufficient for a committal.
In either case, whether the accused is to be tried or the evidence "examined" the preliminaries are the same and consist of:

(1) The preparation of the *Case File*,

(2) *Securing attendance* of parties and witnesses, and

(3) The *recording of evidence* where the written record itself is or may be admissible in evidence.

(1) is a matter of police practice which needs no explanation here, but the others are governed by law.

Note: The C. & Y.P. Act 1969, introduced special considerations as to procedures to be adopted in dealing with any juvenile who appears to have committed an offence (other than homicide) and to be in need of care or control—see p. 184.

SECURING ATTENDANCE OF PARTIES

A. **To Appear at a Magistrates' Court** (whether at a trial or at committal proceedings).

(i) *Prosecutor.* As he is the originator of the proceedings no process is required (or available) to compel his appearance, unless he is also a witness. In the vast majority of cases the prosecution is undertaken by a public official as a "public prosecution", i.e. by the police. A private prosecution is rare. Appearance can, of course, be by legal representation. In summary cases the court may, on a non-appearance of or for the prosecutor, adjourn the trial, or dismiss the information, or if the case is partly heard, proceed with it in the absence of the prosecutor. If it adjourns the trial, the accused cannot be remanded in custody unless he is in custody at the time or fails to enter into a recognizance or to find sureties. (M.C.A. 1952, s. 16.)

(ii) *Defendant.* The appearance of the defendant in the first instance may be by means of

(a) *Arrest**, (in appropriate cases) with or without warrant, which may or may not be followed by bail by the police conditioned for appearance in court, or by

(b) *Summons* to appear.

* A warrant to arrest to answer a charge cannot be issued in respect of a person aged 17 or over unless

(a) the offence is indictable or punishable with imprisonment, or

(b) the defendant's address is not sufficiently established for service of summons. (C.J.A. 1967, s. 24 (1)).

(iii) *Witnesses.* The attendance of witnesses may be secured by:

(a) *Warning to attend,* written or oral as a matter of police practice, or

(b) *Witness Summons,* in the case of a "reluctant witness", i.e. where it appears that he will not *voluntarily* appear or produce document or thing likely to be of material evidence (for prosecution or defence).

(c) *Warrant in first instance,* i.e. to arrest and bring to court where magistrate is satisfied by evidence *on oath* that a summons would be of no avail.

Note: As to appearance of parent or guardian of defendant under 14 see p. 188.

B. **To Appear at the Hearing at a Crown Court.**

The following refers to process during or after committal proceedings, at which attendance has been procured as in 'A' (above).

(i) *Prosecutor.* No process is provided to enforce the attendance personally of the person who instituted proceedings, unless he is a witness. This is because the prosecution is always represented by counsel at the Crown Court.

(ii) *Accused* is committed either:—

(a) *on bail,* fixed by the court and conditioned for his appearance, usually with sureties, or

(b) *in custody,* and conveyed on commitment warrant to prison to await trial. The warrant may be backed for bail, i.e. permit the Governor of the prison to release on bail for trial if the specified sureties are provided. The Governor of a prison has to produce for trial the prisoners in his custody for that purpose and also to prepare a Court Calendar of persons for trial, for which purpose clerks to justices have to inform him of all committals by bail.

(iii) *Witnesses* are required to attend by:—

(a) *Witness orders* served on them at the time if they gave evidence before examining justices, or

(b) *Witness summonses*—issued by a Crown Court in the case of any witnesses not the subject of witness orders.

NOTE: For all practical purposes the witness summons supersedes the subpoena in all criminal trials. It is still applicable to civil cases.

As to the witness orders and witness summonses referred to above, as well as disobedience of such process, see further on p. 58.

THE RECORDING OF EVIDENCE

(before Trial or Hearing)

Introduction. This heading does not relate to the preparation of the file of evidence for the consideration of whether or not a prosecution is justified, for this is the subject of Chapter VII on the "Taking of statements and making reports" and is mainly a matter of police practice. It refers to those records or statements of evidence which by law may be admitted at the trial as evidence of their contents if the provisions of law relating to them have been complied with. It will be noted that all of them become admissible only as exceptions to the "hearsay rule", i.e. as documents to prove the truth of their contents without calling as witnesses the persons who made the statements recorded in them. Such "statements" include:

(a) *any formal confession* or admission made by an accused person.

(b) *depositions* to be taken by a magistrate from witnesses medically certified unfit to attend the hearing.

(c) "*dying declaration*" in a case of a charge arising out of the death of the witness.

(d) *statement by a child under 14 years* in certain cases of sexual or indecent nature.

(e) *certain statements of evidence* under the C.J. Act 1967, i.e. on purely formal matters, the accused not having objected within seven days of the service of the statement upon him.

(f) *evidence by certificate* in certain cases where not disputed, e.g., of service of summons, of quantity of alcohol in blood certified by analyst. This is dealt with in Chapter XI.

NOTE: As to the recording of evidence by one court for use in another, see pp. 163 and 224.

A. Statements by Accused Persons

N.B.—always bear in mind the application of the Judges' Rules, which, with "Taking of statements", is dealt with in Chapter VI. Evidence obtained from an accused by trick (e.g. eavesdropping) or by questionable means is not, for that reason only, inadmissible, but the judge can exclude it (*R.* v. *Kuruma* (1955)) and should exclude it if obtained by conduct of which the Crown should not take advantage (*King* v. *R.* (1968), *R. v. Stewart* (1970)).

In minor summary cases no formal written statement is either required or made of what the defendant said in answer to a question or when told he "would be reported", and a pocket book entry suffices. Procedural problems arise in statements made in connection with serious charges and which amount to *Admissions or Confessions.*

Confessions.—A confession is a statement by the accused that he committed the offence, or from which an inference can be drawn that he committed the offence.

Admissions.—An admission does not go so far—it is an agreement by the accused with some fact or facts which weigh against his innocence but does not amount to a complete confession.

Such statements are admissible in evidence only if given freely and voluntarily, i.e. made without duress or pressure, threat or promise of favour from any person *in a position of authority* with regard to the accused.

That the statement was so made has to be proved by the prosecution beyond reasonable doubt, to which end conformity with the Judges' Rules materially assists, and non-conformity almost certainly condemns to failure.

A person in authority includes the prosecutor, police officers, or other persons having the prisoner in their custody, or engaged in the arrest or prosecution, or otherwise connected with proceedings against him. The employer of the prisoner is not such a person if the crime was not committed against him or his property.

The merest hint of threat or promise can be fatal, as the following cases, in which confessions were excluded, show:

R. v. *Thomas* (1834)

"You had better split and not suffer for them all"

R. v. *Partridge* (1836)

"If you do not confess, we of course can do nothing for you".

R. v. *Thompson* (1893)
"Tell me where the things are and I will be favourable to you"

R. v. *Collier & Morris* (1848)
"It is better for you to tell the truth and save the shame of a search warrant in your house".

Where, however, the inducement is no more than persuasion on religious or moral grounds, and not a promise of material benefit, confessions have been admitted.

R. v. *Gilham* (1828)
"Repent and confess your sins".

R. v. *Sleeman* (1853)
"Tell the truth and don't run your soul into more sin".

As to importance of the Judges' Rules, see p. 94.

B. Depositions of Persons unfit to attend Hearing

Deposition.—This is a written record of the evidence given by a witness *on oath* before a magistrate.

Normally depositions are taken at the hearing at which the magistrates are acting as "examining justices" (i.e. to consider whether or not on the evidence the accused shall be committed for trial) in accordance with the *Magistrates' Courts Rules*, 1968 though once the "examining justices" have been determined a deposition under these rules can be taken outside court, e.g. at a house or a hospital, by them. Any deposition can be taken by *one* justice.

In the following cases a deposition can be taken by *any* justice of the district, because the witness will be unable to attend the hearing, or in the case of a young person it is inadvisable that he should, and, generally, the deposition will be needed before the examining justices commence their duties:

(1) *Person dangerously ill.*—(Mag. Courts Act 1952, s. 41). Justice to be satisfied that:

> (a) person can and will give material information as to an indictable offence, or the person accused of it, and is dangerously ill and unlikely to recover (on information of a doctor), and (b) taking of deposition by examining justice is impracticable.

(2) *Child or young person.*—(C. & Y.P. Act 1933, s. 42).Relates *only* to child or young person against whom an offence of a specified kind (in 1st. Schedule to Act) has been committed. Offences include sexual offences, cruelty, bodily injury, assault, child-stealing, in brothels, used for begging, dangerous performances.

Justice to be satisfied on evidence of doctor, *that appearance in court would involve serious danger to life or health.*

Requisites in both.—

(a) statement added by justice of reason for taking deposition, as well as where, when, and persons present.
(b) must be signed by the justice.
(c) notice has been served on party against whom evidence may be used. (i.e. the accused and in (1) possibly the prosecutor as well) giving reasonable opportunity to attend.
(d) accused or representative (if present) had opportunity to cross examine.

Admissibility at Trial.—Admissible if proved:

(a) The same medical grounds still apply, and in the case of (1) witness is dead or never likely to be able to travel or give evidence, *and*
(b) The requisites (b), (c) and (d) above were complied with.

NOTE. The justice has by law to send deposition to clerk of court dealing with the case. Admissibility in case of deposition (1) above, is dealt with by s.6. of the Criminal Law Amendment Act 1867.

Remember—Depositions apply to Indictable Charges only.

R. v. *Quigley* (1868)
'A' attacked 'B' on December 18th, ran away and was not caught until Jan. 3rd. In the meantime 'B' made a statement purporting to be taken under the 1867 Act and died on Dec. 23rd. The deposition was held to be inadmissible since no notice had been served notwithstanding that 'A' was not available and notice could not be served upon him. In this case, the statement was nevertheless admitted as a dying declaration.

C. Statements of Children

In committal proceedings for sexual or indecency offences a child (under 14) shall not be called as a witness for the prosecution, but any statement in writing of the child is admissible in evidence. (C. & Y.P. Act 1963, s. 27)

This does not apply where:

(a) The defence objects when (or before) the statement is tendered in evidence,
(b) the child is required to attend to identify any person,
(c) it was not possible to obtain such a statement,
(d) the child has already given evidence in a summary trial which has changed to committal proceedings, or
(e) committal proceedings change to a summary trial.

D. Dying Declarations

A "dying declaration" is a statement made by an injured and dying person, who knows that he is dying and has no hope of recovery, as to the circumstances in which his injuries were received. It can be made to any person, no oath is required, and it need not be in writing, or signed, or made in presence of accused, though everything possible should be done (as circumstances permit) to add to its evidential value, e.g.

(a) if accused is present, establishment of his identity may be possible and he should be allowed to ask questions,
(b) witnesses provide useful corroboration,
(c) put everything on record at the time, or as soon as practicable.

The declaration is admissible only on a charge arising out of the death of the declarant, (i.e. murder or manslaughter), and the Judge must be satisfied that:

(a) the declarant was dying and knew it,
(b) he entertained no hope of recovery, and
(c) the declaration relates to the cause of death.

R. v. *Woodcock* (1789)

The principle which admits a dying declaration in evidence is that it is made when the party is at the point of death, every hope is gone, and every motive to falsehood is silenced. The mind is induced by the most powerful considerations to speak the truth, a situation so solemn and so awful in law as to create an obligation equal to that which is imposed by a positive oath administered in a Court of Justice.

R. v. *Mead* (1824)

The declaration must concern the death only. No formalities need be observed in taking a dying declaration made by a person about to die. It may vary from a gasped out "J.R. stabbed me," to a long written statement. Such declaration is admissible only upon the trial of the prisoner for the murder or manslaughter of the declarant. (N.B. Not in a trial for abortion.)

E. Evidence by Written Statement (C.J. Act 1967, s. 9)

NOTE: S. 9 relates to *all* criminal proceedings other than committal proceedings (for which special provisions apply—see p. 56), and applies equally to statements of evidence for the prosecution *and* for the defence. The section also applies to written statements made in Scotland and Northern Ireland (C.J.A. 1972, s. 46).

Principle. A written statement by any person shall, if the following conditions are satisfied, be admissible as evidence to the same extent as oral evidence to that effect by that person would be.

Conditions, referred to above, are

(a) statement purports to be signed by person who made it,

(b) statement contains declaration by maker that it is true to best of his knowledge and belief and that he made the statement knowing that he would be liable to prosecution if he wilfully stated anything known to be false or not believed to be true,†

(c) *before the hearing, a copy of the statement is served by the party adducing the evidence on each of the other parties concerned,

(d) *none of the other parties, or solicitors, *within 7 days* of service of the copy, serve a notice on the adducing party objecting to the statement being tendered in evidence.

† By s.89 an indictable offence punishable by imprisonment for 2 years or a fine, or both.

* (c) and (d) do not apply if the parties agree before or during hearing that the statement shall be admitted in evidence.

Requirements re statement

(a) If maker is under 21, statement must give his age.

(b) If maker cannot read, statement must be read to him before he signs it and be accompanied by a declaration by the person who read it to that effect.

(c) If it refers to any other document as an exhibit, the copy served on another party must be accompanied by a copy of that document or such information as enables the other party to inspect the document or a copy of it.

Service of copy—may be done by:

(a) personal delivery to party or his solicitor,

(b) addressing it to the person and leaving it at his usual or last place of abode or of business or to his solicitor and leaving it at his office,

(c) as in (b) by sending it by registered letter or recorded delivery service,

(d) in the case of a corporate body—as above but to secretary or clerk of that body.

NOTES:

(i) a statement should be served more than 7 days before trial, but if this cannot be done it can still be admitted if other party agrees,

(ii) if no objection within 7 days, but raised at court, the court has discretion whether or not to call the witness,

(iii) the procedure is useful only for formal evidence, i.e. evidence not likely to be disputed, e.g. as to prove plan or produce photographs,

(iv) where a statement has been made admissible by compliance with this section, the party tendering the statement may change his mind and call the witness to give evidence, and the court, too, can require attendance of the witness either on its own account or on application of any party. Except in the case of a magistrates' court the application can be made before the hearing, the powers of the court being exercisable: by any person entitled to sit as a judge of the court.

(v) the form for written statements under s. 9 is provided by the Magistrates' Courts Rules 1968—see App. 2.

(vi) being below the age for criminal liability a child under 10 cannot make a declaration nor, therefore, a written statement for the purpose of this Act. Attendance of the child could perhaps be avoided by procedure for formal admissions (see below) if facts are not in dispute, while in committals for sexual offences, s. 27 of the C. & Y.P. Act 1933, applies—see p. 51.

F. Formal Admission by Other Party (C.J. Act 1967, s. 10)

By s.10 either party to a criminal trial may admit formally any fact of which oral evidence could be given. When such an admission is formally made it is conclusive evidence against the person making it, and can only be withdrawn with the permission of the court.

The admission can be made before or during the hearing. If before it must be in writing, and it is better to seek admissions on facts not likely to be disputed before the trial if by so doing attendance of witnesses as to those facts only can be avoided, e.g. as to such facts as identity of a deceased person, or ownership of property.

The following conditions also apply:

(a) If made in writing shall purport to be signed by the person making it, and if by a body corporate, be signed by a director, manager, secretary, a clerk, or other similar official of that body.

(b) If made on behalf of an individual defendant, must be made by his legal representative; or if made by the individual defendant before the trial, must be approved by his legal representative, whether at the time or subsequently or at the hearing.

NOTES:

(i) A formal admission is conclusive evidence only against the person who made it, and not against a co-defendant.

(ii) The section applies to *all* trials and applies also to committal proceedings and appeals following trial.

(iii) A formal admission can be withdrawn only with leave of the court of trial. In such a case the court can adjourn hearing to allow a witness to prove facts previously admitted.

(iv) This procedure is designed to save time of the court and witnesses and must be distinguished from admissions (and confessions) made by an accused person which have to be proved by the normal rules of evidence (see p. 49).

COMMITTALS FOR TRIAL BY "EXAMINING JUSTICES"

The progress of proceedings in the case of a preliminary hearing by examining justices to determine whether or not an accused person should be committed for trial is dealt with on p. 137. In so far as the carrying out of a committal is concerned the duty of examining justices is to prepare the case for hearing by a Crown Court by:

(a) placing on record the evidence given before them orally by witnesses (deposition).
(b) receiving (and considering where necessary) any written statements of evidence which may have been made by persons who are not called to give evidence before them by virtue of the provisions of the C.J. Act 1967, s. 2.
(c) securing the appearance at the higher court of the parties and essential witnesses.

1. Recording of Evidence

(1) *Depositions*

Where a witness (or an accused person) testifies orally (i.e. not by a previously made statement), his evidence has to be recorded in writing as a deposition. Exceptions—defence witnesses to character only. The law requires that a deposition shall be:

(a) made on oath before a magistrate,
(b) read over to the witness and agreed by him,
(c) made in the presence and hearing of the accused, and
(d) signed or certified by one of the magistrates.

NOTE. It was required that each deposition should be signed by the magistrate, but now by the C.J.A. 1967, s. 7, a certificate ("*Jurat*") signed by an examining magistrate is sufficient proof that *all* the depositions listed in it were taken by him in the presence of the accused. A student should contrast such a deposition (taken under the Magistrates' Courts Rules, r. 5) with those taken under rule 29 (witness dangerously ill) and the C. & Y.P. Act (young person unfit to attend), both dealt with on p. 50. The differences are that in the latter

(a) the accused need not be present, provided reasonable notice has been served on him, and
(b) *any* justice (not necessarily an examining justice) can officiate.

N.B.—As to admissibility of depositions, see note (iv) on p. 57.

A written statement of a witness accepted under s. 2 of the C.J.Act 1967, is a deposition.

(2) *Exhibits*

As each witness produces an article or document admitted as evidence ("exhibit"), the fact is recorded in deposition, the exhibit retained by court (except for good reason otherwise), and given identification label.

NOTE: As to admissibility later of depositions, see "Depositions from persons dangerously ill", p. 50.

2. Acceptance of Written Statements Made by Witnesses

NOTE. The following applies to committal proceedings only. Provisions relating to proceedings other than committals are contained in s. 9 of the C.J.A. 1967 (see p. 52).

C.J. Act 1967, *s.* 2

In committal proceedings a written statement by any person shall, if certain conditions are satisfied, be admitted as evidence to like extent as oral evidence by that person.

The *conditions* are:

(a) statement purports to be signed by person who made it,

(b) statement contains declaration by maker that it is true to best of his knowledge and belief and that he made the statement knowing that he would be liable to prosecution if he wilfully stated anything known to be false or not believed to be true,*

(c) before the statement is tendered in evidence, a copy of it is given to each of the other parties to the proceedings, and

(d) none of the other parties has, before statement is tendered in evidence, objected to this.

* By s. 89 of the Act an indictable offence punishable by 2 years imprisonment or fine or both. As to position with regard to a child under 10, see p. 54.

R. v. *Nott, R.* v. *Baker* (1968)

A party is given a copy statement if it is given to his solicitor. If the solicitor represents two persons he should be given two copies.

Other requirements

(a) if maker is under 21, statement shall give age.

(b) if maker cannot read, statement must be read to him before he signs it and be accompanied by a declaration by the person who read it to this effect.

(c) if it refers to any other document as an exhibit, the copy served on the other party must be accompanied by a copy of that document or such information as enables the other party to inspect the document or a copy of it.

NOTE: The above conditions and requirements are the same as those applying to written statements used in other proceedings under s. 9 (see p. 52) *except* that under s. 2 there is no condition relating to service of copies of statements on other parties and objection not being made within 7 days of service.

Other provisions

(i) Though a statement is admissible the lower court can, on its own motion or on application by either side, require personal attendance of witness instead.

(ii) An accused can be committed without the written statements being considered by the examining justices (see below), but if evidence of contents is required the admissible passages of a statement must be read out by the party tendering the statement, and an oral account given of the parts which are not read out if the court requires this.

(iii) An exhibit identified by a written statement admitted in evidence is to be accepted as if produced and identified by the witness personally.

(iv) A written statement tendered in evidence is admissible in evidence at the trial on indictment (as is a deposition) in the case of a witness conditionally ordered to attend, or dead, insane, too ill to travel or kept out of the way by the accused, but the requirement as regards a deposition that it should be certified as having been taken in the presence of the accused (or counsel) who had full opportunity to cross-examine does not apply to a written statement under s. 2.

(v) Indictments can be framed on written statements just as they can on depositions.

(vi) Where the court proceeds to try summarily an offence which it began to deal with by way of committal for trial, the written statements are not admissible in evidence as depositions taken orally would be, but this does not necessarily mean that oral evidence of the witnesses would have to be taken, for the parties and the court might agree to admit the statements as evidence under s. 9 (see p. 52).

(vii) The maker of a written statement is a witness for the purpose of procuring his attendance at the trial on indictment by witness summons.

"*Hybrid Offences*" i.e. those triable on indictment or summarily. If the prosecution expect a summary trial, they should not serve written statements under s. 2; though they can serve them under s. 9 (which refers to trials and not committals). If, then, the defendant or the court does not agree to a summary trial and there has to be a committal, three courses are possible:

(1) witnesses give depositions in ordinary way, or
(2) proceedings adjourned to permit service of statements by the prosecution, or
(3) serve statements at once by agreement with defence to procure a committal without consideration of evidence under the 1967 Act, s. 1.*

* By this section examining justices can, if certain conditions are satisfied, commit for trial without consideration of the evidence, if all the evidence consists of written statements under s. 2 and the parties agree. (See further on p. 137.)

Statements made outside England & Wales.

Section 2 is extended to cover written statements made in Scotland and Northern Ireland, and also statements made outside the U.K., but in this case the conditions given on p. 56 and "other provision" (iv) on p. 57 do not apply (C.J.A. 1972, s. 46).

3. Securing Appearance of Parties and Witnesses

(1) *Prosecutor*—no process is provided to enforce the personal attendance of the prosecutor where he is not a witness. The prosecution is always legally represented, i.e. by counsel. See also p. 46.

(2) *Accused is committed either*—

(a) *On Bail*, fixed by the court and conditioned for his appearance, usually with sureties, or

(b) *In Custody* and conveyed on commitment warrant to prison to await trial. Warrant may be "backed" for bail. As to remands in custody of young persons, see p. 144.

Governor of prison has to produce prisoner, and prepare court calendars, and for latter reason the justices' clerk has to notify him of committals by bail.

As to process issued by the Crown Court to secure attendance of a defendant, see p. 47.

(3) *Witnesses* (*The Criminal Procedure* (*Attendance of Witnesses*) *Act* 1965 *as amended by the Courts Act* 1971)

(a) *Witness Orders* (s. 1)

(i) Examining justices are required, in respect of each witness examined by the court (except the accused and any defence witness as to his character) to make a "witness order" requiring his attendance at the Crown Court.

(ii) The court of committal will take into account any representations made by the accused or prosecutor that the attendance of any witness at the trial is unnecessary because his evidence is unlikely to be required or to be disputed, in which case the "*witness order*" may be CONDITIONAL i.e. requiring attendance only if notified to do so by the justices' clerk.

R. v. *Collins* (1938)
The accused should not be asked if he is guilty, but if he clearly states his intention of pleading guilty the witnesses should be bound over conditionally.

(iii) When committing the accused for trial, the court must inform him of his right to require the attendance at his trial of any witness in respect of whom a Conditional Witness Order has been made, and the steps he must take to procure such attendance.

(iv) The witness order is given to the witness (as a reminder), with particulars of the court of trial, as soon as practicable after his evidence has been given, usually after he has signed his deposition.

(v) As to disobedience of a witness order, see (c) below.

(b) *Witness Summons* (s. 2)

(i) A witness summons may be issued by the Crown Court requiring a person (who did not apppear at the committal proceedings) to attend to give evidence and produce any document or thing likely to be material evidence.

(ii) The Court may rescind a witness summons if satisfied by its recipient that he cannot give material evidence or supply the document or thing required.

(c) *Disobedience of Order or Summons* (s. 3 and s. 4)

(i) Disobedience of a witness order or witness summons is a contempt of court punishable by the trial court by n/e 3 months imp.

(ii) The court of trial can issue a notice (requiring immediate attendance or at a specified time) for service on any witness subject to a witness order or summons who has failed to attend. The notice may require him to attend not only to give his evidence but also to answer for his disobedience of the witness order or summons.

(iii) A warrant to arrest can be issued in the first instance (i.e. instead of the notice in (ii)) if the court is satisfied that witness has failed to attend without just excuse.

(iv) The warrant can be issued also where the court notice (as in (ii)) has not been complied with.

(v) After arrest, the witness may be remanded in custody or on bail in accordance with the directions on the warrant to attend the court to give evidence and to be dealt with for disobedience to the summons or order.

(d) *Warrants to Arrest to Meet Likely Disobedience* (s. 4)

An arrest warrant to bring a witness before the trial court will be issued by a judge of the High Court if he is satisfied by evidence on oath that the person in respect of whom a witness order or summons is in force is unlikely to comply with it.

N.B.—In the case of a witness against whom a *conditional* witness order or summons is in force and a warrant is applied for, an additional requirement is that the witness must have received the notice requiring him to attend. In the case of a witness summons the Judge must be satisfied that the witness is a material witness.

NOTES:

(a) When a witness arrested by warrant cannot be brought forthwith before the Crown Court named therein a magistrates' court for the place where arrested may commit him to custody or release him on bail (with or without sureties) until he can be brought before the higher court.

(b) If the warrant has been endorsed for bail and the person arrested cannot forthwith be brought before the court named therein, the officer in charge of a police station may release him on bail subject to his entering into the specified recognizance to appear at that court. Otherwise he must be brought before a magistrates' court forthwith.

(c) Where the court issuing the warrant is satisfied that the evidence of the witness can be dispensed with but that he should be dealt with for disobedience of the order or summons, the warrant may be endorsed to that effect. Such a person will be brought before a magistrates' court which must not commit him to custody unless the court named in the warrant is held within seven days of the committal. If such is not the case, the magistrates may, instead of releasing him on bail as in (a) above, commit him in custody to be dealt with by a judge of the high court.

(d) The provisions of s. 4 relating to the issue of a warrant to arrest applies to any person who fails to attend court in compliance with a recognizance entered into by him as it applies to a person who disobeys a witness order or summons, in addition to enforcement of any recognizance entered into.

SUBSEQUENT DUTIES OF JUSTICES' CLERKS (1968 Rules)

(1) As soon as practicable after committal (and before first day of hearing) to send to clerk of trial court:

(a) the information, if in writing.
(b) depositions (and statement of any direction by lower court prohibiting identification of any young witnesses in press, radio, TV).
(c) written statements of witnesses accepted by the court in lieu of oral evidence. (C.J.A. 1967, s. 2).
(d) statements made to the justices by the accused. (See Chapter VIII, p. 138).
(e) all recognizances to attend, including those of sureties.
(f) list of witnesses (with addresses, occupations) served with a conditional witness order and those since notified to attend and date notified.
(g) all exhibits retained by court (on proper form). *Exception.* If D.P.P. is prosecuting all to be sent to him except statements of accused made to the justices, and recognizances relating to the accused. D.P.P. to send them on to court of trial.
(h) documents connected with alibi requirements (see below).

(2) On request of either party to cause notice to be served on "conditional" witness directing attendance, and other party.

(3) Supply copies of depositions as soon as practicable after request by or for accused, if payment made, as well as of information if in writing. If deposition sent on this becomes duty of clerk of court of trial.

NOTIFICATION OF ALIBI (C.J.A. 1967, s. 11)

On a trial *on indictment* evidence in support of an alibi cannot be adduced by the defendant without leave of the court unless he has given notice of particulars of the alibi before the end of 7 days after the close of committal proceedings. Nor can he without the court's leave call any other person to testify as to an alibi *unless:*

(a) the above notice gives name and address of the witness, or, if this is not known, material information to assist in finding the witness,
(b) if name and address is not in notice, the accused (before and after notice) took all reasonable steps to ascertain the name and address,
(c) if name and address is subsequently ascertained or further material information to help to find it is discovered by accused, he forthwith gives notice of this,

(d) if accused is notified by prosecutor that the witness has not been traced by the name or at the address given, he forthwith gives notice of such information as he then has or subsequently receives.

NOTES:

(i) The court will not refuse leave if accused was not told on committal of the requirements.

(ii) Evidence to rebut alibi may be given (subject to directions of the court as to when it shall be given) before or after evidence given to support the alibi.

(iii) Notice of alibi is to be given either in court during committal proceedings or in writing to prosecution solicitor.

(iv) Notice as in (c) or (d) above is to be given to prosecution solicitor.

(v) The period of 7 days excludes Sunday, Xmas Day, Good Friday, bank holiday or any day appointed for public thanksgiving or mourning.

(vi) "*Alibi*" includes defence that by being in a particular place or area at a particular time the accused was not, or was not likely to have been, at the place where the offence was committed at the time it was committed.

Magistrates' Courts Rules 1968

The Court, on deciding to commit a person for trial (unless, having regard to the nature of the case, the Court thinks it unnecessary), is required:

(a) to warn him that he will not be permitted to give or to call evidence as to an alibi unless he gives the required particulars to the court then, or within 7 days to the prosecuting solicitor, and

(b) to give to the accused written notice of the provisions of s. 11 of the 1967 Act concerning the giving of particulars of an alibi (the name and address of the prosecuting solicitor to be included).

In the case of a committal it is the duty of the clerk to the justices to send on to the Crown Court (with the committal papers) a certificate signed by himself that the accused was or was not informed of the requirements of s. 11 and containing any particulars of an alibi given to the court by the accused.

Procedural recommendation. Difficulty will arise if allegations are made that the police acted improperly when interviewing an alibi witness. To avoid this the police should, whenever possible, give the defence solicitor reasonable notice of proposed interview and opportunity to be present. In the case where an accused person is not legally represented it is not suggested that the same facilities should be given to him, but the interview should be in the presence of some independent person. (H.O.C. 212/1967.)

R. v. *Lewis* (1969)

The restrictions of s.11 apply only to evidence of an alibi as to the whereabouts of the accused at the time of the commission of the offence and not to his whereabouts on another occasion.

R. v. *Sullivan* (1970)

The reason for a prescribed period is to give prosecution time to investigate before the trial opens. It may happen that due notice is not given for good reason and this is why a court has discretion in the matter. The mere fact that notice is not given in the prescribed time does not as a general rule of itself justify refusal of leave to call the evidence of alibi.

CORONERS AND INQUESTS

1. Appointment of Coroner

A Coroner is appointed for (or for part of) a County or Borough by the Lord Chancellor on the recommendation of the local authority concerned. Must have medical qualifications or be a barrister or solicitor of 5 or more years standing. Appointment is for life, though the Chancellor can remove from office for gross negligence.

2. Duties of Coroner (Coroners Acts 1887–1954)

To enquire into, and to hold an inquest where necessary in:

(a) all cases of *sudden, violent* or *unnatural death*, or where there is reasonable suspicion of this,

(b) cases of death where Statute requires inquest to be held (see below).

(c) Cases of *Treasure Trove*, i.e. the finding of hidden gold or silver.

Post Mortem. To assist him in determining whether inquest should be held, a coroner can require a post mortem examination to be made.

3. Coroner's Officer

In many forces it is usual to find a police officer specially appointed to act in all cases affecting the coroner (as "Coroner's Officer") but otherwise the duties of coroner's officer as regards a particular incident is generally carried out by the officer dealing with it. In general the duties consist of making the initial report to the coroner, carrying out particular enquiries as he directs, arranging the inquest (attendance of parties, witnesses, jury, etc.), supervising inquest proceedings, and reporting its result.

4. Jurisdiction of Coroner

The enquiry can be conducted only by the coroner in whose district the body (or remains) is, no matter where death occurred, and for this reason a body must not be removed from the district of one coroner to that of another except with prior consent of both. Where there is no body (destroyed or not recoverable) the Secretary of State can direct the holding of an inquest.

5. Inquests

(1) *Discretion of coroner.*—

(a) Cannot hold inquest unless there is reasonable suspicion, that death was unnatural, i.e. against the course of nature.

(b) Discretion whether or not to hold an inquest does not apply to the following cases *in which an inquest must be held*:

- (i) a violent or unnatural death or sudden death where cause of death is unknown.
- (ii) where death occurs in a prison, and
- (iii) where inquest is required by Statute, e.g. child put out to nurse or inmate of mental home, where there is no satisfactory medical evidence as to cause of death.

(2) *Venue.*—May be held anywhere, but not in licensed premises unless no other suitable place available. To be held in public unless considered not in interest of national security to do so. Not on Sunday, nor on Christmas Day, Good Friday or Bank Holidays, unless on grounds of urgency.

(3) *Jury.*—Coroner must have jury in following cases (otherwise it is at his discretion).

- (a) involving murder, manslaughter or infanticide.
- (b) road accident death, i.e. arising out of use of vehicle on a public road.
- (c) when death is one notifiable to a government department, e.g. accident in factory or on railway or by explosives.
- (d) death in circumstances raising issues of public safety, e.g. food poisoning, deaths under anaesthetics.
- (e) deaths in prison or otherwise requiring inquest by statute (as above).

The jury must consist of not less than seven nor more than eleven adult persons. A majority verdict is accepted, if the minority is not more than two jurors.

For qualifications and exemptions from jury service see p. 157.
A person shall not be summoned to act as a juror at inquests in the same coroner's area on more than 3 days (adjournments excepted) in any year.

R. v. *Divine* (1930)
A Coroner's jury ought not to be drawn from a panel so small that the same persons are summoned again and again and become regular jurymen. It is an irregularity justifying the quashing of the inquisition.

(4) *Viewing the Body.*—The Coroner must always view the body before the Inquest but the jury need not do so unless they so desire or unless the Coroner so directs.

> *R.* v. *Haslewood* (1926)
> It the Coroner omits to view the body the inquest is a nullity, the inquisition will be quashed, and a fresh inquest will be ordered.

(5) *Procedure.*—A coroner's court is a court of law, at which the ordinary rules of procedure apply, with the following main exceptions:

(a) There is no accused person,
(b) Evidence inadmissible in any other court may be admitted (e.g. "hearsay"),
(c) Any interested party can question a witness either personally or by legal representative,
(d) There are no addresses to the court,
(e) Verdict of jury is not of "Guilty" or "Not Guilty" but of a finding as to cause of death, and representation can be made additionally in form of "rider".
(f) The verdict cannot change a civil liability, nor can a rider be added except to indicate a recommendation to prevent similar future occurrences in cases of accidents.

N.B. A coroner may impose a fine upon:

(a) *a juror* for non appearance in answer to a summons (after his name has been openly called 3 times at the inquest) or who, without reasonable excuse, refuses to serve as a juror,
(b) *a witness* who does not appear at the inquest in answer to a summons (his name being openly called 3 times) or who refuses, without lawful excuse to answer questions put to him.

The coroner must notify the clerk of the magistrates' court for the area in which the coroner's court was held and which will then be responsible for dealing with the collection of the fine as if it was imposed by the magistrates' court.

(6) *Criminal Proceedings*:

A. *Committal by coroner.*—Coroner has power to commit direct to the Crown Court for trial on charge of murder, manslaughter or infanticide, on such a verdict being returned, but to do this would be exceptional.

B. *Normal procedure.*—

(a) Where case is one of murder, manslaughter, infanticide or causing death by dangerous driving, the coroner will open inquest, take evidence of identification, and then adjourn proceedings.

(b) If a person has been charged with one of these crimes, the same procedure applies but after criminal proceedings have been concluded, the inquest will be resumed as a new inquest. At this final inquest the jury:

(i) cannot charge accused with crime of which he could have been found guilty at his trial nor return a verdict inconsistent with that of the Criminal Court.

(ii) can return verdict of homicide if examining justices have not committed for trial, or have done so for a lesser offence.

(c) In cases of deaths from industrial accidents or diseases the inquest must be adjourned unless an inspector appointed under the Health and Safety at Work etc. Act, 1974 or some other authority responsible for the enforcement of that Act is present. Coroner has to give notice to the inspector at least 4 days before the adjourned inquest.

R. v. *Beresford* (1952)

In this case, the defendant was charged by the police with dangerous driving and summarily convicted before the justices by fine, only to be committed on inquisition for manslaughter when the Coroner resumed his inquest. It was held that where a charge of homicide can be preferred the police should not prefer any lesser charge, but if for some reason such a charge is preferred it should not be proceeded with until the inquest is concluded—the inquest will not be adjourned solely by reason of the institution of such proceedings.

R. v. *Huntbach* (1944)

It is an established rule that suicide is never to be presumed. It is not a probability which determines verdicts but proved facts. If facts cannot be proved an open verdict must be returned.

(7) *Obstructing coroner.*—It is a Common Law offence to destroy, conceal or dispose of a dead body with intent to prevent an inquest being held.

(8) *Exhumation.*—A coroner has power to order disinterment for good and sufficient reason, but this Common Law power is, in practice, used only in matters of urgency, and the usual way is to obtain a licence for exhumation from the Home Secretary under the Burials Act 1857, or an order from the High Court under s. 6 of the Coroners Act 1887.

CHAPTER IV

SUMMONSES AND WARRANTS

(1) INFORMATIONS, COMPLAINTS, ETC.

Information.—An information is a *written or verbal charge or allegation "laid" before a magistrate* that a person has committed an offence to which a penalty is attached, or is suspected of having done so. The finding of guilt on an information is a *conviction.* It is a necessary preliminary to the issue, at the discretion of the magistrate, of:

(i) *A Summons.*—The information need not be in writing or on oath, unless so prescribed, though a sworn written information is generally advisable in an indictable offence.

(ii) *A Warrant.*—The information has to be in writing and on oath.

Any person may lay an information unless the Statute creating the offence provides otherwise. The information should describe the offence in ordinary language and make reference to the appropriate Act and Section or Statutory Instrument.

Complaints.—A complaint is a verbal allegation *"made"* before a Magistrate that a person has committed a breach of the law not being a criminal offence or in which it is required by Statute that proceedings are to be taken by way of complaint. (The proceedings normally culminate in damages or the making of a court order, e.g.—to keep the peace, to destroy or keep under control a dangerous dog, bastardy, etc.).

Affidavits.—An affidavit is any written statement made upon oath before any person duly authorised to administer the Oath, though the term is generally used in connection with sworn statements intended as evidence in civil matters. An example in police practice is a Declaration of Service of a Summons.

Process.—This is the name often given to the legal documents issued to procure attendance or appearance at a court (e.g. *Summons, Warrant* or *Writ*) but has a wider meaning to cover *all* documents issuable by a court as a matter of its procedure (e.g. notice of fine).

(2) SUMMONSES

Definition of a Summons.—"A written order signed by a Justice of the Peace or by the clerk to the justices authenticating the name of the justice on the summons directing the person named therein to appear at a given time, date and court to answer the *complaint* or *information* set out therein (i.e. *Defendant Summons*) or to give evidence or to produce books or documents (i.e *Witness Summons*)."

There are two other types of summons which follow initial proceedings:

(a) *Defaulter's Summons* issued where the offender has failed to pay a fine or costs to secure his attendance for enquiry into his means, in order to decide whether or not he should be committed to prison in default.

(b) *Judgement Summons*—as above in respect of failure to pay in cases of civil debt, income tax, rates, maintenance, etc.

NOTES:

(1) A summons can be issued by a Justice only on what he considers to be an adequate *information* or *complaint*.

(2) If the allegation is of a crime or offence it is called an *information* and the applicant for summons is said to *lay the information*.

(3) An information for a summons in a summary offence should normally be laid within six months of the date of the offence.

(4) If the matter amounts to something which is civil and not criminal in character (e.g. bastardy) or which can only be dealt with by the court by way of an order (e.g. to keep the peace, or destroy a dangerous dog) the preliminary allegation is called "*complaint*" and it is *made* (not "laid").

(5) Neither *information* nor *complaint* need be on oath or in writing but both are generally required in informations for indictable crimes. If information is on oath a warrant for arrest can be issued by court on failure to appear.

(6) A summons is still valid though the justice who issued it has died or ceased to be a justice. The nature of the summons should be explained when serving it personally, and a pocket book entry always be made.

Service of Summonses: Methods

(a) *In General.—In any one of the following ways* a reasonable time before hearing:

(1) *Personal*: handing summons to defendant wherever he may be.

(2) *Non-Personal*: leaving it with someone at defendant's last known or usual place of abode (residence—not "lock up" shop or office).

(3) *By Registered Letter or Recorded Delivery Service.* to last known or usual place of abode, but *not* if:
(i) outside England and Wales.
(ii) witness summons.

N.B.—In the case of (2) and (3), if no acknowledgement of receipt is made by appearance of the defendant or by letter, a further summons has to be served by method (1), for a warrant cannot be issued. As to the issue of a warrant for non-appearance on a magistrates' summons, see p. 134. Compare a witness summons issued by a magistrate with that issued by the High Court in respect of cases before the Crown Court (see p. 59).

Ex parte Williams (1851)
The Justices are the judges of what in the circumstances is a reasonable time for service of summons upon the defendant.

O'Brien v. *Brabner* (1885)
A warrant ought not to be issued when a summons will be equally effectual, except in cases of a very serious nature.

Blake v. *Beech* (1876)
A defendant is entitled to insist on an information and summons in all cases, even when brought before the justices upon a general warrant under the Betting Act.

R. v. *Rhodes Ex parte McVittie* (1915)
"Place of abode" does not include a shop nor a lock up office where the party sought to be served does not reside.

(b) *In Particular.*—

Rates Summons: as above or by ordinary post.

A Company: service on clerk or secretary at the registered office.

A Club: on secretary or other person as Court may direct.

A member of the Armed Forces: if personal service, serve copy on Commanding Officer as well. If by post do it through Commanding Officer, or, in the case of a sailor on board ship, through the Secretary of the Admiralty.

(c) *For or from Scotland.*

By s. 4 of the S.J. (Process) Act 1881 process issued by a magistrates' court in England or Wales and endorsed by a summary court in Scotland (or vice versa) may be served (or executed) within the jurisdiction of the endorsing court as if it were within the jurisdiction of the issuing court. For endorsement proof is needed by the court of the handwriting (or seal) of the person issuing the document (i.e. the justice or the justices' clerk), either on oath or by a solemn declaration before a justice in accordance with the Magistrates' Courts Rules 1968 r. 55 in the form prescribed—which has to be forwarded with the process for service or execution. The same applies to process under the C.J.A. 1972 (1972 Act, s 51.).

(d) *For or from the Isle of Man.*

By virtue of an Order made under s. 40 of the C.J.A.A. 1914 the provisions of the 1881 Act (above) apply also to process to and from the Isle of Man. *H.O.Circ.* No summons received from the Isle of Man should be submitted to a magistrate to be endorsed for service here unless it has been endorsed or stamped at Douglas before despatch to the police in this country.

(e) *Northern Ireland.*

There is no provision for the service of summonses in Northern Ireland.

Proof of Service

Proof of Service may be effected in any one of three ways, by:

1. *Solemn Declaration* made before a Justice on the prescribed form and signed by him, the summons being marked 'A' and endorsed:
   "This is the document marked 'A' referred to in the annexed declaration of P.C. . . . .". Attach declaration to summons. (Only used now for a summons issued in Great Britain outside England and Wales or for hearing by a court other than a magistrates' Court).
2. *Certificate of Service* in prescribed form attached to the summons, or in that form on back of summons (the usual way), but only applicable to a summons issued in England or Wales, and for hearing before a Magistrates' Court only.
3. *Evidence in Court by Officer who served Summons.*—Until introduction of declarations and certificates of service this was the only way to prove service. Not used now, but could still become necessary (e.g. certificate detached and lost).

Non-Receipt of Summons, Etc.

Where a summons has been issued to secure appearance to answer a charge and the Magistrates' Court has begun to hear the case, the summons (but not the information) and all subsequent proceedings are rendered void *if*

(a) the defendant, during or after the trial, makes a statutory declaration that he did not know of the summons or the proceedings until a *date specified* in the declaration which was a date after the hearing had started, and

(b) within 14 days of the specified date the declaration is served on the clerk to the justices (by delivery to him, left at his office, or by registered letter or recorded delivery service to his office. (C.J. Act 1967, s. 24 (3)).

(3) WARRANTS

Definition.—A Warrant is a written authority signed by a Justice directing the person(s) to whom it is addressed to do some act specified therein.

Execution.—A warrant is *executed when the directions of the Warrant have been carried out.*

General Rules

(1) *Possession.*—The warrant must be in possession of the constable *at the time* of executing, to be produced and read over to the prisoner.

Exception—a warrant to *arrest for an offence* provided the warrant was issued in England, Wales or Scotland and is shown to the prisoner as soon as practicable afterwards.

(2) *Duration.*—Warrants remain in force until executed or withdrawn. Death of justice who issued it has no effect.

Exception—A search warrant when it has a time limit expressly stated in it.

(3) *Time*—A warrant must not be executed during the night.

Exception—A warrant to arrest for an offence or to search can be issued and executed *at any time.*
In exceptional cases a warrant may contain a restriction on *when* it can be executed, e.g. under the Pawnbrokers Act 1872, s. 36—"During the hours of business".

Main Kinds of Warrants

The following are the main kinds of warrants:

(1) **To arrest for an offence.**—This includes a warrant in the first instance i.e. instead of a summons, see p. 47, and also a warrant for failure to answer to a summons for an offence, or to answer to bail—see p. 134. Information to be in writing and on oath, but justice may issue summons instead. It authorises arrest and bringing before the court, or releasing on bail (if so backed) to appear at the court.

Horsfield v. *Brown* (1932)

If the warrant of arrest does not charge an offence an arrest is illegal unless the constable has the warrant in his possession at the time, and the Constables' Protection Act 1750 does not absolve the constable from liability. If the constable acts in obedience to the warrant then though the warrant is an unlawful warrant, he is protected by the Statute of 1750 but if the warrant be a lawful warrant and he executes it in an unlawful way, then no action is maintained against the J.P. but is maintainable against the constable.

Execution—special features:

Use of force.—Wide powers to enter and to search premises, and to use reasonable force in effecting any lawful arrest are provided by C.L. Act 1967—see p. 88.

Bail.—Not unless endorsed for bail by the issuing justice and in accordance with the terms of an endorsement. If no bail, the prisoner must be brought before a justice within 24 hours.

(2) **To search premises.**—Information must be in writing and on oath.

Execution—special features:

The warrant may contain special directions as to type of property to be seized, persons to be arrested, but seizure of property not covered by the warrant may be justified on other grounds, e.g. interests of state, seizure of firearm not lawfully possessed, goods believed stolen.

Garfinkel v. *Metro. Police Commissioner* (1971)

In a search under warrant for explosives police officers took leaflets. *Held*—(following *Ghani* v. *Jones* (1970))—where police find goods showing a person to be implicated in some crime other than that to which the warrant was directed, they can remove them provided they act reasonably and detain them no longer than necessary.

In the case of all warrants to search for stolen property there is an inherent authority to break open doors if purpose cannot be effected otherwise, but before resorting to this the constable should make known his office and authority and request admission. The warrant affords protection to the constable although the person arrested later proves his innocence.

Launock v. *Brown* (1819)

No one can justify breaking open another's door to make an arrest unless he first signify to those in the house the cause of his coming and request them to give him admittance.

The Theft Act 1968 provides that a search warrant issued on sworn information by a justice can be executed only by a constable though the information may be sworn by any person. It authorises entry (by force if necessary), search and seizure of any goods believed to be stolen.

(3) **Commitment.**—To this category belong all warrants to commit a person to prison, to a remand home, etc.

(i) For *"Sentence"* from a summary court, *"Committal for trial"* or *"On Remand"* No warrant needed when sentenced from a Crown Court for the accused is in custody.

(ii) *"To Police Cells, etc"*: Where the court has power to impose imprisonment it may instead order that person to be detained for up to 4 days in any police cell, bridewell, or similar place, certified as suitable by the Home Secretary.

There is no legal requirement that a warrant of commitment should be issued for remands for not more than 3 days in police custody (i.e. to cells). A verbal order of the Court is sufficient.

(iii) *"Detention Warrant"*: Where the court has power to commit to prison in default of payment of a sum adjudged to be so paid (e.g. small fines) it may issue a warrant for the defaulter's detention in a police station until 8 a.m. next day, unless the sum be sooner paid. He may be released within 4 hours before 8 a.m. if the officer in charge thinks it expedient to enable the prisoner to go to work or for other sufficient reason.

(iv) *"Detention Order"*: Where the court has power to commit to prison for an offence, it may order ***in writing*** that he be detained at *any* police station up to 8 p.m. that day, but he must not be deprived of reasonable opportunity of returning home the same day.

(v) *"**in Default**"* of payment of fine or costs—authorises arrest and taking to ***prison*** unless the sum due and costs (shown on warrant) are paid. When s. 49 of the C.J.A. 1972 is brought into force a magistrates' court can, instead of issuing a commitment warrant (in default), make a Community Service Order (as to which see p. 181).

Execution—special features:

Part payments can be accepted and the warrant endorsed accordingly (reduces the term of imprisonment). If a person cannot or will not pay in full, power to arrest and take to prison is given (unless paid before). Persons arrested may be lodged in the nearest prison even though not the one named in the warrant. Delay in execution to be considered if the person named is very ill, aged, or pregnant.

(4) **To Distrain (Distress Warrant).**—This is issued as an alternative to commitment on default of payment of a sum due by a court order—usually a distress warrant is issued first and then commitment if money is not paid and there are no goods or not sufficient goods on which to distrain. The warrant may be signed by the clerk to the justices authenticating the name of the justice appearing on it.

Execution—special features:

Authorises seizure and sale of goods to make good the amount due, unless the amount is paid.

Not to be seized: wearing apparel or bedding of the person and family, or implements of trade to the value of £50.

Sale—by auction within the period stated in the warrant, or if none, not earlier than the 6th nor later than 14th day after seizure, unless the person agrees otherwise in writing to an earlier sale.

Goods—to be marked conspicuously

Household goods are not to be taken away without consent until the day of the sale. Goods should not be left on the premises if the seizure is for non payment of rates.

After deducting costs and the amount due on the warrant, balance to be returned to the owner.

Send written account to Clerk of the Court. The officer executing may receive a part payment of the amount due. If no goods (or insufficient) warrant to be endorsed accordingly and returned to Justices' Clerk concerned.

No breaking into premises is authorised and not to be executed at night.

(5) **To eject from premises**—*Ejectment Warrant.*—This requires *two* justices (not one as the others). Issue of warrant follows court proceedings for failure to comply with an order to quit or give up possession.

Execution: *special features*:

Warrants are addressed to constables who by law are responsible for execution. Must be executed between 9 a.m. and 4 p.m.

(6) **Special Provisions** *as to Northern Ireland, Isle of Man & Channel Islands: Warrant to arrest for an offence and Commitment Warrants.*—Such warrants from these places can be executed in England and Wales and vice versa *if backed* (i.e. endorsed) by a local magistrate (in place to be executed) who can only do so if warrant is accompanied by a declaration of handwriting verifying signature of issuing justice. (The declaration for Northern Ireland must be sworn.)

Eire:

There is provision for the execution in Eire of warrants from outside and warrants issued there may be executed in the British Isles (Backing of Warrants (Republic of Ireland) Act 1965, s.1 (1)) if issued by a judicial authority (i.e. a court, judge or justice of a court or peace commissioner) in the Republic of Ireland, and backed by a justice here.

As to Scotland see p. 69.

(7) **To arrest on failure to appear** *at Court* (accused and witnesses).

(a) *At higher courts*

(i) *Accused persons*—see p. 147.
(ii) *Witnesses*—see p. 59.

(b) *At magistrates' courts*
(i) *Defendants* (see p. 134).
(ii) *Witnesses* (see p. 134).

(8) **Care Proceedings.** See p. 184 as to written authority of justice to detain a young person in need of care and control.

Protection of Constable Executing Warrant

If action questioning the legality of a warrant is brought against any constable who acted in accordance with the terms of the warrant the Judge must find for the constable on production and proof of the warrant, even though there may be a defect of jurisdiction in the justices.

Execution of Warrants by Process Servers

The Magistrates' Courts Rules 1968 (as amended by the 1973 Rules) permit a warrant issued by a Justice for the arrest of any person to be executed by "authorised persons" for the police area specified in the warrant. A further amendment of the 1968 regulations authorises civilian process servers, where specified in the warrant, to execute commitment warrants and convey the arrested person to prison or place of detention.

AUTHORISATION TO SEARCH: ISSUED BY CHIEF OFFICER OF POLICE

1. *Theft Act* 1968, s. 26.—A Superintendent of police (or higher rank) has power to issue an authority to search premises for stolen goods, if:

(a) the occupier of the premises has been convicted within the preceding 5 years of:
(i) handling stolen goods, or
(ii) an offence involving dishonesty and punishable with imprisonment;

(b) a person with a conviction of handling stolen goods within the preceding 5 years has occupied the premises within the preceding 12 months.

N.B.—This method is adopted when there is not time to obtain a Justice's warrant and the ends of justice are likely to be defeated by delay. No particular property need be specified in the authority. It does not authorise an arrest but permits seizure of any goods believed to be stolen.

2. *Explosives Act* 1875, s. 73.—Provides that a Police Superintendent may issue his authority to search for illegal explosives *anywhere*.

3. *Official Secrets Act* 1911, s. 9.—A similar authority may be

issued by a Superintendent of Police to search for plans, etc., in case of emergencies.

N.B.—These authorities can be executed at any time, unless there is a special limitation in the particular authority.

NOTE: These are dealt with in more detail in *Police Promotion Handbook No. 1: Criminal Law.*

PROGRESS CHECK No. 3

1. In connection with Crown Courts:
   (a) What are the three "Divisions"?
   (b) Who are or may be judges?
   (c) Define their jurisdiction.
   (d) Where may they be held?
   (e) What classifications apply to locations of Crown Courts?
   (f) Why are crimes classified in respect of trial?
   (g) What rules apply to magistrates sitting with judges?
2. What is meant by (a) Magistrates' Court; (b) Court of Petty Sessions; (c) Occasional Court, and (d) Juvenile Court.
3. What do you know about the office of (a) Recorder; (b) Stipendiary magistrate?
4. What is a "Hybrid" offence?
5. What is meant by "Open Court", and what is the law concerning it?
6. When may a juvenile be dealt with by an "adult" court?
7. What are the differences between a witness summons
   (a) issued by the High Court and
   (b) issued by a Magistrates' Court?
8. What is the procedure adopted to secure the attendance at the higher court of witnesses appearing at the committal proceedings?
9. What is the distinction between a witness summons and a witness order in respect of the appearance of a witness at a higher court?
10. How is a coroner appointed, and what are the duties of his office?
11. When "*must*" inquests be held?
12. When must a coroner be assisted by a jury?
13. What are the main differences of procedure between a coroner's court and a magistrates' court?
14. What procedure is followed concerning holding of inquests in cases being dealt with by police as criminal homicides?
15. Distinguish between an information and a complaint.
16. What is a summons? What types of summonses are there?
17. Explain the various ways in which a summons can be served.

18. What special rules of service apply to summonses for rates, on a company, or a club, or a member of the armed services?
19. What is a "declaration of service"? In what cases must it still be used?
20. What procedure has to be followed to enable a summons issued in England or Wales to be served in Scotland, the Isle of Man or Ireland?
21. What procedure would you follow to enable service to be effected of a summons issued in Scotland?
22. What is a warrant?
23. What are the general rules concerning the execution and duration of warrants?
24. Name the main kinds of warrants, and state, shortly, their purpose.
25. In what circumstances need the warrant not be in the possession of the constable executing it?
26. What is the law concerning the seizure and sale of goods under a Distress Warrant?
27. What is meant by, and what is the purpose of, "backing a warrant"?
28. To what extent is a constable protected by law from civil action taken against him in respect of the execution of a warrant?
29. What is the law with regard to the service or execution in this country of a summons or warrant issued in Eire?
30. In what circumstances can a police authorisation to search be issued under the Theft Act 1968, s. 26?
31. What is a "Dying declaration", and when is it admissible?
32. Distinguish between a confession and an admission.
33. Describe when a written statement from a young person may be read as evidence, and the conditions which render the presence of the young person necessary as a witness.
34. What is a "Deposition"?
35. When may a "deposition" be read at a trial in absence of witness?
36. What are the essential differences between a deposition taken from a person dangerously ill and that taken normally by examining justices?
37. What details must be given to a court if a person wishes to give notice of an alibi?
38. Within what period must notice of alibi be given?
39. What persons may be present in a juvenile court?
40. What is the maximum imprisonment that can be imposed by a magistrates' court?

CHAPTER V

ARREST WITHOUT WARRANT

1. WHAT IS AN ARREST?

In the widest legal sense a person is "arrested" when he is totally deprived of his personal freedom to go where he wishes. A partial restraint on the freedom of movement is not an arrest.

In its application to Criminal Law "arrest" has a more limited meaning, and can be defined as depriving a person of his liberty by taking him into legal custody for the purpose of bringing him before the court on a criminal charge or investigating his liability in respect of a criminal charge.

An arrest can legally be made only when the law *expressly* provides the power, and such is the care with which the law preserves the right to personal liberty that the power is not readily given, and is always made subject to conditions which must apply. If an arrest is made illegally, i.e. without legal authority, an action lies for "false imprisonment" and liability for an assault may also arise.

2. CONSIDERATION WHETHER OR NOT TO ARREST

It is important to note that the law rarely provides that an arrest must be made, but merely permits an arrest, i.e. may arrest. All proceedings can be commenced by summons, so that where a power to arrest is provided (whether with or without warrant) it is an alternative procedure which should be resorted to only when reason exists for it. Among the grounds on which procedure by arrest may be considered more suitable are:

(1) *The gravity of the charge*—and with it the increased likelihood of the accused absconding.

(2) *Interest of the prisoner*—e.g. for own protection or removal from potential physical or moral danger.

(3) *Interest of the public*—e.g. as the only sure way to remove a danger or nuisance to the public, or the risk of the offence being repeated.

(4) *The ends of justice*—e.g. to prevent the prisoner disposing of evidence, stolen property, or warning an accomplice.

(5) *The need for corroboration*—e.g. as to physical condition of accused.

(6) *Summons likely to be ineffectual*—e.g. person of no fixed abode.

(7) *To obtain evidence*—Where possibility is that search might reveal essential evidence (e.g.—stolen property, betting slips).

(8) *To obtain further information*—e.g. verify address, to obtain fingerprints or to pursue enquiries regarding other crimes, etc.

3. POWERS OF ARREST AT COMMON LAW

Prior to the Criminal Law Act 1967, the most extensive powers to arrest without warrant were derived from the Common Law, and based mainly on the Common Law distinction between crimes which were "felonies" and those which were "misdemeanours". The 1967 Act, which abolished this ancient legal distinction (and with it the Common Law powers to arrest for felony), has substituted powers of arrest which are a modernised version of the Common Law powers and apply to "arrestable offences" as defined by the Act. In short, the powers which were formerly Common Law powers and related to felonies have been replaced by statutory powers relating to "arrestable offences". (See p. 84.)

The Criminal Law Revision Committee commented as follows on this proposed change—

> "The new powers of arrest would not differ in practice greatly from the existing powers. They would apply to all offences which are now felonies with a few unimportant exceptions. They would bring in the most serious misdemeanours; with a few exceptions these are offences for which it would seldom be thought necessary to arrest a person without a warrant, but it may be important to be able to do so on occasion. Offences for which the power may be more freely exercised would include obtaining property by false pretences and causing death by dangerous driving, both of which carry five years' imprisonment."

The Common Law powers which remain relate to "breaches of the Peace" and to assaults on or obstructions of the Police.

(1) Breaches of the Peace

A breach of the peace is a disturbance of the public peace by fighting, or by threatened or actual violence to person or property. A serious breach of the peace may well amount to a statutory "arrestable offence" for which the Criminal Law Act 1967 provides an additional power to arrest without warrant (see p. 84), but, **in any case, the common law power to arrest without warrant** applies to *all* breaches of the peace, though it is conditional upon it *being committed within view* and the arrest *being necessary*:

(a) *to prevent the breach occurring or re-occurring*, or

(b) *to quell it during its continuance.*

Green v. *Bartram* (1830) & *Jordan* v. *Gibbon* (1863)

If a person of whom complaint is made has *lawfully* entered the house of another, his refusal to leave on the request of the occupier is not a breach of the peace. Such refusal gives cause for ejecting him, but not for arrest. However, if he attacks the occupier in order to resist ejectment, this will amount to a battery, and is a breach of the peace for which an arrest may be justified.

Timothy v. *Simpson* (1835)

A constable who arrives on the scene after a fracas is over has no powers of arrest on his own account at Common Law unless he fears a repetition. Even where he does not fear a repetition, he may, like any other citizen, lawfully aid a spectator of the affair who is endeavouring to make an arrest, and he may with the authority of such spectator, do the whole work of arresting on the spectator's behalf, or take over a person already properly arrested.

Baynes v. *Brewster* (1841)

'P' kept rapping violently at 'D's' door threatening that he would continue to do so until 'D' had delivered up a certain book. 'D' summoned a policeman to arrest 'P' and 'P' thereupon fled. 'D' pursued him and arrested him. *Held*, that although the conduct was a breach of the peace or likely to lead to a breach of the peace, the arrest on the facts was illegal, because there was nothing to show that 'P' intended to return to continue his unlawful behaviour. An arrest to put an end to such conduct or to prevent the repetition would have been lawful.

Coward v. *Baddeley* (1859)

A man may arrest for a battery committed on himself.

R. v. *Lockley* (1864)

Mere disorderliness like swearing, or quarrelling by words only without any threat of personal hurt, are not sufficient to justify arrest. The arrester must suppose the person to be on the point of committing or actually committing a breach of the peace.

N.B.—The power of arrest without warrant extends to any person and is not limited to constables.

(2) Assaulting, Obstructing or Resisting the Police

The Common Law provides the authority for a constable to arrest without warrant any person who assaults, obstructs or resists him in the *execution of his duty*. The authority should not be taken too literally with regard to an "obstruction in execution of duty" for "obstruction" is not well defined and it is not difficult to provide instances of obstruction which are of a purely technical nature and for which an arrest without warrant might well be difficult to justify in practice or in law. It is best to regard an arrestable obstruction as one involving *physical* interference designed to prevent a constable from, or seriously hinder him in, doing something which was his duty as a constable to do. This interpretation would put "obstruction" more in line with the other grounds for which the Common Law authorises arrest under this heading, for both of them (assault and resistance) imply some degree of physical opposition which the constable should be legally empowered to overcome.

The expression "execution of duty" also needs consideration, for while it covers the carrying out of anything which it is his duty as a constable to do, it does not extend to the doing of something which, though not unlawful, was not his duty as a constable.

The following cases illustrate these points:

R. v. *Roxburgh* (1871)

A constable is not acting in the execution of his duty in expelling a mere trespasser, being no way obliged in law to do so. When assaulted in these circumstances, he might therefore charge the trespasser with common assault, etc., according to the gravity of the injury sustained, but not with assaulting him in the execution of his duty. In practice, the owner, who is entitled to eject the trespasser after first requesting him to leave, should be asked to remove him, and if the trespasser resists, the constable would act under his common law powers to prevent a breach of the peace, and thus be acting in the execution of his duty.

Davis v. *Lisle* (1936)

It is never the duty of a constable to do anything illegal and whereas a constable may not be acting unlawfully, it does not follow that he is acting in the lawful execution of his duty, as would be the case when he is obstructed or assaulted in ejecting a mere trespasser upon the request of a private person. A constable may himself become a trespasser when asked to leave private premises in the course of making enquiries, and is not thereafter acting in the execution of his duty.

Robson v. *Hallett* (1967)

Three constables visited house to enquire about an offence. One invited in—others left on garden path. Occupier told P.C. in the house to leave, whereupon P.C. was assaulted by occupier's son. Other constables entered to assist, and another son entered the fray. Both sons charged with assault police. *Held*—both guilty. Implied leave permitted the walk to the door and leave was given to one to enter. When requested P.C. began to leave—reasonable time should be given to withdraw. He was therefore assaulted in execution of duty. As to the other constables it was impossible to say that they were not acting in execution of duty in going to their colleague's assistance and preventing further breaches of the peace.

Bailey v. *Wilson* (1968)

P.C. walked through open gateway to house to enquire into a reported domestic disturbance. Refused admittance and told to go away. Refused to move from position across threshold, and was punched by B. *Held*—(applying *Davis* v. *Lisle*) P.C. has no right to enter premises without warrant or statutory authority; has no right to enter premises without warrant to make enquiries; if a trespasser he is not acting in execution of duty; unlocked gate is implied licence to go to door of house to seek entry; if any licence to enter is withdrawn a visitor insisting on staying is a trespasser. No assault under Police Act. (*Robson* v. *Hallet* distinguished as in that case no time was given for P.C. to leave as requested.)

NOTE: Assaults and Wounding. An additional power to arrest without warrant at Common Law is sometimes mentioned, namely, to prevent unlawful injury to any person, but this would appear to be an unnecessary addition for the former would amount to a threatened breach of the peace, and the latter to statutory "arrestable offence" (dealt with later).

4. POWER TO ARREST WITHOUT WARRANT BY STATUTE

(1) Introduction

The Criminal Law Act 1967 abolished the common law distinction between felonies and misdemeanours, and, with it, all the common law powers to arrest without warrant for any crime which was a felony. The Act replaced the common law power of arrest for felonies with a statutory power of arrest for any "arrestable offence", a term which covers almost all crimes which were formerly felonies and, as well, a few of the more serious crimes which were called misdemeanours, e.g. obtaining by deception, and causing death by dangerous driving.

Before the passing of the 1967 Act, the only Statute which provided a general power to arrest for a wide range of offences was the Prevention of Offences Act 1851, s. 11 of which provides that any person may arrest without warrant any person who is found committing any indictable offence by night and convey or deliver him to some constable or other peace officer to be dealt with according to law.

Statutory powers to arrest may, therefore, be classified as follows:

(a) *General powers*—as provided by:
  (i) the *Criminal Law Act* 1967 for "arrestable offences", and
  (ii) the *Prevention of Offences Act* 1851 for indictable offences being found committed by night, i.e. between one hour after sunset and one hour before sunrise.

(b) *Powers for specified offences*, i.e. those provided by a particular Statute for the offences it creates.

(2) General Statutory Powers

Statutes. *Prevention of offences Act* 1851, s. 11 (dealt with above).
Criminal Law Act 1967, s. 2 (arrestable offences).

(a) *Arrestable Offences—Definition* (C.L.A. 1967, s. 2)
An "arrestable offence" means any offence for which
  (i) the sentence is fixed by law (i.e. any capital offence), or
  (ii) a person, on first conviction, may be sentenced to imprisonment for 5 years,

and includes *an attempt* to commit such an offence, and any offence stated to be an arrestable offence by any subsequent Statute (as, for example, unlawfully taking a conveyance, made an A.O. by the Theft Act 1968).

R. v. *Spicer* (1970)
The liability to 5 years imprisonment must be by some enactment in order to make the offence an A.O. Such liability by the Common Law only does not make the offence an A.O. because the Common Law is not an enactment.

NOTES:
  (i) The criterion is whether the punishment is provided by law for the offence and not whether it would apply to the particular person committing the offence. For this reason the power of summary arrest applies, for example, to a young person though proceedings in his case would not result in imprisonment.
  (ii) The definition applies to offences created in any future statute unless the Statute expressly provides otherwise.
  (iii) There is no formula by which an offence can be readily identified as an arrestable offence, though minor or comparatively minor offences are clearly excluded. It becomes a matter of memorising them or the most common of them, but the student who has had a good grounding in the old Common Law

principles, i.e. felonies, may find useful the extract from the Report of the Criminal Law Revision Committee (see p. 79, *ante*).

A list of the arrestable offences most commonly met with in police practice is given in Appendix 1 to this Handbook.

(b) *Arrestable offences—Powers of arrest* (C.L.A. 1967, s. 2)

Any Person may arrest without warrant

(i) any one who is or whom he, with reasonable cause, suspects to be, *in the act of committing* an arrestable offence, and

(ii) where an arrestable offence *has been committed*, any one who is, or whom he, with reasonable cause, suspects to be guilty of the offence.

A Constable has the above powers but can also arrest without warrant

(i) where he, with reasonable cause, *suspects* that an arrestable offence has been committed, any one whom he, with reasonable cause, suspects to be guilty of that offence, and

(ii) any person who is, or whom he, with reasonable cause, suspects to be, about to commit an arrestable offence.

NOTE: The power of a constable exceeds that of a civilian in the following ways:

(i) On an arrest of a person on suspicion of his having committed an arrestable offence, the civilian has to know that the offence has in fact been committed, but a constable can arrest if he *reasonably suspects* that an arrestable offence has been committed by the person concerned.

(ii) The civilian does not have the statutory power to arrest a person suspected of being *about to commit* an arrestable offence, though the Common Law power for breaches of the peace may apply, and he has, by s. 3 (see p. 89) legal authority to use reasonable force to prevent crime.

(iii) A civilian is not given the authority to enter and search any place for the purpose of making an arrest, as a constable is, under the Act (see p. 88).

Remember that an "arrestable offence" includes an attempt to commit that offence, and that the above closely parallels the Common Law powers of arrest for felonies, which it replaces.

The following cases precede the 1967 Act but as they applied to the Common Law which the Act replaces, they undoubtedly apply to the existing law. The text has been amended by substituting "arrestable offence" for "felony" where the latter term was used.

Downing v. *Capel* (1867)
"Found committing" extends to "instant pursuit"—if the offender is found in the act, "fresh" or "hot pursuit" is allowed, and arrest will be deemed an immediate one in law although the chase is prolonged. Fresh pursuit starts on the commission of the offence and it must be continuously pressed. It is sufficient if the person arrested has been seen in a position which justified belief that he had committed the offence.

NOTE: This extension of the power to arrest ceases when the "immediate pursuit" is broken off. It does not apply if pursuit is renewed after being broken off.

Lewis (John) & Co., Ltd. v. *Tims* (1952)
After arrest without warrant *by a civilian* the prisoner should be taken as soon as reasonably practicable before a Justice or to a police station (where the officer in charge has power to grant bail). He should not be taken back to the scene of the crime.

Dallison v. *Caffery* (1964)
Whereas a private person has a duty to hand over anyone arrested by him on suspicion of having committed (an arrestable offence) as soon as he reasonably can, a constable has extra powers to do what is reasonable to further investigate the matter by taking the prisoner to his own house or place of work (to search for property or arrange identification) before taking him to a police station or before a magistrate provided the measures taken are reasonable.

McArdle v. *Egan* (1933)
A constable's suspicion may be founded on matters within his own knowledge, including the fact that the person suspected has been previously convicted of similar offences or in statements by another coming in a way which justify him in giving them credit.

Though a civilian has wide powers to arrest it is not likely that these will be used except in the most serious of "arrestable offences". It will happen more often that the civilian will give information or make an accusation to a constable, who will have to consider his own powers of arrest where he considers that the correct procedure is by arrest rather than by summons and immediate action is necessary. In such circumstances it will be for him to decide whether on the evidence available it would be reasonable for him to suspect that the person accused has committed an arrestable offence and act accordingly.

Dumbell v. *Roberts* (1944)

A constable is justified in arresting a person without warrant upon a reasonable suspicion of (an arrestable offence) having been committed and of the person being guilty of it. The police are not called on before acting to have a *prima facie* case for conviction, but have the duty of making such immediate presentable enquiry as the circumstances reasonably permit.

Storehouse v. *Elliott* (1795)

A constable will usually require a private informant to give in charge the person to be arrested. The private informant will then be liable for false imprisonment if the arrest be wrongful, though the constable will be liable as well if the arrest is wrongful on his part.

Hogg v. *Ward* (1858)

An unreasonable charge does not justify a constable in arresting, even though the person making the charge expressly requires him to arrest.

Lister v. *Perryman* (1870)

Information from a person of whom the constable knows nothing, would be regarded very differently from information given by one whom he knows to be a sensible and trustworthy person. The question whether or not it would be reasonable to arrest upon the information received must depend in a great degree on the opinion formed of the position and circumstances of the informant.

If the third party is prepared to prefer the charge, an arrest should be made unless, from the circumstances and evidence (including repute and appearance of the parties, explanation given, advisability of procedure by summons, etc.) the arrest does not appear justified. *If the charge is not clearly frivolous,* the person charging and not the constable will be responsible for the arrest. In such a case, the person preferring the charge should be asked to sign the charge sheet.

(3) Statutory Powers for Specific Offences

Where the offence is not an "arrestable offence" under the provisions of the C.L. Act 1967, a power to arrest exists only if:

(a) the common law applies (i.e. the offence involves a breach of the peace), or

(b) a special power of arrest is applied to that offence by a Statute which makes particular reference to the offence, usually the Statute which creates it.

There are very many of these and there is no "short cut" to assist in identifying them readily. Each statutory authority is limited to a specific offence or to a limited range of offences, and it is necessary for the student not only to memorise them as they occur in the course of his studies, but to learn also the widely varying conditions which are generally applied to them. The following observations, however, might be useful to indicate the kind of limitations generally imposed and to afford grounds for comparison with the much wider powers applying to "arrestable offences".

(a) *In the majority of cases power to arrest is given to Constables only.*

Exceptions:

Any person: Coinage Offences Act 1936
Vagrancy Act 1824.

Constable and specified person:

Game Act 1831 (occupiers of land)
Night Poaching Act 1828 (gamekeepers, owners, occupiers).

(b) *Powers to arrest on reasonable suspicion,* and these are comparatively few, e.g.: offences relating to

Absentees and deserters.
Gaming in public places.
Controlled drugs, official secrets, sexual offences, immigrants.

(c) *It is generally the case that the offender must be "found committing".*

In the following cases it is important to bear in mind that any reference to "offence" now necessarily implies reference to an "offence" not being an "arrestable offence" under the C.L. Act 1967.

Matthews v. *Biddulph* (1841)

When a Statute empowers a police officer to arrest a person only when found committing an offence, he is not empowered to arrest one endeavouring to commit it. The offence must actually be committed and arrest for mere attempt is not justified.

Simmons v. *Millinger* (1846)

The words "found committing" like the phrase "within his view" has the effect of prohibiting arrest upon hearsay information. If, when the officer arrives on the scene, the offence has been committed, however recently, he has no power to arrest on his own account. (This would not prohibit a constable acting in aid of another who was a witness and could arrest by the Statute).

Leete v. *Harte* (1868)

A statute authorising arrest for an offence does not authorise arrest for an attempt to commit the offence unless it expressly provides this.

Isaacs v. *Keech* (1925)

The meaning of the expression "within his view" limits the arrest to things which occur before the arrester's eyes and prevents him from merely acting on information received from other persons.

Stevenson v. *Aubrook* (1941)

Upon complaint received from complainant that a man on a bicycle had indecently exposed himself to her, the police went out in a car and immediately arrested him. It later transpired that he had not exposed himself, though he had indecently fumbled with his trousers.

Held: that the arrest was unlawful because the offence had not actually been committed, the reasonable belief on the part of the police was no defence for the Vagrancy Act 1824 authorises arrest only if "found committing". (HALLETT, J.—was prepared to hold that if the man had been guilty of the offence, the arrest by the police on pursuit would have been lawful even though the police had not themselves found the offence, for they were acting on complaint of the person who had found the offence).

5. AUXILIARY POWERS

(1) To Enter and Search to Effect Arrest

Applicable to Arrestable Offences only

Section 2 (6) of the Criminal Law Act 1967 provides that for the purpose of arresting a person *without warrant* for an arrestable offence a *constable* may enter (if need be, by force) and search any place where that person is or where the constable, with reasonable cause, suspects him to be.

NOTES:

(a) Where force is not needed no complications are likely to arise, for the former Common Law power (which was never well defined) is now based on statutory and clearly stated authority.

(b) Where force is necessary (to gain entry) the qualification "*if need be*" (in s. 2 (6)) raises important considerations, and it is on this aspect that the principles applied to the common law rule will still be relevant.

(c) The common law principles may be briefly stated thus—The breaking into premises (e.g. breaking open doors) should not be undertaken unnecessarily or lightly, but reserved for cases where the urgency of an immediate arrest exists, e.g. essential having regard to the gravity of the charge, or in the interests of public safety or of justice. Where the premises is an occupied dwelling, and circumstances *permit this*, the constable should not use force until he has requested admittance after making it known that he is a constable, stated the reason for his request, and his request has been refused or ignored.

Launock v. *Brown* (1819)

No one can justify breaking open another's door to make an arrest unless he first signify to those in the house the cause of his coming and request them to give him admittance.

(2) To Use Force

Applicable to all lawful arrests

A person may use such force as is reasonable in the circumstances in effecting or assisting in the lawful arrest of offenders or suspected offenders or of persons unlawfully at large (C.L. Act 1967, s. 3).

Note that (a) the authority extends to *any* person making a *lawful* arrest, and to arrests being made by warrant;

(b) what force is "reasonable in the circumstances" will depend on the usual considerations as to gravity of charge, degree of resistance by persons to be arrested and/or others aiding him, etc., and (to express it in another way) be no more than was necessary to effect the arrest.

See also as to calling on public to assist—p. 103.

(3) To Take for Treatment

Applicable to some drunkenness offences

A constable who has power to A.W.W. for drunk and disorderly and simple drunkenness, may, by s. 34 of the C.J. Act 1972 take the person arrested to any place approved by the S.o.S. as a medical treatment centre for alcoholics. The person shall not, by this section, be liable to be detained but the exercise of this power by the police does not preclude the arrested person being charged with any offence.

CHAPTER VI

SUSPECTS AND PRISONERS

1. IDENTIFICATION OF SUSPECTS

NOTE: On this subject the case of *R.* v. *Turnbull and Others* (1976), and the guidance given by the Attorney General (July 1976) are very important; see Appendix 7.

In one sense all police work in investigating a crime is directed towards establishing the identity of the person who committed it. The present subject, however, is limited to the means by which identification might be achieved of a person:

(a) *Who was seen* committing a crime or in circumstances rendering him suspect (e.g. at scene or selling stolen property) *but not recognised*, or

(b) *From evidence left at or near scene* by, or probably by, the perpetrator.

1. *In the case of Witnesses* who saw but did not recognise:

   (1) *To effect an arrest* i.e. as a *suspect* by means of identification by:

      (a) *photographs.*

      (b) *corporal identification* (*informal*).

      (c) circulation of information, obtained from witnesses, in form of:

         (i) *"Identi-Kit" type likeness and/or*

         (ii) *personal description.*

   (2) *To effect identification of suspect in person* i.e. by a formal *identification parade.*

2. From *evidence left behind*:

   (1) *To effect*, or aid in effecting *an arrest*, i.e. identification or leads towards identification provided by "specialists":

      (a) *fingerprints*, etc.

      (b) other marks at scene, to which *scientific aids* might be applied.

      (c) criminal records—*Modus Operandi* section.

   (2) *To identify the suspect when found or after arrest*:

      (a) fingerprints, etc.

      (b) scientific aids.

N.B.—Of all these positive identification is afforded only by fingerprints.

Identification by Photograph

1. *When there is no suspect* it is the practice to allow witnesses to go through all available police photographs (no information of identity being revealed to them).
2. *Where there is a suspect* his photograph is put with others and the following procedure is advised:

(a) When an identification has been made, it is advisable, if there are other witnesses not to proceed with them, but to reserve them for the identification parade.

(b) The suspect's photograph should be shown among *at least eight others* of persons of similar appearance, age, colour.

(c) All photographs must be retained in case their production is required in court for it is customary for prosecution to inform defence if identification is made by photograph.

(d) The officer in charge of the case should not be concerned in these proceedings.

(e) The photographs should be placed on a table in front of the witness and no assistance given except in form of directions of what is to be done, and purpose.

(f) Prison authorities will furnish to the police on request suitable photographs, but only on the understanding that they will be shown to witnesses in such manner as to prevent them from knowing that they represent prisoners (e.g.—by concealing prison number at bottom).

There are two considerations which affect the use of photographs:

(a) The fact that a witness had seen a photograph of the accused prior to an identification parade, should be notified to the defence, who will probably use this to minimise the value of subsequent identification by parade.

(b) Evidence of identification by photograph raises an inference that accused has previous convictions, a factor which could well operate to the prejudice of the accused. (see *R.* v. *Wattam* (1942) later). For this reason reference to such identification is avoided unless defence brings it up.

R. v. *Goss* (1923)
Where corporal identification is not possible, because the accused is not under arrest the fair thing is to show a series of photographs. Once it has been decided to arrest a suspect (and after arrest) his photo must not be shown to any witness who is to identify him (e.g. at any identification parade). To do so is to destroy the value of the identification.

R. v. *Dwyer* (1925)
The constable should not show the photograph of the suspect alone, but mixed with others so as to make a kind of "identification parade" of photographs. It is the duty of the police to behave with exemplary fairness.

R. v. *Haslam* (1925)

If possible the prosecution should not mention the use of photographs to the jury, nor produce the photographs themselves. To do so would be a way of telling the jury that the prisoner had previously been convicted. If the prisoner elicits the matter of the photographs (e.g. by cross examination) evidence and production of them will become admissible, and so they should be available in court.

R. v. *Wattam* (1942)

Reference in evidence to photographs should not be made to the prejudice of the prisoner. If the photo of the accused was not a police photo, and/or it was clearly explained that the photos might be of respectable people, there would be no objection to evidence of it.

Informal Corporal Identification

Where the suspect is known to frequent a public place the opportunity for his identification, unknown to him or any other persons, may be used by taking the witness there for the purpose. This method has been favourably commented on in courts, e.g.—when accused is picked out from a queue or when leaving his place of work, or a cinema, etc. The fairness of the identification must be ensured. The accused must be told there and then that the identification has been made and the witness should be shown to him.

"Identi-kit".—This, and similar equipment, consists in the main of sets of separate drawings, all made on a transparent base. Each set deals with a feature of the head, hairline, face, etc., and contains variations on the same theme, each of a variety of outlines of shapes over a very wide range, from which a witness can, in expert hands, be expected to select the one approaching nearest to what his memory suggested. The transparencies enable the "selected" features to be superimposed on each other to build up the final picture, to which changes can easily be made to reach the result the witness accepts. "Identi-Kit" has to be used by officers trained for the job. It was introduced here from America.

Personal Descriptions.—The taking of particulars relating to personal description, and the reading of such particulars in police publications, is such a common feature of every-day police work that no more should be needed here than to advise students to memorise the main headings of the formula followed in the standard *Description Card*, on which it should be possible to answer any question on this subject. The headings are: (a) Personal descriptions; (b) Peculiarities; (c) Personal habits, and (d) Dress.

Identification Parades

It is the practice in some forces to photograph a parade before proceedings start.

1. *Venue*

(a) A well lighted room with at least two doors (entrance & exit) should be chosen, or three rooms for (1) witnesses before (2) parade room and (3) witnesses after.

(b) A constable to be posted at each door of parade room to prevent any contact between or with witnesses.

2. *Members Forming the Parade*

(a) *Eight or more persons* as similar as possible to the subject in size, build, age and station in life. If two suspects of roughly similar appearance, they may be paraded together with at *least twelve other persons*. Where more than two suspects, or if the two suspects are not of similar appearance, separate parades should be held using different persons on each parade. No police officer should be a member of a parade.

(b) Cancel possibility of deformity aiding identification by best means available, e.g.—accused with one eye—all wear eye pads.

(c) Must not be made aware of the suspect's identity, and care taken to avoid this happening otherwise than by accused's own conduct.

3. *The Accused's Rights*

Suspect must be told that his identity will not be disclosed and of his "rights", namely:

(a) He cannot be compelled to take part.
(b) He can select his own position in the parade at the start and change it, if he wishes, after each witness has left.
(c) He can object to any person paraded with him or to any of the arrangements made.
(d) He can have a solicitor or friend present.

NOTE: Make record of complaint and remedy as well as of changes in position. Advisable to give suspect a copy of the above rights to read beforehand and also to "friend" appearing for him.

4. *The Witnesses*

(a) Must not be allowed to see the accused before the parade.

(b) Must be taken before the parade one at a time.

(c) Must not be told anything about the accused or his identity.

(d) Must not be given any assistance to identify the accused e.g.—by means of photograph, description, etc.

(e) Must in turn be instructed by the officer in charge of the parade, loud enough for all in room to hear, as to correct procedure to indicate identification, i.e. to touch the person and say "This is the man", but a child victim of a sexual assault who prefers not to touch the person, may be allowed to "point out". Everything said by any witness and the accused should be noted.

(f) Must not be told that person "touched" is or is not the suspect.

(g) Who have attended the parade and those awaiting must be kept apart with no means of inter-communication. The officer in charge must be prepared to testify on this.

(h) Who desire to see the prisoner walk or with hat on or off, or hear him speak or say any specified phrase. There is no objection to each member of the parade in turn being asked to comply. Such an occurrence must be reported on.

2. THE JUDGES' RULES

This subject should be studied well. It is undoubtedly one of the most important relating to police procedure. Police officers are expected to know the Rules thoroughly and to act in accordance with them.

History and Object of the Rules

The Rules resulted from the Law that a confession is not admissible in evidence unless made freely and voluntarily, and that it will not be deemed to have been made freely or voluntarily if there was any degree of coercion or inducement from a person in authority.

That a confession or statement was freely made is for the prosecution to prove. If made to a police officer (regarded as a person in authority) special care has to be taken to avoid allegations of compulsion, oppression or persuasion, all of which are so easy to make and so difficult to rebut, particularly in the case of a person in police custody. It was as a result of this difficulty that the Judges' Rules were first formulated in 1912 with regard to the questioning, cautioning, and the taking of statements from persons suspected of crime or in police custody on a criminal charge. In 1964 the old Rules were replaced by new ones approved by the Judges of the Q.B.D. and these are now applicable.

The Rules are not statutory but they have, in effect, the force of law because they are rigidly applied by the Courts.

Taken together, the Rules act as a guide to both police and magistrates, and have the following objects:

1. To standardise procedure in all Forces and for all Courts.
2. To afford safeguard to the police who act in accordance with the rules.
3. To protect a prisoner from improper action and to ensure that statements made by prisoners are voluntarily given.

The Rules

It is important to remember that the rules apply to any offence, i.e. summary or indictable.

Rule 1

When a police officer is trying to discover whether, or by whom, an offence has been committed he is entitled to question any person, whether suspected or not, from whom he thinks that useful information may be obtained. This is so whether or not the person in question has been taken into custody so long as he has not been charged with the offence or informed that he may be prosecuted for it.

This rule upholds the common law principle that every citizen has a duty to help a police officer to discover and arrest offenders. It entitles the free questioning of any person whether or not he has been taken into custody so long as he has not been charged with the offence or told that he may be prosecuted for it. It enables questions to be asked about crimes other than the crime for which the prisoner is in custody and the only limit to such free questioning is provided by the next rule.

R. v. *Buckham* (1964)

It is permissible to question a person in custody, in regard to other offences.

R. v. *Bass* (1953)

Where two or more officers are present at the same interview there is no objection in law to their consulting together when preparing their notes of the interview. A note should be included in the officers' notebooks where this has been done.

R. v. *Brackenbury* (1965)

Arrest on suspicion of committing an offence is normally made by the police officer before he has enough evidence to prefer a charge. Where this applies Rule 1 does not preclude him from questioning the prisoner about that offence until he has enough evidence to prefer the charge.

R. v. *Osborne* (1973)

A police officer is not bound to caution until he has some information that he can put before the court as the beginnings of a case. Also applied in *Walmsley* v. *Young* (1974).

Rule 2

As soon as a police officer has evidence which would afford reasonable grounds for suspecting that a person has committed an offence, he shall caution that person or cause him to be cautioned before putting to him any questions, or further questions, relating to that offence.

The caution shall be in the following terms:

"You are not obliged to say anything unless you wish to do so but what you say may be put into writing and given in evidence."

When after being cautioned a person is being questioned, or elects to make a statement, a record shall be kept of the time and place at which any such questioning or statement began and ended and of the persons present.

A person is deemed to be in custody immediately he is told that he is to be arrested, but this does not preclude questioning him in accordance with the rule. Though it would appear that the constable alone can say when he has evidence for suspecting that a person has committed an offence so as to make a caution necessary, this is not so in practice for in those cases where this rule has not been followed the nature of the answers given must necessarily reveal a point at which the reasonable reaction must have been to caution before proceeding to question further, or even to decide to charge him with the offence.

Care should be taken not to suggest that a suspect's answers to questions can only be used in evidence against him, so as to prevent an innocent person making a statement which might help to clear him of any charge.

> *R.* v. *Prager* (1971)
>
> The non-observance of Rule 2 (caution) might lead to the exclusion of a confession, but this depends on the judge's decision as to whether, breach or no breach of the rule, it has been shown to have been made voluntarily. If so, and there is no valid criticism of the means by which the confession was obtained, the failure to caution can be disregarded.
>
> (*Note.* This case seriously impinges on the legal weight of this Rule—particularly on the decision in *R.* v. *Voisin* (1918) in which it was held that the judge had a discretion to exclude a confession, though voluntary and legally admissible, if the Judges' Rules were not complied with.)

Rule 3

(a) *Where a person is charged with or informed that he may be prosecuted for an offence he shall be cautioned in the following terms:*

> "Do you wish to say anything. You are not obliged to say anything unless you wish to do so but whatever you say will be taken down in writing and may be given in evidence."

(b) *It is only in exceptional cases that questions relating to the offence should be put to the accused person after he has been charged or informed that he may be prosecuted. Such questions may be put where they are necessary for the purpose of preventing or minimising harm or loss to some other person or to the public or for clearing up an ambiguity in a previous answer or statement. Before any such questions are put the accused should be cautioned in these terms:*

> "I wish to put some questions to you about the offence with which you have been charged (or about the offence for which

you may be prosecuted). You are not obliged to answer any of these questions, but if you do the questions and answers will be taken down in writing and may be given in evidence."

R. v. *Collier and Stenning* (1965)
The words in Rule 3 "or informed that he may be prosecuted" apply when during questioning, the suspect is told that he may be prosecuted (i.e. the facts reported by the officer for summons) instead of being arrested for the offence.

Any questions put and answers given relating to the offence must be contemporaneously recorded in full and the record signed by that person or if he refuses by the interrogating officer.

(c) *When such a person is being questioned, or elects to make a statement, a record shall be kept of the time and place at which any questioning or statement began and ended and of the persons present.*

NOTE: Rules 2 and 3 emphasise the need for keeping records of times and places of questioning or taking statements, and all persons who are present. The entries should be made in the police officer's notebook for convenience and is a routine duty which should present no difficulty. In addition a record must also be kept of the times that:

(i) any caution was administered,
(ii) the arrest was made,
(iii) the person was charged,
(iv) intervals were taken during questioning or the making of a statement, including periods for and the nature of refreshments taken.

Rule 4

All written statements made after caution shall be taken in the following manner:

(a) *If a person says that he wants to make a statement he shall be told that it is intended to make a written record of what he says. He shall always be asked whether he wishes to write down himself what he wants to say, if he says that he cannot write or that he would like someone to write it for him, a police officer may offer to write the statement for him, if he accepts the offer the police officer shall before starting, ask the person making the statement to sign, or make his mark to the following:*

"I, ..., wish to make a statement. I want someone to write down what I say. I have been told that I need not say anything unless I wish to do so and that whatever I say may be given in evidence."

(b) *The person writing his own statement shall be allowed to do so without any prompting as distinct from indicating to him what matters are material.*

(c) *The person making the statement, if he is going to write it himself, shall be asked to write out and sign before writing what he wants to say, the following*:

> "I make this statement of my own free will. I have been told I need not say anything unless I wish to do so and that whatever I say may be given in evidence."

(d) *Whenever a police officer writes the statement, he shall take down the exact words spoken by the person making the statement without putting any questions other than such as may be needed to make the statement coherent, intelligible and relevant to the material matters. He shall not prompt him.*

(e) *When the writing of a statement by a police officer is finished, the person making it shall be asked to read it and to make any corrections, alterations or additions he wishes. When he has finished reading it he shall be asked to write and sign or make his mark on the following certificate at the end of the statement*:

> "I have read the above statement and I have been told that I can correct, alter or add anything I wish. This statement is true. I have made it of my own free will."

(f) *If the person who has made a statement refuses to read it or to write the above mentioned certificate at the end of it or to sign it, the senior police officer present shall record on the statement itself, and in the presence of the person making it, what has happened. If the person making the statement cannot read, or refuses to read it, the police officer who has taken it down shall read it over to him and ask him whether he would like to correct, alter or add anything and to put his signature or make his mark at the end. The police officer shall then certify on the statement itself what he has done.*

The statement must be made without fear of prejudice or hope of advantage, and the word "wishes" is *not* intended to mean "agrees" or "is willing" for any reason. It is important that the exact wording of the various cautions should be used.

> *R.* v. *Zaveckas* (1970)
>
> To the question "If I make a statement will you give me bail now?" constable replied "Yes". Though inducement was not held out by the constable, but the result of a query by the accused, this was an inducement and the statement rendered inadmissible.
>
> *R.* v. *Middleton* (1974)
>
> M. admitted a crime of "handling" after he had been told by police that the wife of the man he was "assisting" would be kept in custody and her children put into care. The confession was held inadmissible in this case even though the threat was not to M. or his family.

Rule 5

If at any time after a person has been charged with, or has been informed that he may be prosecuted for an offence a police officer wishes to bring to the notice of that person any written statement made by another person who in respect of the same offence has also been charged or informed that he may be prosecuted he shall hand to that person a true copy of such written statement, but nothing shall be said or done to invite any reply or comment. If that person says that he would like to make a statement in reply, or starts to say something, he shall at once be cautioned or further cautioned as prescribed by Rule 3 (a).

This rule enables a police officer to exercise his discretion whether or not to serve a copy of an accused's statement upon another person or persons charged or likely to be charged with the same offence. It is emphasized that the procedure is only necessary where the investigating officer wishes it (usually to further the investigation) and such statements can be served before a charge is preferred.

Rule 6

Persons other than police officers charged with the duty of investigating offences or charging offenders shall, so far as may be practicable comply with these rules.

Note that this relates to persons not being police officers investigating crimes as a duty, e.g. Post Office investigators and others.

Administrative Directions on Interrogation and the taking of Statements

Published at the same time as the new Judges' Rules were directions under the above heading also approved by the Judges. The following is a summary of them.

1. *Procedure generally*:

(a) For statements under caution *use forms provided* for this. Do not use notebook unless no other suitable means available.

(b) Keep record of times of intervals or refreshment, if any. Note nature of refreshment. No alcohol.

(c) Do not use "official" vocabulary. May give misleading impression of genuineness of statement.

(d) Avoid suggestion that answers can only be used against person, for it might deter innocent person from attempting to clear himself.

2. *Record of interrogation*.—In addition to records required by Rules 2 and 3 as to times and places of questioning and of taking statements and persons present, it is advisable to keep following record as well:

(a) time or times cautions given,

(b) time charge was made and/or person arrested, and

(c) as in 1 (b) above.

If two or more police officers are present get records countersigned by them.

3. *Comfort and refreshment of persons interrogated, etc.*—Reasonable arrangements to be made, and wherever practicable the person questioned or making the statement (and the police officer) to be seated.

4. *Interrogation of young persons* (under 17 years of age).—Whether as suspect or witness, interview, as far as practicable, only in presence of parent or guardian, or some person not a police officer and of same sex as the child, or young person. Not to be arrested or interviewed at school, if this can be avoided, but when essential should be done only with consent and in presence of head teacher, or his nominee.

5. *Foreigners, making statement in own language*:

(a) Interpreter to take down statement in language in which made.

(b) Official translation to be made and proved as an exhibit with the original.

(c) Foreigner should sign statement made as at (a).

It might be unfair to obtain signature to the translation, which, in any case, is of little evidential value if he later disputes accuracy of it.

6. *Written statement of charge.*—In cases of arrest without warrant, when charge is accepted:

(a) give accused written notice of charge, which should:

(i) be in simple language, and

(ii) specify precise offence (if statutory, quote Act and section)

(iii) commence with a form of caution.

(b) if further charge (or modified one) to be made before court appearance:

(i) do it as soon as practicable, and

(ii) give appropriate written notice at same time.

NOTE: in connexion with (b) (i), in cases of difficulty (e.g. on bail) it will be sufficient if the accused is further charged and given notice on surrender to bail and before court.

7. *Facilities for defence—persons in custody.*

Telephone—allow use of to contact solicitor or friends if not reasonably likely to hinder investigation or administration of justice.

Telegram—to be sent at once at his expense.

Letters—supply with writing materials at request, and send by post or otherwise without undue delay.

NOTE: It has been suggested that this provision imposes an absolute requirement to supply writing materials to a person in custody and to send any letters and telegrams he might prepare. The Home Secretary after consulting with the Lord Chief Justice, has indicated that the sending of telegrams and letters should be subject to the same proviso as telephone calls with the person's friends or solicitor. Writing materials should be supplied on request but the sending of letters or telegrams should be subject to the proviso that no hindrance is reasonably likely to be caused to the processes of the investigation or the administration of justice.

Rights—to be informed orally of rights and of facilities available. Notices regarding these to be displayed at convenient and conspicuous places at the police station *and* attention drawn to them.

3. MODE OF ARREST AND HANDLING OF PRISONERS

As to separation of juveniles from adult offenders, see p. 187.

(1) The Arrest

General Principle.—The law does not deal specifically with the manner in which an arrest shall be made, although it provides powers to facilitate an arrest (e.g. to enter premises, to use force and to call for assistance). The general principle is the negative one that a constable must not do anything that cannot be justified by law, e.g. use unnecessary force. The nearest approach to positive directions on this matter come from two sources, both concerned, generally speaking, with the rights of the persons being arrested, *viz:*

(a) *The Judges' Rules* (dealt with on pp. 94–101, *ante*) and

(b) *The case of Christie* v. *Leachinsky* (1947) from which the following principles emerged:

(1) Every person arrested (whether on warrant or not) should be informed of the grounds for his arrest, and after caution, his reply, if any, noted.

(2) If the person is not told the true grounds for his arrest at the time, the arresting officer may be liable for false imprisonment.

(3) The requirement in (1) does not apply if the circumstances are such that the person must know the general nature of the alleged offence for which he is arrested.

(4) Technical or precise language need not be used by the arresting officer if he states in substance the reason why he is making the arrest.

(5) The arrested person cannot complain that he has not been informed of the reason for his arrest, when he himself produced the situation which made it not practicable to inform him, e.g.—a violent or disorderly prisoner.

(6) These principles apply equally to private persons who arrest on suspicion.

Christie v. *Leachinsky* (1947)
Also directed that the charge on which the arrest was made must be preferred though there may be additional charges.

R. v. *Kulynycz* (1970)
The detention of a person improperly arrested because he was not informed of the true ground for arrest may be subsequently rendered lawful when (and from that time) he is told of that ground.

(2) The Use of Force

Force may be used if not greater than necessary for the purpose. In exceptional cases only, extreme force might be justified even if death results, but the crime must be a serious one and extreme force must have been the only course open to the constable after all other practical means had been tried and found to be insufficient. The order should be to begin without show of force, then threatened force if resistance is shown, and only then, if necessary, use such force (and no more) as may be needed, in proportion to the resistance offered. Getting assistance even by waiting for it (if practicable) is better than use of extreme force.

(3) Transport

The question of the use of motor transport is one which has always to be considered, not only when an arrest has to be made but also in the case of the conveyance to the station of a person arrested, for the conducting of an arrested person through public places is to be avoided, so far as is practicable. There will be many cases where use of transport may be impracticable after an arrest without warrant, but in other cases criticism can be expected of any unnecessary handling of prisoners in public view. (See next paragraph and "handcuffs" below).

(4) Members of H.M. Forces

Prisoners in uniform of the Navy, Marines, Army or Air Force, should not, when in custody of the police, be marched through the streets, but should be conveyed by official transport, taxi or other closed vehicle.

(5) Illness of Prisoners

Special care must be taken of prisoners who are or may be ill. Undue risk should not be taken by neglecting to call a doctor or to take the prisoner to the nearest hospital for an immediate check. If a prisoner is unconscious, always do this.

A report should be submitted to the court in the case of persons seriously ill or physically unfit for prison, e.g. pregnant women and persons suffering from serious complaints. The Home Secretary advises a written notification to prison authorities whenever a prisoner appears to be ill when charged at Court, or when his arrest was effected at a hospital.

(6) Assistance by the Public

If a constable in face of resistance requires assistance to effect an arrest, he may call on bystanders "*In the name of the law*" to assist him and they are under a legal obligation to do so. If any such person refuses, he may commit an offence if the conditions indicated below exist. No more should be asked than to subdue and keep subdued, and to send then for transport.

N.B.—Duty of private citizens to assist the Police to arrest or in the execution of duty.—The refusal by a private citizen (when called upon) to assist the police when physical assistance is needed to effect the execution of his duty, e.g. to make an arrest, or quell disorder is a common law offence. It has to be proved that:

1. *There was reasonable necessity for calling on the defendant for assistance.*
2. *When called to assist the defendant refused.*
3. *The defendant had no lawful excuse, nor any physical incapacity.*

Rewards.—In the case of certain crimes (e.g. murder, serious woundings, procuring the miscarriage of any women, rape, burglary, robbery, arson, cattle and sheep stealing, or procuring the same to be done, etc.) a private person who actively assisted in the arrest of the offender may be rewarded by a Judge of the Crown Court and compensated for his expenses, loss of time and for the display of extraordinary diligence or exertion. (Criminal Law Act 1826, s. 28.)

(7) Use of "Appointments"

(a) *The Whistle.*—The use of the whistle needs no comment.

(b) *The Staff.*—This is to be used in extreme cases only, e.g.—when likely to be overpowered by a prisoner or in defence against superior force, technically as a last resort. It should never be displayed unnecessarily. The aim should be to disable without causing serious bodily harm. The fact that the staff was used should be stated in evidence.

(c) *The Handcuffs.*—Handcuffing cannot be justified unless there are special reasons, e.g. likely to abscond or of violent nature, and should be done as unobtrusively as possible.

N.B.—A handcuffed prisoner should not be conveyed in public vehicles. A taxi or private car should be used if a police vehicle is not available.

> *Wright* v. *Court* (1825)
> The right of handcuffing must depend on the nature of the charge and the conduct and temper of the person in custody, and should not be resorted to unless there is fair ground for supposing that violence may be used or an escape attempted. Handcuffing cannot be justified unless it is made to appear there are good special reasons for resorting to it.

(8) Medical Examinations

Often desirable in interests of prisoner, e.g. in charges of a sexual nature, but may be proposed in other cases in search for evidence. In any case can only be made with consent, otherwise it would be an assault. Always record (a) fact of consent or refusal, and (b) the offer (which should be made) to get doctor to represent prisoner as well as the police doctor, and whether this was accepted or refused. Officer may be required to prove consent at later trial.

When consent given, examination to be arranged as quickly as possible. The police doctor to record result of examination in writing and be notified when and where required to testify. (Procedure in connection with drink/driving offences is dealt with in Handbook on *Road Traffic Law and Practice*). For treatment for illness see "Prisoners' Rights", p. 109.

4. SEARCH OF SUSPECTS AND PRISONERS

(1) Suspects

No legal right.—Whatever risks may sometimes be taken, or have to be taken, in the performance of police duties in this direction there exists *no legal right to search a suspect* (or a container or bag with him) without his consent until he has been arrested on a specific charge. The refusal to submit to a search (in circumstances where it would not be unreasonable to expect compliance on the part of an innocent person) may add to the suspicion already existing so as to make it "reasonable" and justify an arrest which can be made on that ground for an arrestable offence. It must also be added that the "risk" attending an unauthorised search can vary from very great to almost negligible according to the circumstances attending it, but no police officer should be unaware of the legal position.

(2) Prisoners: On Arrest

Right of Search.—The right to search a prisoner has long been accepted by the courts, generally on the grounds that it is or may be necessary on one or other, or both of the following grounds:

(1) *The protection of the prisoner, those responsible for his safe custody and as a safeguard against damage or injury to person or property.*

(2) *For the purpose of obtaining and preserving evidence in connection with the crime for which he has been arrested.*

There may, exceptionally, be a need for an immediate search (e.g. suspected possession of firearm) but the general rule is that *a search is better done at the police station,* where there will be privacy, corroboration, less danger of escape and opportunity for search to be made by another officer,

But (a) vigilance is always needed, greater or less according to charge, to ensure prisoner gets rid of nothing before search.

(b) A "look around" the scene is advisable to ensure that nothing of evidential value is being left there, where it is not unlikely that such may be found.

(c) If transport used to convey prisoner—a search of this is also advisable at journey's end.

(3) Prisoners: At the Station

General Rule.—Generally every prisoner who is to be placed in the cells should be searched, as well as those on whom evidence of the charge might be found, but otherwise there is no justification for searching persons being detained, e.g. for failing to answer summons to court or non-payment of fine.

General Principles

(1) Where search is justified it should be made as soon after arrest as possible.

(2) Female to be searched only by a woman, but male officer should be near at hand, though not present.

(3) Search should be made, when evidence may be found, by an officer not in the case, but the arresting officer should be present.

(4) Prisoner should first be asked to "lay out" everything in his clothing or on his person, then asked to ensure that nothing has been overlooked (something found afterwards on search acquires a significance it might not otherwise have had).

(5) Thorough searching should be habitual, as a matter of practice, though the particular case might not demand it.

(6) Search should also be made of property in possession e.g. wallet, case, motorcar.

(7) When two or more prisoners are to be searched it would be done one at a time, and apart from each other.

(8) Consideration has always to be given to the advisability of extending search (in appropriate cases) to the home or lodgings of prisoner, with his consent or a warrant, or written authority to search from Superintendent, (see p. 75)

Records of property found on prisoner or elsewhere

All such property is to be recorded in detail in constable's notebook and the appropriate station records. Property so found is classified and recorded under two headings, i.e.:

(1) *Property subject to charge.*—I.e. all property which is of evidential nature and has to be referred to in evidence. It has, where practicable, to be returned later to the person entitled to it, i.e. owner, loser, or in accordance with order of the court or Police (Property) Act 1897 or the Police (Disposal of Property) Regns. 1975 (see p. 242). The safe custody of this property for production in court is the responsibility of the officer in charge of the case.

(2) *Personal Property.*—i.e. everything other than that recorded as (1) above. It must be itemised and checked in presence of prisoner, and returned to him if he is released on bail or otherwise released from custody. If prisoner is sent to prison it must accompany him and be recorded on the *body receipt* which is signed at the prison.

NOTE: All cash must go to prison, unless special reason otherwise, e.g. good reason to believe it to be proceeds of sale of stolen property.

Leigh v. *Cole* (1853)

Whatever the nature of the charge, a prisoner may be searched who has conducted himself by reason of violence language or conduct, as to render it prudent and right to do as well for his own safety as that of the constable.

Agnew v. *Jobson* (1877) & *Turnbull* v. *Barnett* (1931)

A prisoner may be searched where it is likely that there are on him tools connected with the type of offence he has been alleged to have committed, or other similar articles which may be useful evidence against him.

Bessell v. *Wilson* (1853)

A prisoner may be searched where it is likely that there are on him stolen articles, or instruments of violence.

Latter v. *Braddell* (1881)

The right to search does not include the right to examine the private person of a prisoner (written consent should be obtained when this is done by a doctor).

Elias v. *Pasmore* (1934)

Held, that the police may take all articles which are in the possession or under the control of a person arrested and are material on a charge against the prisoner or any other person. If in a search which might have been improper originally there were matters discovered which showed the complicity of the prisoner in a crime, then the officers would be excused by the result of the search but not justified.

5. CHARGING OF PRISONERS

(1) Acceptance of Charge

As soon as possible after an arrest without warrant the facts of the case must be reported to the officer in charge of the police station for the time being. It is often the practice for the facts of the report to be recited in the presence and hearing of the accused. After consideration of the evidence available, the officer in charge has to make decision on one of three possible courses, viz.:

To refuse the charge.—Evidence not being considered sufficient to sustain the charge. Entry to be made in station record of the charge on which the arrest was made, and the grounds for its refusal. The prisoner must be released without delay with an explanation of the reason.

To delay the charge.—If it appears to the officer in charge that the arrest was justified but that further enquiry is needed and cannot be completed forthwith the prisoner may be released on bail to appear at the police station at a specified time and date later, unless notified in the meantime in writing that his presence is no longer so required. This procedure is often referred to as "Delayed Charge" or "Deferred Charge". (M.C. Act 1952, s. 38). See further on p. 112.

To accept the charge.—When the charge is accepted it must be correctly formulated, and contain a reference to the Act and Section creating the offence.

(2) Charging the Prisoner

The following is the correct procedure:

(a) Usually by the arresting officer, and in presence of officer in charge of the station.

(b) Prepare beforehand the notice of charge to be given to prisoner (see "Judges' Rules", p. 100, *ante*).

(c) Tell prisoner of what is about to take place, and advise him not to say anything until formality, including caution, is concluded.

(d) Charge prisoner by reading it to him (from notice or charge-book) and if necessary explaining it in simple terms, then caution and note (in pocket book) any reply made.

(e) If more than one charge, charge, caution and note reply for each one in turn.

The above procedure with regard to giving written notice, as well as that relating to any modification or amendment of the charge, or the preferring of any additional charge is regulated by the directions from the Home Office approved by H.M. Judges. If the decision to amend or add a charge is reached while the accused is in custody, then he should be charged and given the notice in respect of the new charges, but after release it is a question of getting summonses served or, if there is not sufficient time for this, charging and giving the notice when he surrenders to his bail, and before he appears before the court, in which case the court can and probably would adjourn proceedings on his complaint of lack of notice.

> *Hall* v. *R.* (1971)
> A defendant is under no obligation to comment when informed that he is accused of an offence. Silence of itself does not provide an inference that the accused accepted the truth of what is alleged against him, though exceptional circumstances may justify such an inference.

(3) Arrest on Warrant for an Offence

The procedure on taking a person into custody on a warrant is similar to that of arrest without warrant, i.e. a reading of the warrant, an explanation in simple terms, and the administering of the appropriate caution. The formal charging and cautioning comes later at the police station and is carried out by the officer in charge of the case if latter is a local one, or by the officer who arrives to take custody of him (as escort) if he is to be taken to a court elsewhere.

(4) Prisoners in Cells

Not all prisoners are placed in cells. The decision on this point is one for the officer in charge of the station and is dependant upon the nature of the case, whether bail is to be given, and the length of time of probable detention. If a prisoner is placed in a cell, the following general principles apply:

(a) The appropriate station record is to be made of the fact, as well as of times of supervisory visits, meals and visitors.

(b) A female prisoner must be lodged in the cell used for females, supervised by a female.

(c) precautions may be necessary in the case of some prisoners, e.g. removal of laces, braces, ties, or even boots.

(d) the frequency of visits of inspection (mainly casual but occasionally for greater reassurance) will be governed by local force instructions, as well as circumstances of the case.

See also, "Prisoners' Rights" below.

6. PRISONERS' RIGHTS, ETC.

Police officers responsible for the custody of prisoners must take care to assist so far as is practicable in the exercise by prisoners of any of their "accepted rights", and these should be distinguished from the facilities or privileges which prisoners may claim or request, but on which the officer in charge has to exercise discretion according to the circumstances of particular cases. On this subject the directions issued by the Home Office and approved by H.M. Judges, advise that *persons in custody should not only be told of their rights and facilities available, but that notices of them should be displayed at convenient and conspicuous places at police stations, and the attention of such persons should be drawn to them.*

Rights with a Legal Foundation

Some rights have a *legal foundation*, i.e. they refer to, or are based on, legal principles, e.g.:

(1) *Bail.*—The right to bail (or otherwise) should be explained, and steps taken, including aiding the prisoner where needed (e.g. to get a surety), to secure release on bail as soon as practicable, if bail is being allowed.

(2) *Legal Aid.*—A Home Office circular recommends that leaflets giving information about legal aid and explaining the contribution scheme should be given to defendants in cases where it is desirable in the interests of justice that they should be legally represented. Such leaflets are generally available at police stations for issue to prisoners, or to persons enquiring. If not, the prisoner (or person enquiring) should be given the broad outline as to the availability of legal aid (as given below) and advised to pursue enquiries in this respect with the justices' clerk. Any person may apply for and be granted legal assistance if he is brought, or being brought, or is appearing before a criminal court for an offence, or to be dealt with (e.g. for breach of recognisance) or to pursue an appeal, or to resist an appeal. Application has to be made on the appropriate form to the justices' clerk or made orally to the court. A legal aid order cannot be granted unless the statement of means of the applicant (made by the applicant on a prescribed form) has been taken into consideration. See also p. 101 as to facilities for defence in relation to persons in custody.

(3) *Right to Object to certain Procedures.*—The following procedures may be objected to:

(a) *Examination or Test.* No person can be subjected to a physical examination or test without his consent, and where the matter arises, this should be explained. If agreed to, he should be told of his right to have present a representative of his own (e.g. in medical examination a doctor, or in identification parade a legal representative or friend).

(b) *Taking of fingerprints, etc.* The explanation of his right to refuse should be extended to include reference to the power of the court to order fingerprints to be taken by force, if this applies (see p. 226).

(c) *Cleansing of verminous prisoner.* A filthy and verminous prisoner should, if practicable, be taken to a cleansing centre if his condition is likely to be a nuisance to the public, or if he is to be taken anywhere in a public conveyance (e.g. to court or to prison). The local authority should be able to co-operate in supplying cleansing facilities, but the prisoner must remain all the time in police custody. If prisoner refuses to comply application may be made to the court for an order for forcible cleaning under s. 85 of the Public Health Act 1936.

Rights with semi-legal Foundation

Other rights have a *semi-legal foundation,* being founded on official rules of guidance not having force of law.

(1) *Communications.*—The question of directions (approved by H.M. judges) relating to the facilities which should be provided for the purposes of the prisoner's defence involving the use of telephone, sending of telegrams or letters, and the supply of writing materials has already been discussed (see p. 101). In addition to this it should be borne in mind that:

(i) the fact of arrest should be communicated on request to any person closely connected with prisoner, unless good reason to contrary, and always done (on request or not) in case of a juvenile prisoner, i.e. to parent or guardian.

(ii) interviews should be allowed for purposes of defence, and also, if reasonable and no good reason to contrary, visits by relatives and friends. With regard to interviews and visits care has to be taken to maintain supervision and yet afford reasonable privacy. General rule should be one visitor at a time, reasonable time allowed, and in presence and (except defence solicitor) hearing as well. Note anything said likely to affect course of justice.

(2) *Medical examination for defence.*—Where physical condition is in issue (e.g. influence of drink) or examination might reveal evidence for defence, the prisoner has a right to be afforded facilities for examination (for procedure advised in such cases, see page 104).

(3) *Medical treatment.*—Special care is needed in case of prisoners suffering from (or showing symptoms of) an illness. In all cases doctor should be called and his advice followed, e.g.

as to means of transport, hospital treatment. Special care is needed to avoid the unnecessary committal to prison of persons physically unfit, e.g. pregnant women and persons suffering from illnesses likely soon to end fatally, and in such cases medical evidence on this should be available for the court before which he or she is brought. Information of such medical history should be given to prison authorities *in writing*.

(4) *Aliens.*—Should be allowed to communicate (telephone, telegram, post) with embassy, consulate or legation, and facilities provided. Some countries have required notification by police of detention of any of their nationals (Norway, Sweden, U.S.A., France, Greece, Mexico), and this should be done by quickest means to the nearest place, and facilities for visits provided.

The Demands of Ordinary Welfare

The remaining rights are governed by demands of *ordinary welfare* which need no more than a mention, e.g.:

(a) Meals (three per day, and prisoners can be allowed to purchase own meals, or receive meals supplied from outside).
(b) Ablution and toilet facilities.
(c) Ordinary creature comforts, e.g. warmth and light, and opportunity for exercise in case of protracted detention, as well as any other requested amenity if it appears reasonable, and there is no good reason to contrary, e.g. the purchase of books, magazines, newspapers and smoking requisites. Smoking can be permitted at discretion of officer in charge, and should not be unreasonably denied, although the prisoner should not normally be allowed to have matches with him in a cell, nor smoke there except under supervision.

7. BAIL

Definition.—Bail is a bond or recognisance taken by an authorised person to ensure the attendance of an accused person at an appointed place and time to answer the charge made against him.

Bail (with or without sureties) may be granted:

(1) *by the police.*
(2) *by a court.*

R. v. *Harrow JJ. ex p. Morris* (1972)
There is no authority under which justices (or the police) can require a surety to put down additional security as part of bail (i.e. to put up the money). Bail is a promise to pay.

(1) Bail by the Police

This is given by the Officer in charge of the station or of rank of Inspector or above.

(a) *If Arrested on Warrant* (M.C. Act 1952, s. 93)

No bail by police except:

(i) *When warrant is backed for bail* by issuing justice—bail only in accordance with endorsement.

(ii) *When prisoner is under* 17 *years*—see p. 185.

(b) *If Arrested without Warrant* (M.C. Act 1952, s. 38)

Bail can be granted when an arrest is made without warrant, in the following circumstances:

(i) *After charge.*—If prisoner of or over 17 years of age cannot be brought before court *within* 24 *hours* of arrest the officer in charge of the station (or an inspector or above) *must* enquire into case *and bail* unless good reason otherwise.

(ii) *When charge delayed.*—because it cannot be made until further enquiries have been made, which cannot be completed in reasonable time. Prisoner may be bailed to report back at *police station* at fixed time and date *unless* notified in writing that such attendance is not required.

(iii) *Young persons* (*under* 17).—See p. 185.

(iv) *For offences* (1st schedule of C. & Y.P. Act 1933) *committed against children and young persons.*—An offender *must* be released on bail (with or without sureties), unless his release would:

(a) defeat the ends of justice.

(b) cause injury or danger to the victim of the offence.

(2) Bail by Court

This will occur on *remand* or *committal* for trial. A Magistrates' Court may adjourn the trial or hearing of a case and procure the re-appearance of the accused by remanding him, either in custody (which can be in *police cells* if for not more than 3 days or 24 hours if under 17) or on bail. (See Remand, p. 143).

Objection to bail.—Where an objection is to be made to an application by or on behalf of an accused, consideration has to be given to grounds on which it might be based, e.g.:

(a) The nature and gravity of the charge and the weight of the evidence to support it.

(b) Reasonable grounds to believe that the accused will not surrender to his bail.

(c) That his release would defeat the ends of justice, e.g. danger of interference with witnesses or enquiries to be made.

(d) Whether his release would expose the accused or other persons to danger (e.g.—threat of revenge, etc.).

(e) The likelihood of the accused committing further similar offences whilst at liberty on bail (e.g. danger in respect of the child or young person concerned).

(f) Whether the proposed sureties are likely to have been indemnified by the accused.

(g) Previous convictions, but any magistrate to whom a conviction is revealed in considering whether to bail or not is prohibited from sitting as a justice at his summary trial, including a summary trial arising from proceedings which commenced as committal proceedings (C.J.A. 1967, s. 19).

R. v. *Dyson* (1943)
The Court pointed out that the Justices were entitled if not actually bound to hear evidence of previous convictions when considering whether committal should be in custody or on bail, but advised that when such evidence is given in court, it should be submitted in writing instead of being recited viva voce as there is always the risk that the convictions may become known to the trial jury and prejudice the case against the prisoner.

R. v. *Phillips* (1946)
Nine housebreakings were committed by prisoner during his committal for trial on bail. He had numerous previous convictions for breaking offences. The court said that the test to be applied when considering whether or not to admit an accused person to bail is whether he will appear to stand his trial. The Justices should also refuse bail if the accused is charged with a serious offence such as housebreaking and does not dispute his guilt, and it appears probable that the offences will be repeated if the accused is released.

R. v. *Armstrong* (1951)
Held that it is the duty of the Justices to enquire into the antecedents of a man who is applying to them for bail, and that it is undesirable that a newspaper should disclose such evidence but such publication by itself is not a ground for quashing a conviction.

R. v. *Wharton* (1955)
'W' was sentenced to 5 years imprisonment for robbery, which he committed while on bail in respect of an earlier offence. Leave to appeal against his conviction was refused. Upholding refusal of leave to appeal, the Court said that it had advised over and over again that unless the Justices felt real doubt as to the result of the case, men with bad criminal records should not be granted bail. It was no kindness to the prisoner to do so, as he now had to serve 5 years imprisonment in addition to his sentence for the original offence, as well as the fact that somebody had been robbed and assaulted.

Ex p. Thomas (1956)

Bail is not usually allowed on charges of murder save where the facts point to a verdict of justifiable homicide.

Limitations on Magistrate's Refusal to Grant Bail

The general rule (by s. 18 of the C.J. Act 1967) is that a magistrates' court *must* remand or commit on bail a person aged 17 years or over when the court:

(i) ***adjourns his trial*** for:

(a) a summary offence punishable by n/e 6 months imprisonment,

(b) a hybrid offence punishable summarily by n/e 6 months imprisonment, or

(c) an indictable offence (specified in Schedule I to the M.C. Act 1952) triable summarily to which he has pleaded.

(ii) ***adjourns the proceedings or commits him for trial*** for a summary offence where he or the prosecutor has claimed trial by jury.

Exceptions.—The court can exercise its discretion whether or not to grant bail where the defendant:

(a) fails to enter into a proper recognisance with the court or other person prescribed for the purpose (e.g. a police officer or prison governor),

(b) is unable to produce sufficient and satisfactory sureties as required,

(c) is charged with an offence punishable with 6 months or more imprisonment and has a previous conviction of imprisonment or borstal training,

(d) has failed to comply with the conditions of his bail on a previous occasion,

(e) is charged with an offence which he committed whilst on bail,

(f) is unknown and has to be detained to establish his identity or address,

(g) appears to be of no fixed abode or ordinarily resident outside the U.K.,

(h) is charged with an offence involving an assault on or threat of violence to another; having or possessing a firearm, imitation firearm, an explosive or an offensive weapon; or indecency with or towards a person under 16 years of age,

(i) is likely to commit a further offence if not in custody,

(j) should be remanded or committed for his own protection, or

(k) is required to be remanded for the purpose of obtaining his medical examination and a report for the information of the court.

NOTES:

(i) Where a magistrates' court refuses to remand or commit on bail, the court must give the prisoner a written notice stating the reason for refusal, and inform him of his right to apply to a judge of the High Court for bail, or, in the case of a committal, to the crown court or a High Court judge.

(ii) A justice to whom a defendant's previous conviction/s have been revealed when considering whether or not to grant bail is prohibited from sitting as a Justice at his summary trial. This applies to a justice at any committal proceedings out of which the summary trial arose (s. 19).

(iii) In committing an offender for sentence for an indictable offence tried summarily, with a view to a borstal sentence or for sentence as an incorrigible rogue, a magistrates' court may commit him in custody or on bail (s. 20).

(iv) The court may impose special conditions to bail, i.e., such as it considers likely to result in the offender's surrender to bail or necessary in the interests of justice or the prevention of crime, but the court cannot require the defendant to find sureties in respect of such conditions.

(v) A judge of the High Court is empowered to admit any person to bail or vary the conditions of any bail granted by a magistrates' court, a coroner's court, or crown court.

Powers of A.W.W.

A constable may A.W.W. a person on bail:

(1) if he has reasonable grounds to believe that the person:
- (a) is not likely to surrender to his bailment, or
- (b) is likely to break, is suspected of breaking or has broken any special conditions of his bailment.

(2) if a surety notifies in writing his wish to be relieved of his obligation as such because he believes that the person will not surrender to his bail.

After arrest, the accused must be brought within 24 hours before a justice for that area or the court dealing with the offence. If the justice is satisfied that the reasons for the arrest are valid, he may remand or commit the person in custody, or release him on his original or a new recognisance for bail, with or without sureties.

(3) Sureties

A prisoner may be required to enter into his own recognisance for bail, with or without sureties (i.e. bailsmen). The surety enters into a bond to be guarantor of the prisoner's appearance at court under penalty of forfeiting the amount named in the recognisance but cannot be made responsible for compliance by the accused with any other conditions of the bail. The accused is then in the custody of his surety, who, if he fears his escape or believes that the accused will not surrender to his bail, must notify the police in writing of his wish to be relieved of his obligation and thus avoid possible penalty. The accused is then liable to arrest without warrant. (See above.)

The recognisance of a surety may be entered into before the court, any Magistrates' Clerk, a Justice, an officer of the rank of Inspector or above, or in charge of a police station, or the governor of H.M. Prison, and separately from the recognisance of the principal. If the accused has been taken to prison a prospective surety should be advised by the police to first obtain a certificate from the Clerk of the Court of his ability to pay the amount of the recognisance in the event of forfeiture. A person who has taken the recognisance of a surety at some place other than the prison must send to the Governor a certificate of that fact in the prescribed form. The police, when taking a recognisance from a surety, should require the surety to produce a certificate from the magistrates' clerk showing amount and conditions.

(4) Estreating Bail

If a prisoner fails to surrender to his bail, the surety may be summoned before the court to show why the amount of the recognisance should not be paid as a debt to the Crown. The prisoner is also liable, when re-arrested, to the estreating of his bail.

(5) Personating Bail

It is an arrestable offence to acknowledge in the name of any other person, without lawful authority, any recognisance or bail before any court. (Forgery Act 1861, s. 34.)

(6) Excessive Bail

It is illegal to require excessive bail.

CHAPTER VII

TAKING OF STATEMENTS AND MAKING REPORTS

The persons from whom statements have, or may have to be taken, fall broadly into three classes:

1. *Witnesses*
2. *Suspects*
3. *Prisoners*

WITNESSES' STATEMENTS

A statement is a written record of the information a person has given concerning a matter under investigation. In some cases a statement is taken although the information the person can give (or says he can give) is nil, so as to record that fact. This statement is commonly called a *negative statement* and is taken for a special purpose (see p. 119). In murder enquiries it is the practice to take statements from all persons interviewed.

The purpose for which a statement is taken is important because it may well determine the form in which it is taken, e.g.,

(a) *If it is to assist an enquiry* and not directly for the purpose of placing on record the evidence which the person is expected to give at a trial, then everything which can be elicited which is or might reasonably be useful to that enquiry should be included without regard to the law of evidence.

(b) *If it is to record evidence* which the person will give, if necessary, at a trial, then

(i) the rules of evidence should be applied so far as is possible to exclude inadmissible facts, though there are exceptions to this which will be referred to later; and

(ii) the requirements* of the C.J.A., 1967, ss. 2 and 9 (the admissibility of written statements of witness in evidence), should be borne in mind and applied, so that the taking of a second statement which does conform with the Act, becomes unnecessary

(a) if the evidence is being recorded on a charge for which there would normally be a committal for trial by jury—all statements to comply with s. 2 or

(b) in any case where the evidence being recorded is of a formal nature and/or is unlikely to be disputed—in accordance with s. 9.

* The requirements are that the statement shall purport to be signed by the witness, shall include the age of the witness if under 21, and shall contain a declaration that it was made with full knowledge of criminal liability for any wilful falsehood contained in it—see p. 56 as to written statements in committal proceedings, and p. 52 as to such statements which may be admitted at any trial.

General Principles

Preparation

1. Do everything to make witness at ease and thus foster willingness to tell everything.

2. Statements from females re sexual or indecency offences should if possible be taken by a female officer—otherwise have another constable present.

3. Margin (on original or copy) should be allowed on left hand side.

4. Obtain verbal account first—it facilitates correct sequence and avoidance of omissions.

5. Witness may be questioned on points of ambiguity and obtain all relevant information.

The Taking

6. Always use ink, or a typewriter.

7. Do not take statement in presence of any other person from whom a statement on the same subject is to be taken later.

8. Use actual words of witness. Do not attempt to improve grammar if meaning is clear.

9. If pro-forma not used, commence with information to identify witness (name, address, age, occupation, etc.).

10. If correction is needed do not obliterate or erase words, but strike pen through so that cancellation is clear but words can still be read. Write corrections above and get witness to initial it.

11. Include everything, for or against an accused.

Conclusion

12. Before obtaining signature, it is best, not only to read it to witness, but to allow him to read it as well.

13. Carry out corrections before signature.

14. It is often the practice, after the reading out and signature, to add as a conclusion, "I have read this statement and it is true" or words to that effect, or to invite the witness to write this before adding his signature.

15. Obtain signature as close as practicable to last line and initials or signature at foot of each preceding page.

Endorsements

16. Add endorsement giving particulars of where, when, and by whom taken, and of any other person present, and sign it.

17. It is the practice in some forces to add any observation that might be useful as an indication of the quality of witness or any apparent handicap, e.g. deaf, impediment in speech, reluctant etc.

Particular Points

1. Test on points where memory may be at fault, or to aid it e.g. as to time, day, date.

2. In serious cases (for trial or submission to D.P.P.) do not omit relevant facts because they are or may be inadmissible in evidence, for they may provide useful background for counsel, e.g. source of information, why witness was present, etc.

3. Although there is no objection to a witness recording or making a copy of his statement for his own use, supplying him with a copy is not favoured and can be criticised in important cases.

4. Statements are confidential to police and should not be divulged to third parties except through official channels. Refer request for copies to the Superintendent.

> *Dallison* v. *Caffery* (1964)
>
> There is no duty upon the prosecutor to place before the Court all the evidence known to him, but if the prosecutor has information from a credible witness which is not consistent with the guilt of the accused, or is helpful to him the prosecutor has a duty to make such witness or his statement available to the defence. (Where witnesses' statements were made available to the accused's solicitor immediately on the accused's committal, the action was approved.)

Negative Statements

Persons when interviewed may say that they know nothing about the matter when the constable already has reason to believe they do, but will not help. In serious cases it is advisable to take a "negative" statement, for it may prove most useful later, e.g. should a witness "remember" something and come forward for defence.

A simple denial of guilt does not require the taking of a statement but is a matter of record in the notebook, inclusion in report, and evidence to the court, but when the accused wishes to give an explanation or an account relating to relevant facts a statement should be taken in accordance with the Judges' Rules.

Statements taken from Accused or Suspected Persons

A written statement made by a potential witness is on quite a different footing to that made by a suspected person. In the latter case the statement itself becomes of evidential value, and where it amounts to a confession (or admission) will have to be proved to have been given or made voluntarily, on which conformity or otherwise with the Judges' Rules, and the directions published with them on the taking of statements, will be an important, if not always decisive, factor.

Read the "Judges' Rules" again and the Directions on taking Statements

In addition the following principles apply as matter of practice:

(1) Do not use notebook for statement except in emergency.

(2) Always use ink.

(3) Presence of another officer is advised all the time.

(4) Although paragraphs are permissible in statements of witnesses do not use them here.

(5) If correction necessary do not blot out or erase—strike out with line making cancellation clear but words legible, or if correction being done by person himself advise this.

(6) Get corrections signed or initialled as well at the bottom of each page except the last.

(7) Make record in pocket-book of *relevant* facts affecting the taking of the statement as required by the Judges' Rules and directions, and make one report on these points to accompany statement.

(8) The records relating to questioning of prisoner or accused or taking of statements should be countersigned by all officers present.

THE MAKING OF REPORTS

The making of police reports and the preparation of any file that may be necessary on straightforward matters of common occurrence present no problems, for these are a matter of almost every-day experience. More difficult because experience in it is by no means so common, is the preparation of a file dealing with a serious or complicated issue, which consists of collecting together copies of all statements and documents connected with the enquiry, and the preparation of a covering report. On this we think that no better guidance can be given than is contained in a "Guide of the drawing up of reports, taking of statements, and documentation of papers" issued for the assistance of police officers from the office of the D.P.P. in 1964, for advice given with respect to files sent to the D.P.P. must be equally applicable to all files of a complicated nature which are forwarded for consideration as to the action, or further action, which should be taken. The following is an abstract of the "Guide".

(1) Frontispiece

On this should be entered:

(a) Name, address, age, occupation of each person charged, with aliases (if any) and nationality, if alien.
(b) Offence, or offences charged or alleged.
(c) Court and date, of hearing or remand, and whether bailed.
(d) Police reference No.
(e) Defending solicitor, if known.
(f) Officer in charge of case and his Tel. No.

(2) Reports

This should be prepared as follows:

(a) Begin with a brief outline of nature of offence (and dates).
(b) Follow by parts played by the accused in relation to the offence, and, if more than one accused, in relation to each other as well.
(c) Give narrative account of events condensed to give gist of evidence available, but do not recapitulate whole of witnesses' statements.
(d) Number each paragraph for easy reference later.
(e) Put names of individuals or concerns in *capitals*.
(f) An appreciation of each witness is useful (good, bad, handicapped by deafness, stuttering, etc.) and also opinion of veracity or otherwise, and reasons for opinion.
(g) Describe standing of professional witnesses. ("Dr. Jones" can mean so little).
(h) Views of investigating officer and superiors on issues and personalities are often useful.

(3) Statements

These should be prepared as follows:

(a) Fastened together to form file separate from report.
(b) Assembled in order of reference in report.
(c) Number each page of file consecutively (not statements separately) and provide index as front page, e.g.

JONES, Albert . . . . .Page 1.
ANDERSON, William . . . . .Page 3.

but if more than 12 witnesses make alphabetical index as well.

(d) Use dates as well as days when witness can say this. ("Last Tuesday" is confusing to reader, weeks later). If it is not in statement put note in margin, e.g. (i.e. 17th March).
(e) Verbs in active, not passive, voice, e.g. not "a letter was posted", but "I posted a letter". The latter indicates competency to prove, the former does not.

(f) "Hearsay" can be useful and should not be excluded merely as such, provided it is made clear that it is "hearsay" by words such as "I was told that . . . .".

(g) *Husband and Wife.* Take statements from them though not competent to testify, unless special reason for not doing so. Indicate whether willing to testify or not.

(h) *Marginal notes* are useful where comment is needed, e.g. "no such letter traced" or "See document No. 2." or "Contradicted by statement of Smith, Page 12".

(4) Documents

The following rules should be observed in the preparation of documents:

(a) Send copies of documents referred to, but *not* originals.

(b) Make file of them separate from the report and statement file.

(c) Number document copies on left and consecutive page numbers on right, and list them on a frontispiece, thus:

Document No. *Description* *Page.*

(d) *Cross referencing* is useful, i.e. where reference is made in report or statement to document, insert alongside in the margin reference number of the document concerned and underline the text reference.

(e) *Map or plan,* should have visual scale, and show every place referred to in the files, or the direction to it, but not controversial matters (e.g. an assumed route) which should be pencilled on a copy of the plan or map. Sketch plans are useful even if not to scale, and can be used for the above pencilling in.

(f) *Road Accidents.* Include at least two photographs to show accused driver's approach view. One should show any relevant warning sign.

Also:

(a) Typing should be *double spaced* on one side of paper only

(b) *Three copies* prepared if D.P.P. is concerned, but send only one in first instance.

(c) Always include previous convictions of accused, and antecedents if known.

In addition, *remember* to retain all original documents and exhibits for production in court.

PROGRESS CHECK No. 4

1. What is an arrest? Is there any distinction in law or police practice between an "arrest" and a "detention"?
2. What are the considerations to be borne in mind when considering whether procedure should be by summons or arrest?

3. Explain fully the common law powers to arrest for breaches of the peace.
4. What advice would you give to a young constable about entering premises by force?
5. To what extent is a constable legally justified in using force to effect an arrest?
6. What statutory power to arrest without warrant applies only at night?
7. What directions apply to the conduct of an identification by photograph(s)?
8. What is "Identi-Kit", and of what value is it in relation to the identification of suspects?
9. What are the provisions of the Judges' Rules relating to:
   (a) interrogating persons from whom information might be obtained?
   (b) the point at which a caution becomes necessary in (a)?
   (c) the use of cautions?
   (d) taking of statements after caution?
   (e) statement by a person jointly charged with another person?
   (f) procedure after taking of statement with regard to persons who refuse to sign, or cannot, or refuse to, read it?
10. Write out the administrative directions on interrogation and taking of statements approved by the Judges, and published with the Judges' Rules, in relation to (a) records of interrogation, (b) comfort and refreshments, (c) young persons, (d) foreigners, (e) written statement of charge, and (f) facilities for defence.
11. What principles concerning "mode of arrest" arise from the case of *Christie* v. *Leachinsky* (1947)?
12. What legal principles govern the use of force to effect an arrest?
13. What directions should be borne in mind concerning (a) the transport of prisoners, (b) illness of prisoners, and (c) prisoners in uniform of armed forces?
14. What principles govern the search (a) of a suspect before or at time of arrest, and (b) at the police station?
15. What is meant by (a) personal property and (b) property subject to charge, and what records should be made of them?
16. What general rules of practice apply to a formal search being made at a police station?
17. What courses of action can be taken by the officer whose duty it is to consider whether or not a charge should be "accepted"?
18. What rules apply to "charging" an accused?
19. What considerations apply to the question of whether or not a prisoner should be confined in police cells?

20. Write out the headings under which prisoners may claim their "rights"?
21. Guided by the "headings" required in question 20, run through the "rights" or "facilities" which come under each of them.
22. What is the law and police practice concerning affording bail, or otherwise, to a prisoner by the police?
23. On what grounds might an objection to the grant of bail by a court be made by or on behalf of the police?
24. To what extent is the taking of a statement from a witness governed by the law of evidence?
25. What is meant by a "negative statement", and what considerations of police practice apply to it?
26. Apart from the provisions of the Judges' Rules and the directions approved by H.M. Judges concerning taking of statements, what practical rules of guidance apply?
27. What are the recommendations of the D.P.P. concerning: (a) covering reports, (b) statements, and (c) documents, in files submitted to him?
28. What powers are provided by the Criminal Law Act 1967, with regard to arrest without warrant:
    (a) by a constable
    (b) by any person.
29. When must a Magistrates' Court remand or commit an accused person on bail, and describe any eight exceptions whereby the Court may still exercise its discretion whether to do so.
30. Write out the declaration required to be made by a person making a statement so as to make his statement admissible under ss. 2 and 9 of the C.J.A. 1967.

CHAPTER VIII

COURT PROCEDURE

GENERAL PROCEDURE

General procedure at a trial is common to all courts (though addresses to court are frequently dispensed with in minor summary cases) as follows:

1. Identification of accused.
2. Charging the accused.
3. Taking plea—"Guilty" or "Not Guilty".
4. Address by prosecution, if any, to be made.
5. Presentation of evidence for prosecution.
6. Defence may submit there is no case to answer, if court agrees information is dismissed, if not trial continues.

At this point, order of progress depends on whether Defence

(a)	(b)	(c)
7. addresses court (no witnesses)	7. calls witnesses 8. addresses court	7. addresses court 8. calls witnesses 9. obtains leave for 2nd address 10. if so, prosecution can address 11. Defence—second address
8. Verdict	9. Verdict	12. Verdict

Verdict of "Guilty" is followed by evidence of antecedents and sentence.

NOTE: Either party may, with leave of the Court address the Court for a second time, but where leave is granted to one party it shall not be refused to the other. The defence is always allowed to have the "last word". It is the duty of the prosecution to conclude its case before the defence opens (*R.* v. *Jones* (1972)). As to prosecution evidence introduced at a later stage see p. 130.

Notes on General Procedure

(1) Identification

By calling accused to answer, and question by clerk. "is your name . . . . ?" . . . . .etc.

(a) If a summary offence the case may be dealt with in the absence of accused, if legally represented, or court accepts plea of guilty by letter from the defendant or his solicitor, or by the 1957 procedure (see later).

(b) If indictable the accused must be present, whether the case is dealt with summarily or not.

As to procedure where the accused does not appear to answer the charge—

(a) before a magistrates' court—see p. 134.

(b) on indictment—see p. 146.

(2) Plea

After the charge (or each charge in turn) has been read by the Clerk—the defendant is asked to plead *"Guilty"* or *"Not Guilty"*. Any plea which is conditional or not one of "guilty" is entered as "not guilty", e.g. in a "handling" case, accused may plead guilty (to handling the goods) but qualifies this by saying that he did not know they were stolen, which must be recorded as a "not guilty" plea.

In the case of

(a) *"Guilty" Plea*: court may dispense with evidence for prosecution or require only a summary of facts from the main witness with or without being sworn, or from the person representing the prosecution. After this follows antecedents and sentence.

(b) *"Not Guilty" Plea*: trial proceeds in a formal way.

By the Criminal Justice Act 1967, s. 29, a representative* of a corporation other than a solicitor may enter a plea of guilty or not guilty on its behalf (by letter or in person) before a magistrates' court.

* Duly appointed in writing on behalf of the corporation by the managing director or manager of the corporation to represent it specifically for the purpose of the particular proceedings.

Change of plea

S. (*an infant*) v. *Manchester City Recorder* (1970)

An accused can apply at any time before sentence to change his plea, and the court must then decide whether justice requires this to be done.

R. v. *E. Suffolk JJ, ex p. Harber* (1970)
The above decision applies to a defendant committed for sentence to the Crown Court.

R. v. *Rimmer* (1972) *and R.* v. *Hetherington* (1970)
A plea of guilty is a confession of fact. Confessions are generally admissible in evidence against the accused. Whether a withdrawn plea of guilty should be admitted as a withdrawn confession is a matter for the judge to decide having regard to whether the probative value of the withdrawn plea exceeds its prejudicial effect.

(3) Opening Address

Given by prosecutor or representative who outlines the case for the prosecution, and the facts he seeks to prove by witnesses.

Duncan v. *Toms* (1887)
Where the complainant is the real prosecutor, and is not legally represented he may conduct his own case by examining and re-examining his witnesses and cross-examining the witnesses for the defence, but it is doubtful whether he has the right to make an opening speech.

R. v. *Banks* (1916)
If the defendant pleads "not guilty" on the hearing of a case tried summarily, counsel or solicitor for prosecution (if any) makes an opening address, but should not state any fact which he is not prepared to prove and ought not to press for a conviction but should regard himself as a minister of justice assisting in the administration as an advocate.

(4) Presentation of Evidence

(a) "*Swearing*" *Witnesses*
(Magistrates' Courts Act 1952, s. 78)

Witness must be "Sworn" by:

(a) Taking the "*Oath*" or
(b) Making "*Affirmation*"
(Exception—child of tender years not understanding nature of "oath" see p. 14).

(i) *The Oath.—If no objection is made* the oath is taken upon the New Testament. In such a case the form normally is:

"I swear by Almighty God that the evidence I shall give to the court shall be the truth, the whole truth, and nothing but the truth".

But in a Juvenile Court, or for any witness under 17 years of age in any court, the prescribed oath is:

"I promise before Almighty God to tell the truth, the whole truth and nothing but the truth" (C. & Y.P. Act 1963, s.28).

but the use of either is binding and error in form of oath will not affect validity of evidence on that ground alone. *If objection is made that* the above form is contrary to religious belief of witness, he may be sworn in the manner prescribed by his religion or which he considers binding on his conscience.

> *R.* v. *Palm* (1910)
> The form of oath is permissive and not compulsory. It is not for the Court to ask the witness what form of oath he desires to take, but for the witness to say whether he desires to adopt any other form.

(ii) *Affirmation.*—If the objection is that taking an oath in any form is against religious belief—or that witness has no religious belief—or it is not reasonably practicable without inconvenience or delay to administer the oath in the manner appropriate to his religion—he may make solemn affirmation instead (Oaths Act 1888), or be required to (Oaths Act 1961), e.g.

> "I do solemnly, sincerely and truly declare and affirm that" . . . . etc.

(b) *Examining Witnesses*

Evidence is elicited by examination of witnesses, i.e. by questioning them. Purpose is to elicit evidence in correct sequence of facts without breach of the laws of evidence, and at the right speed. "Examination" is of three kinds, in this order:

(i) *Examination-in-Chief.*—i.e. the questioning of witness by party calling him. In simple summary cases an experienced witness (e.g. a police officer) may be allowed to give evidence directly.

(ii) *Cross-Examination.*—i.e. the questioning by the other side either on evidence already given or to test the credibility of witness (e.g. as to impartiality, character, reliability). The bad character of a witness is admissible to show that his statements on oath should not be believed hence the whole of cross-examination may be devoted to discrediting him, but note that by doing this the defence may make admissible cross-examination of accused as to his own character.

> *Parkin* v. *Moon* (1836)
> Questions asked at this stage of the examination are not confined to matters dealt with in examination-in-chief but must be relevant to the issue unless their object is to test the witness's credit or to challenge his character. Leading questions may always be asked whether the witness is a willing or an adverse one.

> *R.* v. *Burdett* (1855)
> Where two defendants are jointly indicted and a witness for one gives evidence tending to incriminate the other, he may be cross-examined by or on behalf of the other defendant.

R. v. *Hart* (1932)
The right to cross-examine need not always be exercised and failure to do so implies acceptance of the witness's testimony. Cross examination of a truthful witness will often add force to his story and impress the Court.

(iii) *Re-Examination.*—i.e. by the party calling the witness and restricted to new facts elicited by, or to explain doubts raised by, the cross examination. Entirely new evidence cannot be introduced except by leave of the Court.

Webb v. *Catchlove* (1886)
If a police officer is the informant he has the same rights as any other informant but High Court advise that in such cases, the officer should be a mere witness and should not take the position of an advocate.

"*Leading Questions*", i.e., those so framed as to suggest the answer desired (usually answerable by "*yes*" or "*no*") are *not allowed*, except:

(a) On *introductory* and immaterial matters.

(b) To *identify* persons or things.

(c) To assist the *memory* of a witness.

(d) To obtain *contradiction* of what another witness has said.

(e) To a *hostile* witness (see later).

(f) *In cross examination.*

Acerri v. *Petrovi* (1815)
When a question cannot be put except in leading form, the Judge who has a general discretion over the conduct of the trial may allow it to be so put.

Nicholls v. *Dowding & Kempt* (1815)
Questions which either deal with matters not in dispute, or which merely serve to introduce matters which are material and lead the witness to the subject of enquiry are, in general, allowed to be put in leading form without objection.

R. v. *Watson* (1817)
It was held that to identify a person in court as one whom the witness had already described that person might be pointed out to him, and he might be asked in direct terms whether that was the person whom he meant.

(5) Address to Court: Order of Speeches (Magistrates' Courts Rules 1968)

(a) For summary courts, dealt with by Magistrates' Courts Rules 1968, Rule 13, 14.

(b) The general rule is that prosecution and defence is entitled to one speech only, but if a point of law is argued by one side, the other has right to reply.

(c) Prosecution may make its address before calling witnesses, and has no other opportunity except where defence is given "another go" as in (d).

(d) Defence has a choice, for it can:

  (i) Leave the address until after defence witnesses have been called.

  (ii) Make the address without calling witnesses.
  in each case, the score being one speech each, *the prosecution has no right to reply*, but if the choice is

  (iii) to open with an address, then call witnesses,* an address afterwards can only be given with *leave of the court* which, if given, entitles the prosecution to a second address also, to be given before that of the defence.

  * If the only witnesses called are as to character only or the accused in his own defence, the right of the prosecution to reply does not apply. (Criminal Evidence Act 1898, as amended by Criminal Proceedings (Rights of Reply) Act 1964).

(e) The defendant, if not legally represented, is entitled to address the Court in his defence and to examine and re-examine his witnesses, and cross-examine the witnesses for the prosecution.

(6) Rebutting Evidence

After the witnesses for the defence have given evidence, the evidence in the case is closed and the general rule is that the prosecution cannot afterwards support its case by additional evidence because of an unexpected defence, but there are exceptions, e.g.:

> *R.* v. *Harris* (1927)
> If any matter arises in the defence which no human ingenuity can foresee, there is no reason why the matter which so arose may not be answered by contrary evidence on the part of the Crown.
>
> *R.* v. *Liddle* (1928)
> The Judge has a discretion to allow such evidence when a point is raised by the defence which could not be dealt with otherwise.

Evidence for the defence is usually sought to be rebutted either by anticipation in calling the evidence-in-chief in the first instance or by cross-examination of the witnesses for the defence.

Rebutting evidence after the evidence for the defence has been adduced, is unusual. It must be strictly in reply to the defence set up and which should have formed no part of the prosecutor's original case. The evidence is to be evidence in reply and will not extend to proof of some fact necessary to support the crown case which was omitted when calling evidence.

> *R.* v. *Doran* (1972)
>
> During the defence case prosecution learned of two witnesses present in court who could give material evidence. Leave of court obtained. D appealed on ground that the prosecution could not call evidence after the close of the case, unless it was in the nature of rebutting evidence. *Held:*—The rule as to calling evidence after the close of the prosecution was properly stated, but there may be exceptions to the rule, and the question in each case was whether it was right and proper to serve the ends of justice that further evidence should be admitted. The judge has a right to admit such evidence.

(7) Verdict

Magistrates decide on law and fact. The jury decides on the facts alone. Both may retire to consider their verdict. A finding of guilt—conviction. If "not guilty" the information is dismissed, and (on indictment) prisoner is discharged or acquitted.

(8) Antecedents

In simple cases, just matter of previous convictions, if any. In others more may be required, but not in any way as detailed as at higher courts.

(9) Sentence

The decision as to what form the sentence shall take is entirely one for the court (i.e. magistrates, chairman, recorder or judge) though counsel do often make pleas concerning it.

> *R.* v. *Black* (1963)
>
> A Jury has no power to decide the question of punishment but may make a recommendation to mercy. Such a rider to their verdict must be a spontaneous act of the Jury not invited by the Judge or Counsel in the case.
>
> *R.* v. *Church* (1970)
>
> A trial comes to a conclusion when sentence is passed.

In connection with sentencing the following have relevance:

(i) *Taking admitted other offences into consideration.* In determining sentence other similar untried offences may be taken into consideration if the accused admits them, wishes them to be dealt with in this way, and the prosecution consents. This subject is included in the "Crime" syllabus and, therefore, in Handbook No. 1.

(ii) *The following extensions of court powers provided by the Powers of Criminal Courts Act* 1973.

(a) *Deferment of sentence.* A court may defer passing sentence for a maximum period of six months so as to be able to have regard in determining sentence, to the conduct of the defendant after conviction (including any reparation made) or to any change in circumstances. The following main points apply:

(i) One deferment having been made, there can be no further deferment.

(ii) The offender must consent and the court must be satisfied (having regard to the offence and the character and circumstances of the offender) that this would be in the interests of justice.

(iii) If the offender is convicted of any offence in G.B. during the period of deferment, the "deferring" court can pass sentence before the normal expiration of the deferment period.

(iv) The offender may be brought back to the court at the end of the period (or by virtue of (iii) above) by summons or warrant.

(v) Nothing in this section affects the power of the Crown Court to bind over to come up for judgment when called upon, or the power of any court to defer passing sentence for any purpose for which it may do so lawfully apart from this section.

(vi) If sentence is deferred a magistrates' court is not obliged to remand the offender. A summons or warrant can be issued for securing reappearance. (s. 1).

(b) *Deprivation of property used for crime.* Where a person is convicted of an offence punishable on indictment with not less than 2 years imprisonment the Court, if satisfied that any property which was in his possession or under his control at the time of his arrest

(*i*) has been used for committing (or facilitating commission*) of any offence, or

(ii) was intended by him to be used for that purpose, can make an order depriving him of his rights, if any, in the property, and the property shall be taken into the possession of the police (if not already so possessed). The Police (Property) Act 1897 (see p. 242) applies to police possession of such property except that

(*i*) no application can be made by any claimant after 6 months from the date the order was made, and

(*ii*) no such application can succeed unless the claimant satisfies the court either that he had not consented to the offender possessing the property or that he did not know, and had no reason to suspect, that the property was likely to be used for the purpose stated above. (s. 43)

(*Note:* In Scotland such property is liable to forfeiture and to be disposed of as the court directs.)

* includes taking steps (after the offence was committed) to dispose of the property or to avoid arrest or detention.

NOTE: Disqualification. A person convicted by Crown Court of an offence punishable by two years (or more) imprisonment, or who has been committed there for sentence on such an offence by a magistrates' court, may be ordered to be disqualified for holding or obtaining a driving licence, for as long as the court thinks fit, if the court is satisfied that a motor vehicle was used

(a) *BY* the person convicted or anyone else

(*b*) *FOR* the purpose of committing or of facilitating the commission of the offence in question.

(*Powers of Criminal Courts Act* 1973, s. 44).

(c) *Power of magistrates' court to re-open case*:

(i) A magistrates' court may vary† or rescind a sentence or other order imposed or made by it, and

(ii) where there is a finding of guilty on a "Not Guilty" plea, or the court has dealt with the case in the absence of the accused, and it later appears to the court that in the interests of justice that the case should be heard by different justices, the court may so direct.

Conditions: The power must be exercised within 14 days, and only by a court constituted in same manner as the original court, or where that court comprised three or more justices, by a court which consists of or comprises a majority of those justices. (C.J.A. 1972, s. 41).

† Where a sentence is varied it takes effect from the beginning of the day on which it was originally imposed or made unless the court otherwise directs.

(iii) *The following provision of the Courts Act* 1971.

Power to vary or rescind sentence—Crown Court. A sentence imposed by the Crown Court can be varied or rescinded by that court within 28 days. In the case of joint defendants the sentence on any one of them may be varied or rescinded not later than 28 days from the conclusion of the trial or 56 days from the day sentence was passed, whichever is the shorter period. In such a case the court must be constituted as it was when the sentence was imposed, except that where justices were sitting the court may act without them. (s. 11)

PROCEDURE IN PARTICULAR COURTS

Having learned the general procedure of trial, it should be easy enough to associate with a particular court any departure from the general rules applicable to it. e.g.

(1) Magistrates' Courts

(a) *Effect of non-appearance of accused.*

As to special procedure by which certain summary cases can be heard in the absence of the defendant on pleas of guilty, see p. 141. In other cases at first hearing or adjournment, the following applies—

If on bail—the court can issue warrant for arrest (M.C.A. 1952, s. 97).

If on summons (prosecutor appearing) the court may either

(i) proceed in absence, or

(ii) issue warrant* for arrest and adjourn hearing if information for summons was made on oath,

provided in each case that the court is satisfied that the summons was served within reasonable time before trial,† or accused has previously appeared to answer the information. (M.C.A. 1952, s. 15).

* If the case is part heard or accused has been convicted on pleading guilty no warrant is to be issued unless court considers it unreasonable by reason of the gravity of the offence, to continue the trial in the absence of the accused.

By s. 24 (2) of the C.J.A. 1967 a warrant cannot be issued in respect of a defendant aged 17 years or over unless—

(i) the offence is punishable with imprisonment, or

(ii) the court, having convicted, propose to impose disqualification.

† The requirement of the M.C. Rules (r. 82), that if summons was served otherwise than personally it must be proved to have come to the defendant's knowledge does not apply in cases triable summarily only. See also p. 163.

(b) *Non-appearance of witness.*

On the failure of a witness to attend court after summons, a warrant to arrest and bring him before the court may be issued *if* the court is satisfied by evidence on oath that—

(i) the witness is a material witness,

(ii) the summons was duly served and reasonable conduct money was tendered to him, *and*

(iii) there is no just excuse for the failure to attend.

Summary Offences

(a) *Offence triable summarily only.*

The following apply to simple straightforward cases.

(i) Though the defendant may sometimes be absent from the hearing, s. 26 of the C.J.A. 1967 provides that a magistrates' court cannot in the absence of the accused sentence him to imprisonment (suspended sentence or otherwise) or to detention in a detention centre, or, except after an adjournment and notice to defendant, impose any disqualification.

(ii) *Opening Address*—not given, generally.

(iii) *Examination-in-chief*—an experienced witness may be allowed to give evidence directly—i.e. without leading the witness (e.g.—a police officer).

(iv) *Address to Court*—not usual, unless defendant represented, or is plea in mitigation of penalty.

(v) *Antecedents*—no more than previous convictions needed (though local practice varies on this point).

(b) *Summary Offence (with right to claim trial by jury) by person 17 years or over.*

i.e. when liable to more than three months imprisonment—but note the following exceptions, where accused cannot claim trial by jury as of right, although liable to this punishment:

(i) "Incorrigible rogue", committed only for sentence.

(ii) Male living wholly or partly on earnings of prostitution;

(iii) Female exercising control over a prostitute for gain;

(iv) Soliciting by male for an immoral purpose other than a legal homosexual act.

(v) Assault cases.

After charge and before plea, the clerk informs accused of his right. If he does not claim trial by jury proceedings as in (a) above. If he does, magistrates carry on as "examining justices" (see below, p. 137). There are a few cases in which the accused can claim right of trial by jury although the penalty does not exceed three months imprisonment as stated above, e.g.

(i) Cruelty by painful experiments on living animals;

(ii) Certain offences under the Explosives Act 1875, s. 92 and

(iii) The Conspiracy and Protection of Property Act 1875, s.9.

Indictable Offences triable summarily with Consent

Certain offences are triable summarily with consent (Magistrates' Courts Act 1952, s.19).

Persons of 17 years or over may waive their right to claim trial by jury in respect of indictable offences listed in the First Schedule to the Magistrates' Courts Act 1952 (see Appendix 4), but this is qualified as follows:

(a) Prosecution can ask the justices to commit, having regard to nature of charge, circumstances, antecedents of accused. If justices agree accused loses his right to choose summary trial.

(b) Magistrates are required to consider any representations made by or on behalf of the accused and the prosecutor before deciding to deal summarily with such an offence.

(c) Ordinarily, however, after charge and before plea, accused is told by the clerk that the case is triable by jury but it can be dealt with by the court below if he consents to this, but that the court may on a finding of guilt commit him to a Crown Court for sentence, if it considers that he should be given greater punishment than that which it can inflict. If he consents trial follows normal pattern except that:

(i) Accused must be present. The accused must be asked personally how he pleads (*R.* v. *Wakefield JJ, ex p. Butterworth* (1970)).

(ii) *Antecedents*—in view of heavier penalty more detailed information is required.

(iii) *Sentence.*

After conviction, the accused must or may be committed for sentence:

(a) If Court consider that a greater penalty should be given than that which it can impose.

(b) If Court considers that he should undergo Borstal Training and he is aged from 15 to 21 years.

(c) If convicted as an incorrigible rogue and the circumstances are to be examined before sentence up to 12 months imprisonment is imposed.

N.B.—In the above cases committal may be in custody, or on bail (C.J. Act 1967, s. 56). As to committals in custody of young persons, see p. 144.

(iv) During hearing Court may decide on grounds of seriousness not to continue a summary trial, but to act as examining justices to commit case for trial.

Offences by Persons of 17 years and over which are both "Summary and Indictable"

Certain offences committed by persons of 17 years and over are both "summary and indictable" (Magistrates' Courts Act 1952, ss.18, 25 and 29). This applies to those offences for which the Act specifies varying punishment according to whether conviction is summarily or on indictment, e.g. dangerous driving, drink/driving offences, possessing offensive weapons (Prevention of Crimes Act 1953). Because of their "in between" nature these offences are often called "hybrid offences". In these offences, the choice between summary trial and trial by jury rests with the prosecution in the first instance, but later the decision may become one for the magistrates (or the accused if summarily liable to more than 3 months imprisonment), as follows:

(i) If the prosecutor does not at the outset apply for summary trial, the case *must* start as though indictable. (*N.B.*—It is not for the prosecution to apply for trial by jury).

(ii) If the Court commences to enquire into the case as examining justices, it may at any time during the proceedings after hearing representations made by either the prosecutor or the accused (and it is proper to do so having regard to the nature of the case) *change to summary trial.* If liable summarily to imprisonment exceeding 3 months the defendant must then be given the opportunity to claim his right to trial by jury, which he may still do. If he waives this right, he must be told that the Court may still commit him to the crown court for sentence if he is 17 years or over and the nature of the offence and his previous character makes it seem that greater punishment is merited than the Summary Court can impose. Once the Court changes to summary trial as above, they cannot again revert to proceeding again as examining justices.

(iii) *The Prosecutor* at the outset, may "*apply for summary trial*", and the Court may at any time before the conclusion of the evidence for the prosecution, discontinue the summary trial and proceed as "examining justices" *N.B.*—Committal to for sentence as above does not apply in this case.

(2) Examining Justices

Committals for Trial

Note that the justices are "examining" from the outset where:

(a) the charge is one which has to go for trial, or

(b) the accused, having a choice, has not agreed to summary trial.

(c) the charge is one of the few "hybrid" ones (e.g. dangerous driving), though in this case the proceedings can change to summary trial if court decides to do so of itself, or on application of prosecution or accused. A summary hearing of an indictable offence can change to a committal for trial during hearing if justices before end of case for prosecution so decide, in which case witnesses already examined will have to be recalled to depose if depositions have not been taken from them.

Procedure—

A. Normal Procedure

Under the Magistrates' Courts Act 1952, in cases where the procedure under the C.J.A. 1967 (see later) is not used—

(a) Accused must be present during whole hearing.*

(b) Depositions are taken (see Chapter III, p. 55).

(c) After decision to commit (which has to be taken after evidence of prosecution normally), charge (in writing) has to be read to accused and explained to him in ordinary language.

(d) After charging, accused must be cautioned in the words of rule 4 of the M.C. Rules 1968, or words to same effect.

(e) Main points of the caution are:

 (i) You will be able to give evidence and call witnesses.

 (ii) Do you wish to say anything in answer to charge? Not bound to—nothing to hope from any promise, or to fear from any threat made to induce confession of guilt.

 (iii) Anything said will be taken down and may be given in evidence at trial.

(f) After caution evidence may be given for defence, though usually reserved.

(g) Committal for trial, by securing attendance of parties and witnesses. (See Chapter III, p. 58).

* By s. 45 of the C.J.A. 1972 the examining justices may allow evidence to be given in the absence of the accused if they consider that, by reason of his conduct, it is not practicable for evidence to be given in his presence, or he cannot be present for reasons of health but is legally represented and has given consent to evidence being given in his absence.

B. Procedure under C.J.A. 1967, *s.* 1

(Committal for trial without consideration of evidence).

Under the law as it existed prior to 1.1.68 the examining justices had to hear the evidence of all witnesses for the prosecution to decide whether the evidence justified putting the defendant on trial on indictment (as in A.) After 1.1.68 an alternative procedure for committal was provided by the C.J.A. 1967, s. 1, which enables

(i) written statements of evidence of a witness to be accepted as evidence without calling the witness to give evidence orally, and

(ii) when certain conditions are fulfilled the defendant to be committed for trial without the evidence against him (in the form of written statements of the witnesses) being considered by the examining justices.

Committal without hearing evidence (1967, s. 1).—The conditions applicable are:

(i) The prosecution have not taken the initiative in calling any of their witnesses to give evidence orally and the defendant has not objected to the prosecution witnesses' written statements being tendered in evidence under section 2.

(ii) The defendant does not call any witnesses to give evidence orally and does not give evidence orally himself.

(iii) The defendant does not tender any written statements in evidence or, if he does, the prosecution does not object to their being tendered in evidence.

(iv) The defendant does not submit that the evidence does not disclose a prima facie case.

(v) The defendant is legally represented.

Where there is more than one defendant the conditions must be satisfied in respect of each defendant.

Committals of young persons

A person under 17 charged with an offence which cannot be tried summarily may be committed for trial under s. 1 in like manner as a person over that age. (C.J.A. 1972, s. 44).

Acceptance of written statements (*C.J. Act*, 1967, s. 2).—For the provisions of s. 2, see p. 56.

The effect of s. 2 (acceptance of the written statement of a witness in committal proceedings) upon the normal procedure under the 1952 Act is that

(i) the written statement will take the place of the deposition which would have been taken at the hearing if the witness gave oral evidence, and

(ii) the appearance of the witness at the trial will be by way of witness summons and not witness order (see p. 47).

As to which court committal should be made, see p. 37.

NOTES

1. On decision not to commit for trial, accused is discharged. Not having been "in peril" of conviction subsequent defence of "autrefois acquit" cannot apply.
2. One justice required though usually two or more.
3. Examining Justices sit in open court unless there are special reasons to hear all or part of proceedings "in camera" (see p. 44).
4. Defence has right to cross-examine prosecution witnesses making depositions.
5. Committal for trial (or sentence) of person 17–20, if not on bail, should be to a remand centre, if available.

Publication of Reports of Committal Proceedings *(C.J. Act 1967 ss. 3 and 4)*

(*a*) *Restrictions*

General.—The effect of s. 3 is broadly, that during a "restricted period" only "permitted facts" relating to committal proceedings can be published in writing or print or broadcast within G.B. unless the defendant, or one of them where there is more than one applies to the court for its order to authorise publication of a full report.

The court must explain to a defendant, if not represented, that he has the right to have full publicity given to the case (unless the court hears the case in camera).

NOTES

(i) G.B. includes Scotland but not N. Ireland.

(ii) "Broadcast" covers radio and television services for general reception.

(iii) "To publish" is to make public by distribution of the report either separately or as part of a newspaper or periodical.

(iv) Breach of the section is a summary offence. (Fine n/e £500).

"Permitted Facts".—i.e. those which can be reported to the defendant (or the last of them if more than one) is finally dealt with, i.e. proceedings are concluded against him, or all of them, if more than one defendant, as illustrated below.

Result of proceedings	*Restricted period ends*
(i) No one committed for trial, e.g.:—prisoner discharged or no case to answer.	When this decision is announced.
(ii) Defendant (or one of them) is committed for trial.	When trial (at higher court) of defendant (or last of them) has been concluded.
(iii) Where proceedings commencing as "committal" change to summary trial.	As soon as court ceases to act as examining justices.

Exception. Where, in the case of joint defendants, the court commits one (or some) but deals summarily with the other or others, a report can be published in full of the case tried summarily.

"Permitted Facts".—i.e. those which can be reported to the public at any time are—

(a) the names of the court and examining justices;

(b) the names, occupations and addresses of the parties and witnesses, ages—of defendant(s) and witnesses only;

(c) the offence(s) charged and charge(s) on which any defendant was committed for trial, as well as particulars of the court to which committed and of bail, if any;

(d) the names of counsel and solicitors;

(e) the decision of the court to commit, or on the disposal of the charges against any defendants not committed;

(f) if committal is adjourned, the date and place to which adjourned and particulars of bail;

(g) whether legal aid was granted to the defendant(s).

Prosecutions

(a) No prosecution except by or with consent of the Attorney General.

(b) Liability is limited to the publisher, proprietor or editor of a newspaper or periodical, and in the case of a broadcast, the corporation and the person responsible for broadcasting or editing the programme.

(c) Certain of the particulars which are lawfully permitted by this Act to be published or broadcast at any time (see para. (3) *ante*), may still remain prohibited from publication by other statutes, e.g. the C. & Y.P. Acts (see p. 41), and the Judicial Proceedings (Regulation of Reports) Act 1926 which restricts the reporting of court proceedings involving matter likely to be injurious to public morals.

(b) Notices to be Posted at or near Court

Section 4 required the court to post up a public notice at or near the courthouse on the day of (or day after) the conclusion of any committal proceedings. The notice must state the name, age and address of each defendant, particulars of the charge(s) and the court to which committed or the fact that he was discharged (if such was the case). The section does not specify how long the notice should remain exhibited, but the recommendation is that it should be at least 2 or 3 days.

> *R.* v. *Blackpool JJ, ex p. Beaverbrook Newspapers* (1971)
> Where the defendant is one of several defendants and applies for an order lifting restriction on press reporting of the committal, the magistrates must make the order and cannot limit the order to those parts of the proceedings which affect the applicant. The lifting of the restriction applies not only to the applicant but also those charged jointly with him at the time and those who may subsequently be joined in the same committal proceedings.

(3) Magistrates' Courts Act and Rules of 1957 and 1958

Procedure for accepting plea of "guilty" from absent defendant

This does not apply:

(i) To *Juvenile* Courts.

(ii) To *Indictable Offences.*

(iii) To *Summary Offences*—triable by jury, or those in which an order can be made on complaint e.g. dangerous dog, or any disqualification must be made.

(A) Procedure before Hearing

(i) *By Prosecutor.*—Service of following forms with summons:

(a) **Statement of effect of the** *Statute*.

(b) Statement of Facts alleged in support of charge. *Note*: As the Rules provide that if summons is not served personally the case cannot be heard in absence unless there is an acknowledgement of receipt from defendant, the practice is to serve also:

(c) A form on which to plead guilty and state any mitigating facts (returnable direct to the Magistrates' Clerk), and

(d) A form on which to acknowledge receipt of summons (returnable to the Prosecutor)
Clerk to be notified by police when forms (a) and (b) have been served,

(e) Previous Conviction Form (if any) (See p. 143).

(ii) *By Defendant.*—If he intends to plead guilty and not appear he must notify clerk accordingly (form (c) above). He can, before hearing, withdraw "guilty" plea by notifying the clerk accordingly.

NOTE: A plea of guilty by letter may be made only by the accused himself or by a solicitor acting on his behalf, but the Criminal Justice Act 1967, s. 29, enables a director or the secretary of a corporation to enter a plea of guilty by letter on behalf of the corporation and the court can accept the notification without strict proof of signature and deal with the case as though it had been received from an individual defendant.

(iii) *By Clerk to the Justices.*—To notify prosecutor of:

(a) receipt of "guilty" plea.

(b) withdrawal of such plea (procedure then is by appearance of parties and witnesses in usual way).

(B) Procedure at Hearing

Application.—This arises if a plea of guilty is received and not withdrawn. Case can be heard in absence of prosecutor, defendant and witnesses provided service of summons and forms (a) and (b) is proved (certificate of service will do) and "guilty" plea has been received (Form c). If court decides not to proceed in absence of defendant it may adjourn for a normal hearing in his presence by notifying him of the adjournment or issuing a new summons.

To be read to court:

(a) Proof of Service of the Summons and the statement of the effect of the Statute.

(b) the "*statement of facts*"

(c) mitigating facts sent in by defendant. (read by the clerk).

The court cannot sentence a defendant to imprisonment in his absence nor, except on resumption of the case after its adjournment to enable him to attend:

(a) hear evidence of facts not in the "Statement of Facts", or

(b) impose any disqualification.

The notice of adjournment served on the defendant must state the reason for the adjournment.

NOTE: The above is the legal method. In practice, summary courts do, in minor cases, deal with cases in absence of defendant, if prosecution agrees and defendant has acknowledged receipt of summons (e.g. by letter pleading guilty). As to guilty plea case dealt with by court without knowledge that accused is under 17, see p. 43.

Proof of Previous Convictions

Until the 1957 Act a previous conviction unless admitted, could only be proved by fingerprint evidence, or by:

(a) Documentary evidence from the convicting court (i.e. certified copy of the court Register) and

(b) Evidence of identity, i.e. that the defendant present is the person referred to in the document by witness who was present at the conviction.

This still applies at Crown Courts and to all convictions of indictable crime, but in a summary case (not a juvenile court) if it is proved that not less than 7 days previous to the hearing a notice was served on the defendant in proper form and manner specifying the convictions of *Summary Offences* proposed to be put to the court on his conviction, the court may take account of these convictions even if the accused is not present, as if he had appeared and admitted them. *Summary Offence* includes "hybrid offence" i.e. one triable either on indictment or summarily. The format is prescribed by the 1968 Rules. Service to be personal or sending by registered post or recorded delivery service. The proof of service is by declaration or certificate of service.

(4) Adjournments and Remands

For this subject see also under "Bail", Chapter VI, p. 111.

(A) Before and during Hearing

(a) *Where accused is not in custody of the court.*—In such cases (i.e. those triable summarily only, and initiated on summons) any adjournment is at discretion of court (no time limits applying), subject to representations by or on behalf of prosecutor and accused as to a suitable date. If no date is fixed (adjourned sine die) the court must be satisfied when hearing is resumed that both parties have had adequate notice of its resumption. There is no duty to remand accused but Court can do so.

(b) *Where Accused is in Custody of the Court.*—i.e. where:

(i) the accused appears after arrest on *any* charge, or

(ii) the proceedings are before "examining justices", or

(iii) the charge is of indictable crime or a hybrid offence being dealt with as indictable offence, then the question of *remand* of the accused arises. *Persons aged 17 years or more must be remanded.* With regard to persons under that age the court has a discretion.

Remand.—This is the procedure whereby the re-appearance of the accused at an adjourned hearing is secured, and may be by

(a) *an order that he shall be kept in custody.* If for less than 3 clear days may be committed to custody of constable (i.e. to approved police cell). The following important provisions relating to young persons apply:–

C. & Y.P. Act 1969, *s.* 23.

(i) The remand to police cells can, in the case of a person under 17, be for not more than 24 hours.

(ii) With regard to the following persons, i.e.

(a) a person *under 14* charged with or convicted of homicide, or

(b) a person under 17 years but not under 10 years of age charged with or convicted of *any* offence,

any remand, or committal for trial or for sentence, otherwise than on bail, must be a committal to the care of the L.A. of the area in which he habitually resides or where the (or one) offence was committed.

Exception. If the person is *14*† *to 16* and the court certifies him to be of such unruly character that he cannot safely be committed to the care of the L.A., then he shall be committed to a remand centre, if available,—otherwise to prison.

Note. S. 23 does not apply to committal for borstal sentence.

† The Home Secretary has power to increase the minimum age.

C.J. Act 1948, *s.* 27. (substituted by C. & Y.P. Act 1969)

When an accused person not less than 17 but under 21 is committed for trial or for sentence, and not on bail, the remand must be to a remand centre, if available—otherwise to prison.

(b) *release on bail* (with or without sureties), which may be to a fixed date, or *continuous*, i.e. to appear at each and every adjourned hearing.

NOTE: If bail is permitted but not entered into at court, recognizances may be fixed by the court and the accused remanded in custody until recognizances are concluded.

Duration of Remand: Such a remand is not to exceed *eight clear days*, unless:

(a) it is on bail and accused and prosecutor agree to longer period, or

(b) the court is not properly constituted to deal with the case (e.g. one justice) and adjournment is to the next sitting of the proper court.

B. After Conviction and before Sentence

(Magistrates' Courts Act 1952 as amended by the Criminal Justice Act 1967, s. 30.)

Purpose of adjournment:

(a) Enquiries to be made to enable court to determine best way to deal with case (s.14), or

(b) When offence is punishable by imprisonment, for physical or mental examination or report (s.26).

Duration.—For not more than four weeks at one time but three weeks only if the defendant is remanded in custody.

Notes re. s.26 (i) If in custody full report on case and accused to be sent to prison doctor.

(ii) If on bail recognizances may secure reporting to named doctor or institution (or residence there).

(iii) In case of juvenile a Juvenile Court can extend period of remand conditional on appearances of accused before the court or a justice once in each period of 21 days.

General Notes

(a) A remand must be to a fixed date and time.

(b) After first remand, court can make further remands, substitute a new remand for a "continuous" one, or enlarge recognizances, giving notice to parties.

(c) If by *illness or accident* accused cannot appear, court can further remand in absence, and increase recognizances.

(d) Deserters and absentees can be remanded for reasonable period to await escort.

(e) The 3 day remand to custody of constable could be verbal under old law and has not been expressly changed.

(5) Proceedings in the Crown Court.

NOTE: By s. 7 of the Courts Act 1971 (and Crown Court Rules 1971) the trial of a person committed by a magistrates' court shall not begin until the expiration of 14 days from the date of committal except with his consent and that of the prosecution, and, unless the Crown Court otherwise orders, shall begin not later than the expiration of 8 weeks from the date of committal.

The progress of a case is the same as that outlined at the beginning of this chapter as being common to all courts, but the following special feature should be noted.

(a) The Indictment. (*Administration of Justice* (*Miscellaneous Provisions*) *Act* 1933 *and the Indictments* (*Procedure*) *Rules* 1971).

The proceedings before a Crown Court are founded on an indictment which replaces the "information" which is the basis in magistrates' courts. An indictment is the officially prepared document which sets out the charge or charges on which a person is to be tried before the Crown Court. Each charge is called a "count". Other counts may be added or substituted if they can be charged in the same indictment, and a charge of having a previous conviction can be included even though this is not included in the committal charges or any direction as to an indictment by a High Court Judge. The first step towards completing an indictment is to prefer a bill of indictment. This bill is preferred before the Crown Court by the prosecution delivering it to the Appropriate Officer (A.O.) of the Court, unless, with the assent of the prosecution, the bill is prepared by or for the A.O. When the defendant has been committed for trial the bill must be prepared within 28 days of the date of committal or such longer period as the judge of the Crown Court may allow. Subject to the Court being satisfied that all proper preliminaries have been complied with the bill is signed by the clerk to the court and then becomes an indictment.

By the 1933 Act no bill of indictment shall be preferred unless either:

(a) the person charged has been committed for trial by examining justices (or coroner), or

(b) the bill is preferred by the direction or with the consent of a Judge of the High Court on application to him for such a direction.

An application for a direction of the High Court Judge (under (b)) can be made on the following grounds:

(i) the accused was so violent and disorderly that it was a practical impossibility for depositions to be taken in committal proceedings (on a certificate of a magistrate to this effect), or

(ii) where there have been no committal proceedings or the

examining justices have refused to commit for trial (by any person who has a desire to prosecute).

The Indictments (Procedure) Rules 1971, specify the procedures for such applications and the evidence and documents which have to be submitted with applications made to the Judge of the High Court.

(b) Arraignment

This is the name given to the first three steps of general procedure (identification, charge and plea) and is effected by—

(i) calling the prisoner by name to the bar of the court,

(ii) reading the indictment to him—the jury may be told in general terms what the charges are,

(iii) asking him whether he is guilty or not of the offence charged.

The arraignment is not complete until the prisoner has pleaded.

Failure to plead. If the accused "stands mute of malice" or will not plead or answer directly to the indictment, the court will direct the charge to proceed as on "not guilty" plea.

(c) Non-Appearance

(i) *Of accused.*

Where an indictment has been signed the Crown Court can issue a summons for the appearance of the person charged or issue a warrant for his arrest. Where the defendant has entered a recognizance condition for his appearance and he fails to appear the Court may issue a warrant for arrest (without prejudice to the recognizance). Such warrants are sometimes called "Bench Warrants". Such a warrant may be endorsed (by the Crown Court) for bail, in which case (unless the Court otherwise directs) the arrested person must be taken to a police station, where the officer in charge must release him from custody if he and any sureties required by the endorsement *and approved by the officer* enter into the recognizances stipulated by the endorsement. If the warrant is not endorsed for bail (or if the bail endorsement is not fulfilled by release on bail by the police) the person arrested must be forthwith brought before either the Crown Court or a magistrates' court. In the latter event the magistrates' court must commit the person in custody or release him on bail until he can be brought, or appear, before the Crown Court at the time and date appointed by the Crown Court. If the warrant is endorsed for bail but the person in custody is unable to satisfy the conditions of the endorsement the magistrates' court may vary those conditions if it is satisfied that it is proper to do so. Process under this section may be served or executed in same way as process issued under the Magistrates' Courts Act 1952. The court and any justice of the peace may act in pursuance of this section whether or not the offence was committed or the arrest made in the court's (or magistrate's) jurisdiction. (Courts Act 1971, s. 13).

R. v. *Johal and Ram* (1972)

There is no rule of law precluding amendment of an indictment after arraignment, either by adding a new count or otherwise. The question in each case, for the judge to decide, is whether, having regard to the interval between arraignment and amendment, the amendment would be likely to prejudice the defendant.

(ii) *Of witnesses.*—See p. 47.

(d) The Plea

The accused may—

(i) *Plead Guilty*. In such a case counsel for the prosecution will put the facts of the case briefly to the court, and then call evidence of the prisoner's antecedents. The prisoner or his counsel may then address the court in mitigation of sentence. A change of plea to one of "not guilty" can be made, with leave of the court, before sentence but not afterwards.

Where a plea of guilty follows a committal at which evidence was not considered (see p. 138) no evidence will have been made available to the public at the committal proceedings or at the trial. In these circumstances the recommendation is that it would be in the public interest for the prosecution to give a fairly full account of the facts of the case after the defendant has pleaded guilty.

(ii) *Plead Not Guilty* which may or may not be combined with:—

(a) *A "demurrer"* which is a written objection made before plea admitting the facts alleged but asserting that they do not amount to the crime charged in the indictment. If his demurrer fails the accused cannot himself then plead "not guilty" (the facts being admitted) but the court may allow him to "plead over", i.e. enter a plea of "not guilty" even though the demurrer has failed.

(b) *"Special plea in bar"* which may include a plea of:—
autrefois acquit, i.e. that he has been tried and acquitted by a competent court for the same offence on a previous occasion, or

autrefois convict, i.e. that he has been tried, convicted and sentenced by a competent court for the same offence on a previous occasion.

NOTES:

The pleas that an acquittal or a conviction is a bar to a second indictment for the same offence is dependent on the principle of law that a man should not be put in peril twice for the same offence.

Another special plea (of rare occurrence) is a "plea to the jurisdiction of the court", i.e. that the court is not competent to try the case or lacks jurisdiction.

(iii) *Plead not guilty of the offence charged, but guilty of another offence of which he could be found guilty on the indictment.* (see later). The judge would not allow the prosecution to accept a plea to the lesser offence unless the evidence warranted this. If a plea of guilty to another offence is accepted so that the accused is not tried for the offence charged, the conviction on the plea of guilty is an acquittal of the offence charged. This applies whether or not two or more offences are separately charged in distinct counts.

(e) Addresses (or speeches)

These are made in proper order during the course of the trial to the jury, except where points of law or procedure are being argued.

(f) Presence of the accused

The accused should normally be present throughout the trial but in a long trial in which there are several accused, the court may permit the hearing to continue in the absence of one or more of them if satisfied that this would not prejudice their defence.

(g) The "summing up"

At the close of the defence and before verdict, the Judge sums up the evidence and explains the law involved for the guidance of the jury, leaving all questions of fact arising from the evidence to the jury. He may express an opinion as to the facts, but the jury are not bound to follow it. He would not direct the jury that it was open to them to give an alternative verdict of a lesser offence (see later) unless the evidence warranted this.

(h) The verdict

It is for the jury to return the verdict, and they can (and generally do) retire to consider it. On return to court, it is not for the jury to volunteer their verdict but for the clerk of the court to ask for it, the spokesman for the jury being its foreman. On a verdict of "guilty" it is the practice of the clerk to reassure the court of the unanimity of the verdict by asking, "and is that the verdict of you all?". In the case where the return of a majority verdict has been allowed (see p. 162) the foreman has to state in open court the number of jurors for and against the verdict of "found guilty".

A jury may find the prisoner—

(i) not guilty;

(ii) guilty (on all counts of the indictment) with or without a recommendation to mercy;

(iii) guilty of the attempt;

(iv) guilty on some counts but not on others;

(v) guilty of an alternative offence (not made the subject of a count in the indictment)—see later;

(vi) unfitness to plead, or

(vii) Special verdicts, *viz.*:—

(a) not guilty by reason of insanity;

(b) on the facts alone from which the court will draw the legal inference from those facts, e.g., autrefois acquit, autrefois convict, whether it is murder or manslaughter.

If the jury fail to agree upon their verdict, the judge will discharge them and the prisoner will be tried again by another jury at that or the next sitting of the court. It is usual for the prosecution to offer no further evidence if a jury fails to agree on a second trial and the prisoner will then be discharged.

A "majority verdict" of guilty or not guilty may now be accepted by the court subject to the conditions prescribed by the Juries Act 1974, s. 17. See "Juries", p. 157

> *R.* v. *Dickson* (1967)
>
> During trial accused changed his plea to "Guilty" but no verdict was taken from the jury. *Held*:—Trial was a nullity. If, on arraignment, accused pleads guilty he is never in charge of the jury, and there is no jury verdict, but on a plea of not guilty he is in charge of a jury and can be convicted or discharged only by verdict of the jury.

(i) Alternative Verdicts

By the C.L. Act, 1967, s. 6, a person tried on indictment for any offence, *except treason or murder*, can be found (or plead) guilty of—

(i) any lesser offence which by its nature is part of, or included (either expressly or by implication) in the offence charged, e.g., a verdict of indecent assault on a charge of rape. (*Exception*—Murder, see (v) p. 151).

(ii) any offence of which he could have been found guilty if specifically charged with the lesser offence for which he was found guilty in (i) above, e.g., a person charged with incest could be convicted of unlawful sexual intercourse with girl under 16 years but if originally charged with the latter offence could have been convicted of indecent assault, therefore a person charged with incest could be convicted of indecent assault.

(iii) an attempt to commit the full offence with which charged. (A person charged with an attempt in the original indictment (or with an assault or other act preliminary to an offence, e.g. assault with intent to rob) may be convicted of the attempt even though the evidence showed him to be guilty of the full offence—subject to the discretion of the court that he should be indicted for the full offence before another jury).

(iv) an offence expressly provided by statute as an alternative, i.e. on the charge of one there can be conviction of the other. The following are the alternative convictions for which there is specific statutory authority:—

Offence charged.	*Alternative conviction*
Murder	Manslaughter, causing grievous bodily harm with intent, infanticide, child destruction, abetting suicide.
Manslaughter	Child destruction
Cause death by dangerous driving.	Dangerous driving
Infanticide	Child destruction, cruelty to child.
Child destruction	Abortion
Abortion	Child destruction
Poisoning to endanger life.	Administering poison with intent to injure.
Cause grievous bodily harm with intent.	Cause grievous bodily harm, common assault.
Unlawful wounding	Common assault.
Wounding with intent	Unlawful wounding, common assault.
Indecent assault.	Common assault.
Theft	Take conveyance without consent.
Rape	Procure by threats, by false pretences or by drugs, indecent assault.
Sexual intercourse with with girl under 16.	Indecent assault common assault.
Incest (by man)	Intercourse with girl under 13 or under 16. Indecent assault (if girl under 16).
Riot	Unlawful assembly. Rout.

N.B. Where an alternative offence is not included in that charged in the indictment nor specifically authorised in any statute, the prosecution will have to include it as a second count in the indictment in order to obtain a conviction, e.g. concealment of birth on a charge of murder, infanticide or child destruction, and assault with intent to rob on a charge of robbery.

(v) *Murder.*—The general rule that a person may be convicted of any such lesser offence included in that charged does *not apply on a charge of murder*, for which the only alternative verdicts are—

(i) manslaughter;

(ii) causing grievous bodily harm with intent to do so;

(iii) wounding with intent to cause grievous bodily harm;

(iv) verdicts specifically provided for by statute, i.e., infanticide, child destruction or abetting suicide;

(v) giving assistance to a person guilty of murder;

(vi) attempt to commit murder, or

(vii) attempt to commit any of the offences in (ii) to (v) above.

Treason—The procedure in trials for treason or misprision of treason is the same as that for murder.

(j) Sentence or acquittal

On a finding of "guilty" it is the general rule, when the accused is undefended, for the judge before passing sentence, to invite him whether he has anything to say. It is a matter for the judge's discretion whether he also does this when the accused is defended. As the accused is always in the custody of the court of trial on indictment, on a verdict of "not guilty" he is formally "discharged" (i.e. acquitted). A sentence or order imposed by the Crown Court begins from the beginning of the day on which it was imposed unless the Court directs otherwise.

(k) Solicitors—right of audience

The Lord Chancellor may direct that solicitors may appear as legal representatives in the Crown Court, and the direction may limit this to specified areas, circuits or places. In exercising this power the Lord Chancellor has to pay regard to any shortage of counsel in any area, any rights of audience formerly exercised by solicitors at courts of Q.S. in the area, and any other circumstances affecting the public interest. (Courts Act 1971, s. 12.)

WITNESSES

(1) Interference with Witnesses

It is a common law offence to commit, or conspire to commit, acts designed to pervert or prevent the true course of justice, or its administration, and this would include hindering, dissuading, or preventing the attendance of any witness subpoenaed, summoned or ordered to attend court. Another such offence is "contempt of court", and this might cover other kinds of serious interference with witnesses, e.g. intimidation. An attempt to persuade a witness to give false evidence of a material nature would amount to "subornation of perjury", still another offence at common law. Witnesses are "privileged" against arrest on *civil* process for a reasonable time before and after the trial.

(2) Difficult Witnesses

(a) *Adverse Witness*.—i.e. one whose evidence is unfavourable to the side which calls him. The party which calls such a witness is not entitled to cross-examine or otherwise to attempt to discredit him unless he is deemed to be "hostile" (see below).

(b) *Unwilling Witnesses* (sometimes called "*Reluctant*").—

(i) *At Magistrates' Court*: Refusal to be sworn, to give evidence or to produce any document without just excuse can be met by committal in custody by the court for up to 7 days, or until the witness agrees to testify, or produce such documents.

(ii) *At Higher Courts*: May be committed to prison (as above) for a contempt of court.

(c) *Hostile Witness*.—i.e. one who shows himself opposed to the party calling him, not merely because evidence is unfavourable, but for other additional reasons, e.g. his manner, or behaviour in the box, his refusal to give proper answers tending to show that he is unwilling to speak the truth, not giving full answers, or evidence contrary to that previously given by him. The court on application may permit such a witness to be treated as "hostile" in which case he may be:

(i) cross-examined by own party, and asked "leading questions".

(ii) confronted with his previous inconsistent statement and asked whether he did or did not make it. If he denies this, proof may be given that he did in fact make it. The proof of the earlier statement is not evidence of the facts stated therein, but is evidence only to discredit the story which the witness now tells.

Greenough v. *Eccles* (1859)
A witness is not adverse merely because his testimony is unfavourable to the party calling him. To be adverse so as to entitle the party calling him to prove that he has made another statement inconsistent with his present testimony, such witness must in the opinion of the Judge be hostile.

R. v. *James* (1954)
It would appear that a change of story may be sufficient without other signs of hostility.

R. v. *Fraser & Warren* (1956)
A witness for the prosecution may turn hostile and be unwilling to give evidence against the defendant. Where the prosecution counsel has in his possession a statement

which is contradictory to the evidence given by a witness called by the prosecution, he should show it to the Judge and ask to cross examine the witness as hostile. With the permission of the Judge the witness may then be cross examined as to the previous statement and if necessary witnesses may be called to prove the making of the statement and its contents. On the prosecution counsel failing to do so, the Judge acts quite rightly in calling for the statement and himself cross examining on it.

R. v. *Mann* (1972)

Where a witness denies or does not admit that he has made a statement inconsistent with his present testimony, evidence may be given that he did in fact make it. The previous statement is not evidence of the facts it contains, but is only relevant to show the unreliability of the witness.

(d) *Disorderly Witness.*—A magistrate can direct removal from Court, or order to find sureties for his good behaviour any person who is either obstructive, insulting, disrespectful, or disorderly. The magistrate is not empowered to deal summarily with such contempt of court, but may commit the offender to prison in default of finding such sureties.

(e) *Deaf & Dumb Witness.*—suitable interpreters will be provided upon application to the nearest National Institute for the Deaf to assist the court with witnesses not fully expert in the manual alphabet or who have an incomplete knowledge of the alphabet owing to their disability.

(f) *Child Witness.*—The court may be cleared (excluding officials of Court and Press) when a child or young person is required to testify (e.g. in indecency cases). A child (not being a child in arms) must not be allowed in Court unless he is the accused or for the purpose of giving evidence.

(g) *Witnesses for the Defence.*—when so requested by a Prison Governor on behalf of a prisoner awaiting trial the Police should assist, so far as is practicable, in obtaining attendance of defence witnesses. It is the duty of a police officer entrusted with the enquiries in a criminal case to bring before the Court, so far as he is able, the whole facts of the case, and not merely those points which make for a conviction.

(3) Witnesses in Prison, etc.

The production of an inmate of a prison, borstal institution detention centre, and remand centre to appear as a prosecution witness may generally be authorised by the person in charge of the establishment without reference to the Home Office. Applications should be sent direct to the governor of the establishment where the inmate is detained.

(4) Refreshing Memory

This is permitted if from note made at time of incident, or as soon after as practicable while memory still fresh. Source of reference (e.g. notebook) becomes liable to inspection by the other party, if used. A constable witness should always have his notebook with him because the advocate for the accused may wish to see it, though he would not technically be entitled to this if it had not been used to refresh the memory and no subpoena had been issued in respect of it. However, it would be unwise to refuse except on good grounds and then a direction should be sought from the court and this direction is usually sought before acceding to the request.

Gregory v. *Tavernor* (1833)
The opposite party is entitled to see any document so used and cross-examine upon it without making it his evidence, but if he cross-examines as to other parts of the document not used by the witness he makes them his evidence.

Burton v. *Plummer* (1834)
A witness may not refresh his memory with a copy of an instrument, unless the copy were made by himself, or in his presence, and he knew it to be correct.

Burgess v. *Bennett* (1872)
When a diary is used by a witness to refresh his memory, the cross examining counsel is not entitled to inspect the whole of the diary, but only such parts as refer to the subject matter of the case.

R. v. *Bryant* (1946)
A witness may read any document he pleases before he enters the box, but once in it he may refresh his memory only from a document written so shortly after the events that they were then fresh in his mind.

R. v. *Bass* (1953)
If two or more constables make notes about the same matter, there will be no objection to their consulting together providing that a note is made that this has been done.

Refreshing memory out of court from statements supplied by police

The general rule is that a witness may refresh his memory, while in the witness box, by reference to a document he made (or was made under his direction) soon after the event. As a witness is entitled to a copy of any statement he had made to the police there is nothing to prevent him refreshing his memory right up to the moment he enters the court. There is no rule to prevent a witness seeing a statement he had made at some time reasonably close to the event on which he is to testify. It would be wrong however for the police to permit or arrange for several witnesses to be shown their statements so as to enable them to compare one with another what they had said. (*R.* v. *Richardson* (1971)).

It is desirable that defence be informed of what has been done (*Worley* v. *Bentley* (1976)).

(5) Witnesses "Out of Court"

(i) *At Magistrates' Courts.*—Court can order this on application of either party. If before the hearing, *all* witnesses remain out until required to testify. If application made during a hearing, those not examined at that point are required to leave the court. Disobedience is punishable as contempt but evidence of the witness is still admissible.

(ii) *At the Crown Court.*—It is the practice for witnesses in a case, to remain outside the court until called to give evidence, after which a witness may remain in court.

> *Chandler* v. *Horne* (1842)
> If a witness disobeys an order to leave and remains in court, his evidence will not be rendered inadmissible for that reason but is a matter for observation on his evidence and he may be punished for contempt.

(6) Recalling a Witness

Court can recall at any time. A party can do so only with permission of court on good grounds. The witness is subject to examination again only on such new facts as would be admissible to rebut a "surprise" defence, for court will not normally allow prosecution to give rebutting evidence after it has closed its case, unless the defence is one which could not readily have been anticipated.

> *Adams* v. *Bankart* (1835)
> The permission to recall a witness is entirely in the discretion of the Judge.
>
> *R.* v. *Holden* (1838)
> In a criminal case, the Judge has the right to call and examine any witness whose evidence may be likely to bring out the truth and it is in his discretion whether or not questions by the prosecution or defence to any witness so called should be permitted.
>
> *R.* v. *Cliburn* (1898)
> The evidence of a witness so recalled after the close of the case for the defence should be such as would be admissible only as rebutting evidence.

(7) Character of Witness

Cross-examination of a witness as to bad character is allowed because it affects the credit of the witness which is for the jury to assess. The cross examination of a witness may be wholly devoted to discrediting him and not confined to general reputation. Previous convictions may be put to him, and proved against him if he denies them. Note, however, that where defence attacks character of prosecutor or the witnesses the accused renders himself liable to cross-examination as to his own character if he gives evidence—see p. 30.

R. v. *Carey & Williams* (1968)

Where a prosecution witness is of bad character there is no legal duty on the court or the prosecution to reveal this to the jury.

R. v. *Oliva* (1965)

Where the prosecution chose not to call witnesses because they were considered unreliable, it was held that where the evidence of a witness is capable of belief it is a duty of the prosecution to call the witness—in the interests of justice and in fairness to the accused.

(8) Use of the Welsh language

The Welsh Language Act 1967, provides that any party, witness or other person who wishes to speak the Welsh language may do so in any legal proceedings in Wales providing, in the case of a Crown Court the prescribed notice is given so that arrangements can be made for interpretation. (s. 1).

NOTE:

The Act enables specified government departments by order to prescribe Welsh versions (in whole or part) of any statutory forms or pro formas specified by any enactment for public or other official use. The order will prescribe conditions authenticating the use or production of the Welsh version of the document and where any discrepancy between the English and Welsh text is questioned, the English text must be the one accepted (ss. 2 and 3).

JURIES (Juries Act 1974)

(1) Qualifications

Every person is liable to serve as a juror if he or she:

(a) is not under 18 nor more than 65, and is registered as a parliamentary or local government elector, and

(b) has been ordinarily resident in the U.K., Channel Islands or the Isle of Man for at least five years since reaching the age of 13,

but not if he is for the time being disqualified or ineligible for such service. (s. 1).

(2) Ineligibility, disqualification and exemptions

(a) *Ineligible:*

(i) *Persons connected with the judiciary* including judges, recorders, magistrates, justices, registrars and assistant registrars of any court or tribunal—including in the latter case its Chairman (or Vice) and President (or Vice), and *any person who has been ineligible under this heading at any time.*

(ii) *Others concerned with administration of justice,* including barristers* and solicitors* and their clerks, members of a police force or a police authority, special constables, civilians employed for police purposes by a police authority or employed in a forensic laboratory, officers of any prison, remand centre, detention centre, borstal institution, probation home or hostel, justices' clerks and their assistants, coroners and their deputies or assistants; and any *person who at any time within the last ten years* has been ineligible under this heading.

(iii) *The clergy* and any vowed members of a religious order living in a monastery, convent, or other religious community.

(iv) *The mentally ill* being resident in a hospital or other institution or regularly attended by a doctor; a person adjudged under the Mental Health Act 1959 to be incapable of managing his own affairs or is under guardianship under that Act.

* whether in actual practice as such or not.

(b) *Disqualified.* Any person who has been at any time sentenced in the U.K., the Channel Islands or the Isle of Man:

(i) to imprisonment for life or for a term of 5 years or more, or

(ii) to be detained during H.M. pleasure or pleasure of Governor of N. Ireland.

Also any person in the last ten years in the above named places has:

(i) served any part of a sentence of imprisonment or detention being for a term of 3 months or more, or

(ii) been detained in a borstal institution.

(c) *Excusable as of right:*

(i) *Parliament.* Peers and peeresses and officers of the

House of Lords and members and officers of the House of Commons.

(ii) *The Forces.* Full time serving members of H.M. Forces, the W.R.N.S., the Queen Alexandra's R.N.N.S., or any voluntary aid detachment serving with the Royal Navy. (*Note:* Where the commanding officer certifies that it would be prejudicial to the service for the member to be absent from duty and this is presented to the officer issuing the jury summons, there is no obligation on that member of the Forces to attend.)

(iii) *Medical and other similar professions.*—If practising their professions and registered as such—doctors, dentists, nurses, midwives, veterinary surgeons and practitioners, chemists. (1st. Schedule)

(3) Summoning Jurors

The Lord Chancellor (through Circuit administrators) is responsible for summoning jurors to all courts (except coroners Courts) and for determining the occasions on which they are to attend and the number to be summoned. There is no restriction on the places at which a juror may be required to serve, but in making arrangements regard has to be paid to the convenience of the persons summoned; their places of residence; and the desirability of selecting jurors within reasonable travelling distance. Jurors are summoned by notice in writing sent by post or delivered by hand. Every summons must be accompaned by a notice in writing indicating the provisions of the Act relating to qualifications, disqualifications and ineligibilities of persons serving on a jury in a criminal case. Proof of service is by a certificate signed by the appropriate officer (A.O.) of proper posting (prepaid) and correct address. The summons can be withdrawn or altered by a notice served in the same way as the summons. "Appropriate officer" (A.O.) means the person designated for the particular duty by the Lord Chancellor. (S. 2)

(4) The Panels of Jurors (s. 5)

Lists (called "panels") of persons summoned as jurors (with additional information, e.g. dates of attendance) are prepared in accordance with the directions of the Lord Chancellor. Any party to proceedings, or his representative, is entitled to reasonable facilities to inspect the panel (up to the end of the trial concerned), and this right can be extended by the Court to any other person.

(5) Making Up the Number in Extreme Cases (s. 6)

Where the number of summoned jurors available appears to be insufficient the Court may require persons in the court or its vicinity (who are qualified or who, though not qualified, appear to the Court to be responsible and suitable persons) to be summoned (without written notice) to make up a full jury. The names of these persons are added to the panel. The liability to serve as a juror under this section applies even though the name of the person does not appear in the register of electors.

(6) Attendance and Excusals (s. 7)

The person summoned shall attend on the days directed by the summons or by the A.O., and is liable to serve in the High Court, Crown Court or County Court held at (or in the vicinity of) the place to which he is summoned. The Court (or the A.O. for good reason) can excuse from attendance any person summoned. Appeal against a refusal to excuse by the A.O. lies to the Crown Court.

(7) The Ballot and Swearing (s. 11)

The jury in a particular case is to be selected by ballot in open court from the panel (or part of it) of jurors summoned to attend at that time and place. Balloting does not apply to jurors summoned under s. 6. Jurors are to be sworn singly.

(8) Juries of One Sex and Special Juries Abolished (Courts Act 1971, s. 35 and s. 40)

The provisions of s. 1 of the Sex Disqualification (Removal) Act 1919, which enabled a judge to order that a jury be comprised of men only, or of women only, were repealed by this Act. Special juries are also abolished.

(9) Exemption for Previous Jury Service (s. 8)

The Court or A.O. shall excuse if satisfied that the person has served on a jury* or attended to serve, within 2 years ending with the date on which the summons was served, or that a Court has excused him for a period of years not yet expired. A juror attending in answer to a summons is entitled to a certificate from the A.O. recording that he has so attended.

* Not being a coroner's jury.

(10) Offences (s. 20)

(a) Failure to attend in compliance with summons†, or

(b) After attending in compliance being not available when called on or being unfit for service by reason of drink or drug. (Fine n/e £100).

The offence is punishable on summary conviction or as if the offence were a criminal contempt of court committed in the face of the court. It is a defence to show "reasonable cause".

†Not to apply unless the summons was duly served not later than 14 days before the date fixed for attendance.

(c) (i) false representation to avoid jury service of self or another (£100).

(ii) knowingly to serve on jury while disqualified or ineligible (£400).

(11) Swearing of the Jury

When in the jury-box each juror takes the oath as follows, "I swear by Almighty God that I will well and truly try the several issues joined between our Sovereign Lady, the Queen and the prisoner at the bar and a true verdict give according to the evidence". A juror is not at liberty to leave the box without permission of the court. The jury may be allowed to disperse at any stage before the Judge's summing up, but subject only to an undertaking not to discuss or allow themselves to be spoken to on any subject connected with the trial or to disclose what has occurred in the jury room. It is a contempt of court to do otherwise.

(12) Challenges to Jurors (s. 12)

The accused is informed by the Clerk of the Court that he has a right to object to or challenge any of the jurors as they are called upon to be sworn.

The prosecution or the defence may challenge—

(i) *The array*, i.e. the whole jury, but must specify in writing the grounds for doing so, e.g. some default or partiality of the Sheriff, (rare).

(ii) *The Polls*, i.e. a challenge to particular jurors, which may be:—

(a) *Peremptory*, i.e. without the need to show cause or reason but is restricted to seven jurors, or

(b) *For cause*, i.e. reason for each objection must be shown, e.g.:—some defect in the juror such as suspicion of partiality or bias, being a relative of either party or known to be of weak mental intellect.

R. v. *Page* (1965)
When the accused is not allowed his full number of peremptory challenges of jurors, the trial will be declared a nullity on appeal and a "venire de novo" ordered.

(13) Verdicts

The Juries Act 1974, s. 16 provides that (subject to the discretion of the court to discharge a jury in any case where a juror is unable to continue and order a trial anew) if a juror dies or has to be discharged through illness or any other reason the trial can continue and a verdict arrived at if the number of jurors is not reduced below 9. On a trial for murder or any capital charge the prosecution and the accused must consent to it in writing.

To consider their verdict, the members of the jury usually withdraw to a private room, where no intercourse with other persons is permitted, and where, when their deliberations are protracted, food and other necessaries are provided. If they fail to agree among themselves they are discharged by the judge and the case can be tried anew before a fresh jury.

(14) Majority Verdicts (s. 17)

The verdict of a jury *in criminal proceedings* need not be unanimous and a majority verdict of "guilty" or "not guilty" may be returned:—

(i) by at least 10 jurors out of the normal jury of 12;
(ii) by at least 10 jurors out of 11;
(iii) by at least 9 jurors out of 10.

But will not be accepted by the court *Unless*:—

(i) the foreman of the jury states in open court the actual numbers of jurors for or against the majority verdict of finding the accused "guilty". (If the verdict is "not guilty" a jury is not required to say how many disagreed) *and*
(ii) the jury has had at least 2 hours or more, as thought by the court to be reasonable having regard to the complexity of the case, for deliberation of their verdict.

N.B. If the trial has continued with 9 jurors, the verdict must be unanimous.

Majority verdicts apply to all other jury verdicts in criminal proceedings, *viz*:—a "special verdict" of not guilty by reason of insanity; unfit to plead, whether the accused is mute of malice or by visitation of God, and special pleas in bar, see p. 148.

By s. 17 of the C.J. Act 1967 the judge may order a verdict of "not guilty" to be recorded against a defendant who pleads "not guilty" in any case in which the prosecution offers no evidence against him. This procedure can be followed without putting the defendant in charge of a jury to ask for a formal verdict and has the same effect as any other acquittal by the court which allows for the awarding of costs.

In Scotland where there are normally 15 jurors and where a trial may continue if the number is not reduced below 12, a majority verdict must be supported by at least 8 jurors. (Administration of Justice (Scotland) Act 1933).

R. v. *Elia* (1968)
The words of the section are not mandatory, though they should generally be followed. If a jury says they are hopelessly divided it would be idle to make them wait for the full two hours to announce their inability to reach a decision.

VOIDANCE BY DEFENDANT OF PROCEEDINGS TAKEN IN ABSENCE

(C.J.A. 1967, s. 24)

Where a magistrates' court has begun to try or has tried a summary offence in the absence of the defendant who had been summoned to appear, the defendant may make a statutory declaration that he did not know of the summons or proceedings until a date (specified) after the court had begun to try the case. If he serves the declaration on the clerk of the court within 14 days of the day he has declared to be that on which he became aware of the proceedings, the summons and all subsequent proceedings automatically become void. Process can be re-issued on the original information. The annulment of proceedings does not render illegal anything done by the court or its officers or the police before receipt of the declaration. It is an offence to make a false declaration. (C.J. Act 1967, s. 89.)

EVIDENCE (PROCEEDINGS IN OTHER JURISDICTIONS) ACT 1975

This Act enables evidence to be obtained and recorded by a court in the place where it exercises jurisdiction at the request of and for use in a court in another jurisdiction, even abroad. It authorises certain courts in the U.K. to take this action either

(a) on behalf of each other in both criminal and civil proceedings, or

(b) on behalf of a court outside the U.K., but in this case only where the evidence relates to criminal proceedings which have already been instituted.

The U.K. courts concerned are the High Court (England and Wales), the Court of Session (Scotland), and the High Court of Justice in Northern Ireland. Political offences are excluded and the Perjury Act 1911, has been amended to include evidence given and taken under the provisions of this Act. Procedures will be governed by Regulations to be made under the Act.

CHAPTER IX

CONSEQUENCES OF CONVICTION

General.—When a case is proved (plea or verdict of "Guilty") the court has to decide what the consequence shall be, unless the sentence is one "fixed" by law for the specific crime or verdict. Such "fixed" penalties are:

Death Penalty. For treason, piracy on the high seas accompanied by acts endangering life of person on board the ship, setting fire to or destroying any ships belonging to H.M. The Queen, or vessels of war.

Life Imprisonment. Murder, except in the case of a person under 18 when committing the crime.

Detention during H.M. Pleasure. Murder by persons under 18, and on special verdict of "Not guilty by reason of insanity".

In all other cases the law provides a variety of courses from which choice can be made *having regard to the circumstances of the particular case, including the nature of the charge, and the character of the accused* (i.e. to make the punishment fit the offender as well as the crime).

KINDS OF SENTENCES

The sentences which can be imposed or applied by the court can, perhaps be best summarised as follows:

1. *Not involving punishment.*—

(1) by *Binding Over* e.g. to keep the Peace.

(2) by *Order of Discharge*, either

(a) Absolutely or (b) conditionally.

(3) By making a *Probation Order.*

2. *Pecuniary penalty,* i.e.—by *fine* in which can be included any order constituting financial disadvantage, e.g. compensation, restitution.

3. *Detention or Imprisonment.*—

(1) *Prison Sentence* (which may be in addition to, or instead of, a fine) including a "suspended" sentence.

(2) Detention in Police Cells.

(3) In case of persons under 21, *detention* in

(a) *Detention Centre,* or

(b) *Borstal.*

(4) To protect the public from a persistent offender by imposing an "extended" term of imprisonment (on indictment only after certain previous convictions—see p. 175).

(5) Community service—see p. 181.

N.B.—3 (3) above (detention of persons under 21) is dealt with later in Chapter X.

SENTENCES NOT INVOLVING PUNISHMENT

1. Binding Over

A Binding Over (with or without sureties), is a recognisance entered into:

(a) *To Keep the Peace* (Common Law), and/or

(b) *To be of Good Behaviour* (Justices of the Peace Act 1361).

It may be required by a criminal court of a person who or whose case is before it (J. of P. Act 1968, s. 1).

(i) *Without Conviction*

A summary court may require a person to enter into recognisances (usually for a period up to 12 months) as a preventive measure, if there are grounds to believe that he is likely to commit a breach of the peace in respect of any complainant in particular, or by his conduct in general—rioters, night revellers, peeping toms, etc.

Failure to comply with such a requirement renders the person liable to imprisonment for a term of not exceeding six months. On failure to comply with the conditions of the recognisance (may be on complaint of surety) the principal becomes liable to appear before the court (by summons or warrant) and his recognisance may be forfeited or a new one ordered.

Such a Binding Over is not a "conviction" as he has not been charged with any offence, but there is a right of appeal.

(ii) *After Conviction*

(a) *By Statute.*—Instead of or in addition to any other punishment, on conviction of any indictable offence (except murder) within specified Acts (i.e. Offences Against the Persons Act 1861, Forgery Act 1913 and Coinage Offences Act 1936). Failure to find sureties (if required by the court) makes him liable to imprisonment for up to one year.

(b) *At Common Law.*—In addition to or in substitution for any other punishment for conviction of any indictable offence. A court may on conviction on indictment "bind over" to come up for judgment when called upon. A Binding Over on indictment is regarded in law as a previous conviction on indictment for all purposes.

R. v. *Ossett JJ. ex p. Tebb* (1972).
Where there has been a binding over to keep the peace, the court cannot order a forfeiture of the recognizance except

on proceedings for this purpose initiated by way of complaint against the person concerned in accordance with sections 43 and 45 of the Magistrates' Courts Act 1952.

2. Absolute or Conditional Discharge

If the court thinks punishment inexpedient and probation order not appropriate it can make an *Order*:

(a) *Discharging* offender *absolutely*, or

(b) *Discharging* him subject to *condition* that he commits no offence during a stated period, not to exceed 3 years (which is to be explained in ordinary language to offender).

If further offence is committed within period of the order he can be brought back to the court to be sentenced for the original offence, in the same way as in the case of an offender on probation (see p. 168) except that in this case reference to a Supervising Court will not apply.

NOTE: If offender is subsequently sentenced for original offence by virtue of offending again, the original "discharge" ceases to have further effect.

Important. By the Powers of Criminal Courts Act 1973, s. 13, neither *discharge* (absolute or conditional) nor *probation* constitute a conviction for any purpose for which a previous conviction is required to be proved, unless the offender by breach of a condition or further offence, is dealt with again for the original offence and convicted. Probation or discharge can, however, be referred to in the general antecedents of an accused person as a "finding of guilt". In connection with this subject it should be noted that the C.J.A. 1967, s. 51, provides that probation or discharge on a charge under the R.T.A. 1972, is a conviction for the purpose of disqualification and/or endorsement of a driving licence and will count towards the "totting-up" procedure when disqualification is imposed for a subsequent offence.

3. Probation and after care (Powers of Criminal Courts Act 1973)

This service operates through "probation and after-care committees" appointed for "probation and after-care areas" which comprise one or more petty sessional divisions.

The committee consists of justices of the peace for the area who co-opt non-justices with after-care knowledge and experience, the latter not to exceed one-third of the committee. The Lord Chancellor may appoint judges of the High Court and additional justices who have sat in a Crown Court to be members of the committee.

Probation officers are appointed by committees and work under the direction and control of the Probation and After-Care Department of the Home Office which undertakes responsibilities for the central training of the service and periodic inspections (50% grant in aid as in the case of the police service). The primary function of the probation officer is the supervision of offenders under probation orders, but they now also include duties—

(a) under supervision orders made in matrimonial proceedings under the C. & Y.P. Acts in respect of children,
(b) concerning money payment supervision orders in respect of fines imposed by magistrates' courts,
(c) of making social enquiries concerning adults appearing before magistrates' courts, e.g. matrimonial cases or in guardianship or adoption, and in respect of offenders appearing for the first time before the court accused of an offence punishable by imprisonment,
(d) of conciliation work in matrimonial cases,
(e) relating to the voluntary or compulsory after-care of persons released (or on licence) from prisons, borstals, detention centres and approved schools concerning their problems of, employment, obtaining money, finding accommodation returning home and general rehabilitation.

Probation (which can now be applied only to an offender aged 17 years or more) involves making an order under s. 2 requiring an offender to be under the supervision of a probation officer of the petty sessional area of residence (the magistrates' court which becomes the "supervising Court") *for not less than one or more than three years*. The court may *also* add further requirements to secure good conduct during the probation period, including:

(a) residence in *approved probation hostel* or *Home* or any other institution specified in the order for not more than 12 months. (If place not an "Approved" one the Home Secretary to be informed).
(b) submission to *mental treatment* (on medical evidence that this is needed):
    (i) at hospital (resident or out-patient), or
    (ii) under care of named doctor. (s 3)

Attendance at a Day Training Centre

A probation order may include a requirement that the offender shall attend at a specified day training centre, if the S. o. S. has notified the availability of such a centre in the petty sessions area in which the offender resides, or will reside, but this does not apply if the order includes a requirement for the treatment of the offender for a mental condition. Such a requirement obliges the offender to attend the Centre as directed by the probation officer (on not more than 60 days) and there to comply with instructions given by or for the person in charge of the Centre. Training at the Centre is regulated by rules made by the S. o. S. References to attendance at a Centre include attendance elsewhere to receive training as directed by the person in charge of the Centre.

Supervising Court, can:

(a) amend order by cancelling any requirement or adding new one (but not reduce or expand probation period beyond 3 years from date of original order or the hostel residence to more than 12 months). The amendment cannot be such as to make the probationer submit to mental treatment unless made within 3 months of the date of the original order.

(b) where probationer moves to another district, make court of that district the "supervising court".

NOTES:

1. Terms of probation to be explained by trial court.
2. Order can be made only if the offender agrees.
3. A Supervising Court can, on application made by the probation officer or probationer—
   (a) discharge (i.e. cancel) the order unless the Crown court making the order reserves this power to itself; or
   (b) substitute the probation order for one of conditional discharge for the same period;
   (c) cancel the residence requirement at hostel or other institution of the order, if any.
4. Court can accept a surety for good behaviour when making an order of probation.

Breach of Probation Requirement

(a) *If Order was made by Magistrates' Court.*—Supervising Court or Court of conviction can:

(i) deal with offender for original offence, as if just convicted of it. (Probation order ceases unless new probation order made.)

(ii) impose fine up to £50 (order continues), or

(iii) if under 21, order attendance at Attendance Centre (Order continues).

Appearance of probationer can be by summons or warrant issued by justice of either district, i.e. where order made or at Supervising Court.

(b) *Order made at Crown Court.*—Justice of supervising court district can issue summons or warrant for appearance of probationer who has to be committed in custody or on bail (with or without sureties) to the court at which placed on probation which may deal with him as if just convicted of original offence or impose a fine n/e £50, leaving the probation order in force.

(c) *Order made at any court.* When ss. (3) (b), (6) (b) and (10) of the Powers of Courts Act 1973 are brought into force the court, on a charge of failure to comply with a probation order requirement, may make a Community Service Order instead of dealing with the charge in any other way, and without prejudice to the continuance of the probation order.

N.B.—Refusal to comply with requirement to submit to mental treatment not to be a "breach" if court considers refusal reasonable.

Commission of Further Offence (*s.* 8.)

If during probation period the probationer is convicted of an offence, he becomes liable to be dealt with for the original offence but the question is what court can so deal with it.

In the case of an *Order made by a Magistrates' Court* it can be dealt with by the court before which the second conviction takes place if:

(a) It is the court which made the original order, or the Supervising Court, or
(b) In the case of another Magistrates' Court the consent of the original court or supervising court has been obtained, or
(c) It is a Crown Court.

If (b) does not apply, then the probationer has, after conviction for second offence, to appear (by summons or warrant) before the original (or supervising) Magistrates' Court (see later).

In the case of an *Order made by the Crown Court* it can be dealt with only at such a court, by appearance direct by summons or warrant from that Court or by committal (in custody or on bail) from the magistrates' court before which he stands convicted or the supervising court before which he can be brought for the purpose.

H. O. Circ. 177/66:—As soon as the police of the area of the Court before which the new charge is to be heard become aware through pre-trial enquiries that the offender is the subject of a current probation order (or of an order for conditional discharge) they should inform the clerk of that court accordingly. This should be done whether proceedings are instituted by arrest or summons. The clerk will in conjunction with the probation officer if necessary, contact the original or supervising court to obtain consent that both offences should be dealt with together in the event of a conviction on the new charge.

If time is short it might be advisable to remand the case to await a reply from the original court in order that the whole matter may be completed before the accused is sentenced. If for any reason this procedure is not followed the police bringing the new charge remain responsible for taking the necessary steps to ensure that the matter is brought before the original or supervising Court in the event of a conviction.

PECUNIARY PENALTIES

Pecuniary penalties which the Courts may impose, include fines costs, damages and compensation.

Fines

(1) Up to the maximum specified for the particular offence, which may be additional to imprisonment where the statute so provides.

(2) The maximum fines which may be imposed by a Magistrates' Court are—

  (a) for an offence punishable by imprisonment where no fine is specified .... n/e £100

  (b) for an indictable offence tried summarily when committed by:—

    (i) an adult .... n/e £400

    (ii) a young person (14 to 17 years).......... n/e £50

(3) On a child (under 14 years) for any offence .... n/e £10

Costs and Compensation

In addition to a fine, discharge or probation order, the court can order payment of costs and make a compensation order.

Compensation (Powers of Criminal Courts Act, ss. 35–38).

Main Rule. A court by whom a person is convicted of an offence may, *in addition to* dealing with him in any other way*, make a Compensation Order (C.O.) requiring him to pay compensation for any personal injury, loss or damage resulting from that offence† or an offence taken into consideration (t.i.c.) in determining sentence. The court must have regard to the offender's means before making the order, and in determining the amount to be paid (s. 1). An order cannot be made where there is no evidence of damage (*R.* v. *Sharkey* (1976)).

* but it cannot combine a criminal bankruptcy with a C.O.

† where property subject to a charge under the Theft Act 1968, is recovered, any damage to the property occurring while it was out of the owner's possession is deemed to have resulted from the offence, however and by whomsoever caused. "Resulting from" can cover a wide range of consequences, e.g. in an assault case it could include damage to clothing caused by the assault even though a charge of criminal damage has not been made.

(a) *Exceptions.* No C.O. can be made in respect of:

(i) loss by dependants in consequence of the death of a person, or

(ii) injury, loss or damage due to a motor vehicle road accident, except such damage as is treated (as above) as resulting from an offence under the Theft Act 1968.

(b) *Limits of amounts ordered to be paid.*

(i) *In a magistrates' court.* Maximum for *each* offence of which convicted is £400, and for any or all offence(s) t.i.c. with that offence at the time the amount is not to exceed the difference (if any) between £400 and the amount (or total amount) ordered to be paid for the offence of which convicted, i.e. the total amount of the C.O. for the offence and that or those for the offence(s) t.i.c. with it cannot exceed £400.

(ii) *Higher Courts*—no legal limitation imposed.

(c) *Suspension and appeals.* A C.O. made by a magistrates' court has to be suspended until the period allowed for appeal (usually 28 days) has expired. Where notice of appeal is properly given it is suspended until the appeal has been determined. A C.O. in respect of offence(s) t.i.c. ceases to have effect if there is a successful appeal against the offence (or all the offences) of which person was convicted. An appeal lies against a C.O. made for an offence t.i.c. as if it were part of the sentence imposed for that offence (s. 2).

(d) *Review of Orders.* The magistrates' court responsible for enforcing the C.O. can, on application of the offender, discharge the order or reduce the amount payable under it, if the C.O. has not been fully complied with and

(i) the property connected with the C.O. has been recovered, or

(ii) it appears to the court from civil proceedings taken that the loss, damage or injury was in fact less than the amount for which the order was made (s. 3).

NOTES:

A C.O. is enforceable in the same way as any other order made for the payment of money. The Court can direct settlement of a C.O. by instalments or allow time to pay. In the application of money received by the justices' clerk from the offender under a C.O. the discharge of the C.O. takes precedence over any order as to costs.

Restitution

Section 28 of the Theft Act 1968, enables restitution to be ordered by the court in relation to property stolen or obtained by deception or blackmail. This subject is dealt with in Handbook No. 1. Section 6 of the C.J.A. 1972 amends s. 28 of the 1968 Act in the following respects:

(a) An order for payment to be made to a person out of money taken from the offender on his arrest can be made without an application being made by that person or on his behalf.

(b) An order for restitution can be made for an offence t.i.c. as well as for the offence of which convicted, and in such a case an appeal lies against the order as if it were part of the sentence for that offence.

(c) The order has to be suspended pending the determination of an appeal, except where the court waives the suspension because it is satisfied that the title to the goods is not in dispute.

Criminal Bankruptcy (Powers of Criminal Courts Act, ss. 39–41).

A Crown Court can make a criminal bankruptcy order on conviction of an offence involving loss or damage to property to the amount of £15,000 or more, provided that proceedings have established liability for the loss and the evidence has been sufficient to identify the victims and their respective losses. The order will constitute an "act of bankruptcy" within the meaning of the Bankruptcy Act 1914.

NOTES:

(i) The court may order that any pecuniary penalty imposed on a child or young person be paid by the parent or guardian, and must do so in the case of a child unless the parent or guardian cannot be found or did not conduce to the commission of the offence.

(ii) Sums ordered to be paid as a parent or guardian under (i) above are enforceable in the civil courts or by attachment of earnings.

(iii) For enforcement and collection of payment of fines, etc. see App. 3.

(iv) Wherever a sum of money is ordered to be paid the court can allow time to pay or order payment by instalments.

DETENTION OR IMPRISONMENT

1. Imprisonment—as to suspended sentences see p. 177.

(a) *Maximum.*—This is specified by the law relating to the crime.

Indictment: Life or during H.M. Pleasure.

Summarily: Six months normally (single or in aggregate), but for indictable offences may be twelve months in aggregate.

(b) *Minimum.*—

Indictment: None. e.g. for one day to mean immediate release.

Summarily: 5 days, but can order detention for lesser period in "approved" police cells.

(c) *Remission*—applies only to "determinate" sentences, and not to sentences of life imprisonment or during H.M. Pleasure. On sentences of so many months or years (exceeding one month) the period of remission is based on marks earned for good conduct, etc., but cannot exceed one-third of sentence. Release on account of remission is a complete release without question of licence or conditions. Release earlier than is justified by remission entitlement may be ordered by the Secretary of State under the C.J.A. 1967 (see p. 208) but such releases are always "on licence." There may be releases on licence instead of complete releases on remission where remission has not been earned. Half of sentence may be remitted for any person under 17 when the detention order was made. (Detention Centre (Amendment) Rules 1975).

(d) *Restrictions* (*also applicable to suspended sentence*)

(a) Not on person under 17. (Powers of Criminal Courts Act, 1973, s. 19).

(b) Not on person under 21 unless no other method of dealing with him is considered by the court to be appropriate, having regard to circumstances and the character and mental condition of the offender

(c) Not on person of or over 21 not previously sentenced to imprisonment, unless no other course appropriate. A sentence of imprisonment (unless fixed by law) shall not be imposed on a person who has attained the age of 21 and has not previously been sentenced to imprisonment unless the court is of opinion that no other method of dealing with him is appropriate, and for the purpose of determining this point the court must obtain and consider information about the circumstances and take into account any information before it relevant to his character and physical and mental condition. Where a magistrates' court does impose imprisonment it must state the reason for its opinion that no other method of dealing with the case is appropriate, and cause this to be specified in the warrant of commitment and entered in the court register. (s. 20).

NOTE:

The age of the person is to be deemed that which it appears to the court to be after considering available evidence. A previous suspended sentence not put into effect is to be disregarded. Because a sentence of imprisonment cannot be imposed in the above circumstances, it follows that a suspended sentence cannot be imposed either. "Sentence of imprisonment" does not include a committal or attachment for contempt of court.

(d) The Criminal Justice Act 1967, s. 26 prohibits a magistrates' court from sentencing a person *in his absence* to *imprisonment, detention in a detention centre* or *order a suspended sentence* for a previous offence to take effect on his further conviction. If the court so wishes, it can adjourn the case after conviction and before sentence to secure presence by service upon him of a notice of adjournment stating the reason for the adjournment. A warrant for his arrest will be issued if he fails to comply with the notice.

(e) *Unrepresented offender.*—A sentence of imprisonment, Borstal training, or of detention in a detention centre cannot be imposed on a person who is not legally represented and who has not been sentenced previously to that punishment*, unless either

  (i) his application for legal aid was refused because it did not appear that his means were such that he required such aid, or

  (ii) having been informed of his right to apply for legal aid and having had an opportunity to do so, he refused or failed to apply. (s. 21).

* In any part of the U.K., but does not include a suspended sentence which has not taken effect.

NOTE: A person is to be regarded as having legally represented if (and only if) he had had the assistance of counsel or solicitor to represent him at the court at some time after verdict and before sentence.

NOTES:

(i) Imprisonment may be made alternative to payment of fine, or, where statute so provides, additional to fine.

(ii) Any time spent in custody before or after committal for trial or sentence (including time on remand between magistrates' court hearings) is deducted from a sentence of imprisonment imposed by any court in England and Wales (C.J.A. 1967, s. 67).

Exceptions. This does not apply to time spent in custody by an offender who is subsequently sentenced for the original offence following a further conviction for an offence† committed during the period that he had been—

(a) placed on probation,

† including a breach of the requirements of a probation order.

(b) made subject to conditional discharge,

(c) subject to a suspended sentence.

(iii) Corporal punishment for offences by prisoners against prison discipline is prohibited (s. 65).

2. Detention for Short Periods in Police Cells, etc. (M.C. Act 1952)

Where imprisonment can be imposed (therefore not person under 17), the court may instead *order Detention*:

(a) For period *not exceeding four days* in place certified as suitable by Home Secretary (e.g. police cell). Not a female unless under supervision of a woman.

(b) Until *not later than* 8 *p.m. same day* in court precincts or at police station—but not to such late hour as would deprive him of reasonable opportunity of getting home the same day. This and (a) above are exceptions to the general legal requirement that all sentences of imprisonment of 6 months or less shall be suspended sentences.

For detention at police station of a fine defaulter, etc., see "Warrants", p. 71.

3. Extended Sentences of Imprisonment (Powers of Criminal Courts Act 1973, ss. 28 and 29)

Sentences of "corrective training" and "preventive detention" for the punishment of persistent offenders were abolished in 1967 but, instead, if certain conditions are fulfilled, there may be imposed an extended sentence of imprisonment, i.e. one which exceeds the sentence which would otherwise have been imposed for the offence. The court must be satisfied, by reason of his previous conduct and of the likelihood of his committing further offences, that it is expedient to protect the public from the offender for a substantial time.

The other requirements are as follows—

(a) convicted on indictment of an offence punishable by two years imprisonment or more.

(b) The offence was committed within three years of either:—

  (i) a conviction (on indictment or summarily) of an offence punishable on indictment by 2 years imp. or more, or

  (ii) his final release* from prison after serving a sentence of imprisonment, corrective training or preventive detention following conviction for such an offence.

  * Includes release on licence but not a temporary release.

(c) Three previous occasions on which convicted *on indictment* since the age of 21 of offences punishable on indictment with imprisonment for 2 years or more.

(d) The total length of sentences (imprisonment, C.T. or P.D.) for the three occasions as in (c) not less than 5 years.

(e) On one of the three occasions (in (c)) there was a sentence of P.D., *or*, if not,

(i) on at least two of the occasions there was a sentence of imprisonment (other than a suspended sentence not put into effect) or of C.T. *and*

(ii) *one* of the two was for 3 years or more for *one* offence *or* both were for 2 years or more for *one offence*

Remember. Each of the above (a) to (e) must apply.

Limits upon extensions of sentences.

It is important to remember that the section simply empowers a court to impose a longer sentence than it would have done if the provisions of the section had not applied. For example in a case (carrying a maximum of 10 years) in which the sentence would normally have been say, 6 years, the Court can extend it under this section (where the conditions apply) to a term not exceeding 10 years, i.e. the maximum. If the normal maximum for the offence is 10 years or more the extension of the sentence cannot be taken beyond that maximum, but in the case of any offence carrying less than 10 years as a normal maximum, that maximum can be exceeded as follows—

Normal Maximum:	*Sentence can be extended to a maximum of:*
Less than 5 years.	5 years
5 or more, but less than 10 years	10 years

An extended sentence certificate has to be issued by the Court which imposes an extended term of imprisonment. The certificate has to state that the extended term was imposed by the Court. It is attached to the Court order of committal and sent with it to the Governor of the prison.

Notice of previous convictions

Section 29 provides that no account shall be taken by the court of any previous conviction or sentence unless notice has been given to the offender at least *three days* before the later sentence is passed on him. In practice, therefore, the notice of convictions or sentences to be proved should be served as soon as practicable, and the offender invited (on a separate form) to acknowledge service and to state whether he admits the convictions or sentences (or both) set out therein. Forms of the notice, of the acknowledgment of service by the accused and of the certificate of service are given in H.O. Circular 149/1967. The court may adjourn a case to enable the notice to be served (or to allow the required 3 days to elapse after service of notice) in compliance with s. 29. A certificate of service must be completed and attached to the copy of the notice which has been served, together with any acknowledgement of service and of convictions signed by the accused.

Such a certificate of service purporting to be signed by a constable or by a prison officer is evidence of service and of the contents of the notice (s. 29 (4)). It is for the police to establish from records the liability of an accused person to s. 28 and to initiate and procure service of the notice. If in prison the notice may be served by a prison officer; two copies of the notice and one of the acknowledgment being sent to the Governor to enable this to be done and a certified copy returned.

Certificate of Prison Governor. A certificate purporting to be signed by a Prison Governor to the effect that a prisoner was finally released on a specified day after serving a specified sentence, or that a prisoner had not been finally released on a specified date after serving sentence is evidence of these matters. In the case of a prisoner released before 1/10/67 or where the fact that a prisoner had not been finally released from prison when he committed the offence has to be established, the Governor of the prison will provide the police, on request, with the certificate required. See also "Release on licence" p. 208.

Proof of qualifying convictions, etc.

Proof of the qualifying convictions and sentences will require production of—

(a) copy of the Notice served on the accused,

(b) acknowledgment form signed by the accused,

(c) certificate of service signed by the serving officer,

and may require production of:—

(d) certificate signed by the prison Governor.

The police will be ready to prove the previous convictions formally *Only if* the offender will not sign the acknowledgment form in (b) or has withdrawn his signed admission before the hearing. As to proof of previous convictions, see Chapter XI. The advance copy of the accused's antecedents sent to the Clerk of the Court should indicate which previous convictions it is intended to prove, and the last paragraph should state that "notice in pursuance of s. 29 of the Powers of Criminal Courts Act 1973, has been served upon the prisoner".

4. Suspended Sentences of Imprisonment

By s. 22 of the Powers of Criminal Courts Act 1973 a court (as an alternative to sending an offender to serve an immediate sentence of imprisonment) may make an order suspending for a specified period of *at least one but no more than two years* (the "operational period") any sentence of imprisonment* *n/e 2 years* then imposed by it for any one offence.

A suspended sentence must not be imposed unless it appears to the court that the case is one in which the court would have imposed a sentence of imprisonment if the power to suspend were absent. Where a sentence is suspended the court shall not make a probation order in respect of another offence of which he was convicted at the same time, but (*R.* v. *King*, 1970) there is nothing to prevent a suspended sentence and a fine being imposed for the same offence.

NOTE: See also suspended sentence supervision orders (p. 180). in respect of suspension of a prison sentence of more than six months.

> *R.* v. *Sapiano* (1968); *R.* v. *Hammond* (1969).
> A suspended sentence should not be passed on the same occasion as a sentence of imprisonment which is to take effect immediately, or be made consecutive to a sentence of imprisonment already being served.

The court must explain to the offender, when made subject to a suspended sentence, the extent of his liability if he should again be convicted of an offence punishable with imprisonment during the period of suspension.

Procedure

(i) A sentence of imprisonment (suspended as above) will not become effective unless the offender commits in G.B. during the "operational period" another offence punishable with imprisonment. If so, a court so authorised* must, on re-conviction, order the original term to take effect immediately and either concurrently with or consecutive to any other term of imprisonment imposed by that or another court unless, for reasons stated by the court, it would be unjust to do so.

When the court is of the opinion that mitigating circumstances exist, and it does not by order impose the original term of imprisonment unaltered, it may deal with the suspended sentence by—

(a) ordering that it shall take effect by imposing imprisonment for a lesser term than the "suspended sentence", or
(b) making no order in respect of the suspended sentence (which continues in suspension), or
(c) vary the "operational period" so as to extend it for a period of n/e 2 years from the date of variation.

The clerk of the court which deals with a suspended sentence should notify the Court which passed the sentence of the manner it had been dealt with. A right of appeal lies against the decision.

* The authorised courts are—any magistrates' court if the suspended sentence was passed by a magistrates' court; and the Crown Court in respect of a suspended sentence imposed by *any* court.

(ii) If an offender who is subject to a suspended sentence is convicted by a magistrates' court of an offence punishable with imprisonment, the court should commit him in custody or on bail to the Crown Court which passed the suspended sentence, but if this would be likely to cause hardship to the defendant, he may be committed to be dealt with by another more convenient Crown Court centre.

(iii) Where the magistrates' court does not commit as in (ii), it must give written notice of the conviction to the clerk of the higher court concerned, (this must also be done by any court in Scotland after reconvicting such an offender of an offence punishable with imprisonment).

NOTE: The police, in practice, will notify the reconvicting court at the same time of the reconviction that the offender is subject to an suspended sentence, but if this is not done because it was not known at the time or, where the reconviction takes place in Scotland, the police bring notice of the reconviction to the court which passed the suspended sentence for such action as it may wish to take. (H.O. Circ.)

(iv) A judge or justice having jurisdiction* may issue a summons or warrant (enforceable in Scotland) to bring such an offender before the court by which the suspended sentence was passed. A justice of the peace shall not issue—

(i) *A summons*—except on information†, or

(ii) *A warrant*—except on sworn information† in writing. Where the offender cannot be brought forthwith before the suspending Crown Court, the warrant may require him to be brought before a magistrates' court when (subject to the conditions referred to in (ii) ante) he may be committed in custody or on bail to some other more convenient court.

* means a judge of the Crown Court which passed the suspended sentence, and if passed by a magistrates' court—a justice of the area for which the court acts.

† includes a notice from a court of the reconviction of the offender sent to the clerk of the court which passed the suspended sentence.

NOTES:

(a) An offender sentenced to borstal training cannot be dealt with by the court in respect of a suspended sentence to which he might be subject unless the more recent conviction is quashed on appeal.

(b) A suspended sentence is not a conviction of imprisonment which disqualifies for or involves loss of office or forfeiture of pension until it has taken effect by order of a court and then counts as imprisonment for all purposes of law.

(c) A court which orders a suspended sentence to take effect may direct detention in a detention centre in lieu of imprisonment if—

(i) the sentence is for a term n/e 6 months,

(ii) that court would have had power to order such detention if it had then convicted him of the original offence (i.e. detention of offenders under 21 years).

The court order will include the direction (to run concurrent with or consecutive to any other term for which the offender is liable to be detained there) and the court which passes the suspended sentence must be notified accordingly.

(d) A court cannot pass a suspended sentence on a person committed as an incorrigible rogue, that being a status and not an offence (*R.* v. *Theophile* [1975]).

(e) A person subject to a suspended sentence may be particularly tempted on that account to give false particulars of himself on subsequent arrest. A fingerprint check (where applicable) should be made as quickly as possible. If not practicable (consent refused, etc.) send form C.4/74 to C.R.O. as soon as possible for descriptive search, and then, if and when fingerprints are obtained, send form and a further C.4/74 (cross reference to the earlier one) for fingerprint search.

5. Suspended Sentence Supervision Order

(1) *The Order.*

(i) Where for a single offence a sentence of imprisonment *for more than six months* is imposed but suspended the court may make a Supervision Order (S.O.) placing the offender under the supervision of a supervising officer for a period specified—not to exceed the operational period of the suspended sentence. (Powers of Criminal Courts, s. 26).

(ii) When an offender already subject to a suspended sentence (S.S.) has been convicted of another offence, and the court deals with the case other than by ordering the S.S. to take effect (i.e. by varying the operative period of the S.S. or making the order with respect to it), the court can make a S.O. (including an S.O. to replace an extension order) for the period, or the extended period, of the operational period of the S.S. (26 (10)).

NOTES:

(a) Unlike a probation order the consent of the offender is not needed.

(b) The order is designed to cover the case where the court in suspending the sentence, considers that the offender would benefit from supervision and that this might help him not to commit another offence.

(c) The S.O. specifies the petty sessions area in which the offender resides or will reside, and the supervising officer is the probation officer for that area (P.O.). On making an S.O. the court must explain its effect to the offender in ordinary language.

(d) The offender must keep in touch with the P.O. as instructed by him and must notify the P.O. of any change of address.

(e) The court provides copies of the S.O. for the P.O. and the offender, and has to send a copy to the clerk of the magistrates' court specified in the S.O. (if it is in another court) together with documents and information relating to the case.

(f) A S.O. ceases to have effect if, before the end of the period specified in it, the court orders that the suspended sentence shall have effect, or the order is discharged or replaced by the court on application by the P.O. or the offender.

(2) *Breach of requirement.* A justice can issue a summons or warrant to secure the appearance of the offender to answer a charge of breach of any requirement of the S.O. before the court specified in the S.O. Penalty for such a breach without reasonable excuse is a fine n/e £50.

6. Community Service Orders (Powers of Criminal Courts Act 1973, ss. 14–17)

(1) *Making an order* (s. 15). On conviction of an offence punishable with imprisonment the court can, if the offender is 17 or over, make a Community Service Order (C.S.O.) instead of dealing with him in any other way*. The Order requires him to perform unpaid work for such number of hours (not less in total than 40 or more than 240†) as the Order specifies.

* but this does not bar an order for costs, disqualification, or (under this Act) compensation, restitution, deprivation of property used for crimes, bankruptcy, or disqualification when vehicle is used for crime.

† May be varied by order of the S.o.S. If there is more than one order, not concurrent, maximum hours of the aggregate is not to exceed this figure.

Conditions precedent

(a) the offender must consent and there must be available in the petty sessions area where the offender resides (or will reside) facilities for community work—notified to the court by the S.o.S.

(b) The court must be satisfied that the offender is a suitable person to perform work under the order (having regard to the report or evidence of the probation officer), and that provision can be made for him to do such work.

NOTES:

(i) Copies of the order, etc., to be given and sent as for Supervision Orders (see p. 180).

(ii) The order specifies the petty sessions area in which the offender resides or will reside.

(iii) The duties of the "relevant officer" (R.O.) are to be discharged by the probation officer of the court area specified or by a person appointed for these duties by the area's probation or after-care committee.

(iv) Before making the order the court must explain to the offender its purpose and effect (particularly the provisions of s. 16), the consequences of failure to comply, and the power of the court to review the order on application by the offender or a probation officer.

(v) "Offence punishable by imprisonment" can be construed without regard to restriction on imprisonment of young offenders.

(2) *Obligations of the offender* (s. 15)

(a) To report to the R.O. and notify him of any change of address.

(b) To perform such work and at such times as the R.O. may direct for the number of hours specified in the order.

NOTES:

(i) Work is to be performed during 12 months from date of order.

(ii) Instructions by the R.O. must, as far as practicable, avoid conflict with the offenders' religious belief and interference with the times of his normal work or attendances at school or other educational establishment.

(iii) A Home Office circular indicates that the kinds or types of work envisaged are activities which involve direct help to individuals (e.g. decorating homes of elderly and handicapped people) and those which help the community at large, e.g. helping to construct a community centre, or to build an adventure playground.

(3) *Breach of requirements* (*including failure to work satisfactorily* (s. 16). A justice of the area specified in the order can issue a summons or warrant to procure appearance before a magistrates' court of the area, which can impose a fine of up to £50, or

revoke the order and deal with the offender for the original offence, unless the order was made by a Crown Court, in which case the magistrates' court has to commit the offender (custody or bail) to the Crown Court. In the case of such a committal the lower court must send to the Crown Court a certificate signed by a justice giving particulars of the failure of the offender to comply, and any other information deemed desirable. Such a certificate is admissible before the Crown Court as evidence of that failure, which is for the court and not the jury to determine. The Crown Court can fine up to £50 or deal with the case as if the order had not been made.

(4) *Amendment and revocation* (s. 17). On application of the offender or the R.O. the court can (a) extend the twelve months limit or, if the order was made by a magistrates' court, (b) revoke the order and deal with the offender for the original offence. If order was made by a Crown Court the offender must be committed (and the necessary particulars sent) to that court which can act as in (a) or (b) above.

(5) *General.*

(a) Appeals from decisions of the magistrates' court lie to Crown Court.

(b) If the offender changes his address to another court area and arrangements for community work exist in that area, the court named in the order can substitute the other court as the supervising court and send on to it copies of documents and relevant information.

(c) The S.o.S. may make rules regulating the performance of community work and, in particular, as to maximum daily hours, recording of time worked, payment of expenses, and keeping records of work done.

(d) Where the amendment or revocation is proposed by a Magistrates' Court, other than on the application of the offender, the court shall summon him to appear or may issue a warrant on non-appearance.

CHAPTER X

EVIDENCE AND PROCEDURE—RELATING TO YOUNG PERSONS

(NOTE: *Where not otherwise stated date references are to the various Acts relating to Children and Young Persons—abbreviations used include L.A.—Local Authority; S. o S.—Secretary of State*).

PROCEEDINGS GENERALLY

1. Legal Presumptions—see p. 2.

2. Liability to Court Proceedings.

(1) *Criminal Proceedings*—

(a) Under 10—cannot commit any offence (1933 s. 50).

(b) 10 or more—liable to prosecution for any offence, but:

(i) a male under 14 is presumed incapable of sexual intercourse;

(ii) if under 17 care proceedings become an alternative to prosecution, except in case of homicide;

(iii) The S. o S. can, under 1969, s. 4, specify an age below which a child cannot be charged with any offence other than homicide.

(iv) In the case of a person aged 13 years or more but not 17 no care proceedings nor proceedings for any offence shall be begun unless the prosecution has (in addition to notifying the local authority) given notice of the proceedings to the probation officer for the court area. (1969, s. 34 (2)).

(2) *Care Proceedings* (which relate to persons of *any age* under 17)—cannot be taken in respect of a person of 16 who is or was married. See also (iv) above.

3. Arrest or Detention—With Warrant.

(1) *For Care Proceedings* (1969, s. 28)—A justice can authorise in writing the detaining and taking to a place of safety of a person under 17 if satisfied on reasonable grounds that the person is one in respect of whom any one of the "care conditions" (other than the "offence condition"—see p. 192) applies, or he is about to leave the country in contravention of the law relating to juvenile entertainers going abroad. The authorisation will specify the maximum period (not to

exceed 28 days) for detention in the place of safety. For subsequent action see para. 5, below.

(2) *For an offence.*—The law relating to the issue of a warrant for an offence in respect of a young person above prosecutable age is the same as that relating to an adult. For procedure after arrest see para. 5, below.

(3) *Special Warrant for Removal under* 1933, *s.* 40.—Such a warrant authorises a constable to search for a person under 17 (who need not be named in the warrant) who is believed to have been subjected to assault, cruelty, neglect, or against whom an offence in the 1st Schedule of the 1933 Act (see p. 17) has been committed and to remove him to a place of safety until he can be brought before a juvenile court, which must be done within 28 days, as specified in the warrant. The warrant authorises entry by force and may direct the constable to be accompanied by a doctor.

4. Arrest or Detention Without Warrant, etc.

(1) *For Care Proceedings*—any constable may detain a person under 17 as respects whom he reasonably believes that one of the care conditions (other than the "offence" or "education" conditions—see p. 192) is satisfied, or that an offence under 1933, s. 10 (vagrant taking child from place to place) is being committed.

(2) *For an offence*—the powers given to A.W.W. by law are not affected by the age of the alleged offender, but subsequent procedures are, see below. The exclusion of the "offence condition" in (1) above is because it was not intended that powers of arrest without warrant for an offence should be extended.

5. Procedure after Arrest or Detention (Persons under 17).

(1) *Arrest without warrant.* (1969, s. 28).

(a) *Nature of arrest.* Section 28 applies where a constable *without warrant* has

(i) detained any person under 17 with a view to care proceedings (as in 4 (1) above) being taken, or

(ii) arrested a child under 10 years of age for any offence except homicide.

(b) *Procedure.* In such a case the constable must as soon as practicable secure that the case is enquired into by a police inspector (or higher rank) or the police officer in charge of a police station, who, after enquiry, must either:—

(i) release the person, or

(ii) if he considers further detention necessary in the person's own interests, or, in the case of an arrested child (under (ii) above), because of the nature of the alleged offence, he must arrange for detention in a place of safety *and* inform him *and* take practicable steps to inform his parent or guardian of his right to apply to a justice for release.

* As to a child charged with homicide, or a young person charged with *any* offence, see (b) below.

NOTE: No detention is to be continued longer than 8 days commencing on day of detention or arrest. If during this period the person or child applies to a justice for release, the justice must direct forthwith release unless he considers further detention advisable in the person's own interests or, in the case of an arrested child, because of the nature of the offence.

(2) *Arrest with or without warrant.* (1969, s. 29, as amended by C.J.A. 1972, s. 43).

(a) *Nature of arrest.* Section 29 applies where a constable, with or without warrant, has arrested a person who cannot be brought immediately before a magistrates' court and who:

(i) appears to be a child (under 14), where the arrest has been made for homicide, or

(ii) appears to be a young person (under 17) who is not under 10 years of age, where the arrest has been made for any offence.

(b) *Procedure.* The police officer in charge of the police station to which he is brought (or an Inspector or higher rank) must forthwith enquire into the case and release him unless he considers detention to be justified on one of the following grounds:

(i) he considers it necessary in person's own interests, or

(ii) he has reason to believe the offence to be homicide or other grave crime, or if released (where arrest was without warrant) he would fail to appear to answer any charge made.

Exception—Where the police have decided to prosecute, the young person shall not be released as above unless he or his parent or guardian enters a recognizance (with or without sureties) for such an amount as the police officer referred to above considers will secure attendance at hearing. The recognizance may be conditioned for the appearance of the parent or guardian at the hearing as well as to alleged offender.

NOTE: It will be possible, of course, to release on bail under the M.C. Act 1952, s. 38 (to report at a police station on a specified date unless notified to the contrary) —see p. 112.

(2) *Action to be taken—Not released from custody*—The enquiring officer (as above), if he does not release the person, shall make arrangements for him to be taken into care by the L.A. and detained by the L.A., unless he certifies that this is impracticable, or that the person is of such unruly character as to make this inappropriate, in which case he must be brought before the court within 72 hours unless within that period a police inspector (or higher rank) certifies to the court that by reason of illness or accident this cannot be done (s. 29 (5)). Such a certificate must be produced to the court to which the person is first brought (s. 29 (3)).

NOTE: When brought before the court (or certificate produced instead) the court, if not proceeding to hear the case, must order release except

(a) where the arrest was on warrant,

(b) further detention considered to be in person's own interest, or

(c) the possible charge is homicide or grave crime, or release would defeat ends of justice, or, if arrested without warrant, he would fail to appear to answer any charge,

in which case the court shall remand. If remand is not on bail the court must inform the person (unless legally represented) of the right to apply to a judge of the High Court for bail and, if not legally represented or his counsel or solicitor requests, give him written notice stating the reason for the remand being otherwise than on bail (s. 29 (6)).

(3) *Notifications to be made of arrest or detention*—

(a) Where a person under 17 is arrested all practicable steps must be taken to inform a parent or guardian *by the person who made the arrest* (1933, s. 34).

(b) the person who detains a person under 1969, s. 2 (see above) must as soon as practicable afterwards inform him of the reason for it and take practicable steps to inform the parent or guardian of the detention and the reason for it. (1969 s. 28 (3)).

See para. 7 below as to duty to notify L.A. as to proposed prosecution.

(4) *Interrogation*—See p. 99.

(5) *Segregation etc.*—Arrangements are to be made for preventing a person under 17 while detained at a police station, being conveyed to and from court, or waiting before or after attendance at a court, from associating with an adult (not being a relative) who is charged with any offence (other

than jointly with the young person) and for ensuring that a girl while so detained, being conveyed or waiting, is under the care of a woman. (1933 s. 31).

(6) *Fingerprinting*—not to be under 14 years see p. 226.

6. Right to Take Proceedings.

(a) *Care proceedings*—see p. 191.

(b) *Criminal proceedings*—as for adults.

7. Preliminaries to Proceedings. It is the duty of the person who decides to lay an information for an offence against a person appearing to be under 17 to notify this to the L.A. where the young person is habitually resident, or, if this does not apply, the L.A. of the area where the alleged offence was committed. (1969, s. 5 (8)). No prosecution can be begun unless the prosecutor has (in addition to the foregoing requirements of s. 5 (8)) given notice of the proceedings to the probation officer of the court area (1969, s. 34 (2)). As to care proceedings see p. 191.

8. Court Proceedings (For "care proceedings" in particular see p. 191).

(a) *Welfare*—Every court dealing with a child should have regard to its welfare and, where necessary, take steps to remove him from undesirable surroundings and to secure proper supervision for education and training (1933, s. 44).

(b) *Presumption of Age*—

(i) Where any person brought before any court, otherwise than as witness, appears to be under 17 the Court shall enquire as to age and take any evidence available on this. The age presumed or declared by the court shall be deemed to be the true age for the purposes of the Children and Young Persons Acts;

(ii) On any charge for any offence against the Children and Young Persons Acts or mentioned in the Schedule to the 1933 Act (see p. 17) it is alleged that the person by or in respect of whom the offence was committed was under 17 or was under or had reached any specified age, and he appears to the court to have been under 17 or under or over the specified age at the time of the offence, he shall be presumed to have been so unless the contrary is proved (1933, s. 99).

(c) *Attendance of parent or guardian*—The court has power to require attendance at hearing and must do so where presence is considered desirable, unless satisfied that this would be unreasonable, (1933, s. 34). See p. 187 as to notifications to be made to parent or guardian.

(d) *Absence of Young Person—Schedule I offences*—A person under 17 on whom an offence under 1933, Schedule I is alleged need not be present when the case is being heard, if the court is satisfied that this is not essential to the just hearing of the case (1933, s. 41).

(e) *Segregation—see para.* 5 (5).

(f) *Young witnesses*—need not be sworn, if, of tender years, see p. 14. Court may be cleared in certain cases, see p. 154. As to depositions and admissibility of statements in specified circumstances, see p. 50. See also (d) above.

(g) *Remands*—see p. 143.

(h) *Publication of Particulars*—

(i) *Newspaper reports (including Scottish newspapers).*—

No newspaper report of any proceedings in a juvenile court shall reveal the name, address or school, or include any thing calculated to lead to the identification of any person under 17 concerned in those proceedings as the subject of the proceedings or as a witness therein, nor shall any picture be published in any newspaper as being (or including) the picture of such a person (S. £50).

Exception

Where the court or the S. o S. by Order has dispensed with the requirements in any case this section will not apply to publication in accordance with the dispensation given. The dispensation can be given in any case if considered necessary to avoid injustice to the young person* (1933 s. 49).

* Change effected by 1969 s. 10.

Extensions of the above by 1969 *s.* 10.

The above restrictions apply also to the following proceedings in *juvenile courts:*

A person who is 17 (*but not* 18) in respect of whom the proceedings are taken (e.g. attain age of 18 during the proceedings). *A person of any age,* in respect of whom 1969, Part I proceedings are taken, e.g. supervision or care order proceedings, or removal to borstal from care of L.A., as well as to proceedings in an *adult* court in respect of supervision orders relating to *persons* 18 *or over,* but a court announcement must be made.

Appeals—Where restrictions apply to the original hearing they apply also to subsequent appeals.

Announcement—Where proceedings to which restrictions on reporting apply are taken otherwise than in a juvenile court the court must announce during the proceedings the fact that restrictions do apply (1969, s. 10).

(ii) *Notice under C.J.A.* 1967, *s.* 4.

This section requires a notice to be exhibited in a court-house giving particulars of committals or persons discharged. S. 10 of the 1969 Act provides that such a notice shall not include the name or address of a person under 17 unless the justices consider it should in order to avoid injustice to him.

9. "Sentence" on "Conviction".

(1) *The words "sentence" and "conviction"*—shall not be used in relation to young persons dealt with summarily. If used in any enactment in relation to a young person they shall be construed as a finding of guilt or an order made, respectively (1933, s. 59).

(2) *Murder*—A person convicted of murder committed when under 18 years cannot be sentenced to death or life imprisonment, but may be ordered to be detained during H.M. Pleasure, in such a place and on such conditions as the S. o S. directs (1933, s. 53).

(3) *Grave Crimes*—Where a person under 17 is convicted *on indictment* of an offence ordinarily carrying a maximum of 14 years imprisonment or more (not being a fixed penalty) the court can, if no other method of dealing with the case appears suitable, impose a term of imprisonment in such place and under such conditions as the S. o S. directs (1933, s. 53).

NOTE: the need for consideration of such a sentence is one of grounds on which a young person can be sent for trial instead of being dealt with summarily.

(4) The following *Orders* (see (1) above)—can be made by a court when dealing with a person under 17 found guilty of an offence (i.e. in criminal proceedings):

	Order	*Remarks*
(a)	Care Order	If offence is punishable by imprisonment as an adult (1969 s. 7).
(b)	Supervision Order	See p. 195.
(c)	Binding over:	
	(i) of offender	See p. 165.
	(ii) of parent or guardian	With consent only (1969 s. 7).
(d)	Discharge, absolute or conditional	See p. 166.
(e)	Hospital or Guardianship Order.	Under the Mental Health Act 1959.
(f)	Fine/Compensation	See p. 170.

Order	*Remarks*
(g) If a Centre is available	
(i) Attendance Centre Order	See p. 198.
(ii) Detention Centre Order	See p. 197.
(h) Borstal.	If 15, 1969 Act permits this age to be raised first to 16, then to 17 if S. o S. makes orders to this effect.

NOTE: A person under 17 cannot be sent to prison by a Crown Court or a Magistrates' Court. No court can impose a sentence of imprisonment on a person under 21 unless no other sentence is appropriate (Powers of Criminal Courts Act 1973, s. 19).

CARE PROCEEDINGS

Establishment of Community Homes

The 1969 Act introduced provisions for the establishment as soon as practicable of Community Homes for the accommodation of children in care of local authorities and for whom no other provision can be made (e.g. with foster parents, or parent, guardian relative or friend) or is suitable. In the meantime the L.A. will make use of accommodation available at former Approved Schools or Remand Homes, until these cease to exist as such. The L.A.'s in each "Planning Area" (created by an Order of the S. o S.) will act together to establish a Children's Regional Planning Committee, on which each L.A. is represented and "specialists" may be co-opted as members. The C.R.P.C. is to submit for the approval of the S. o S. a "regional plan" for the provision by the L.A.'s of community homes for their region ("Controlled Community Homes") and the inclusion in the scheme of homes provided by voluntary and consenting organisations, in the management of which the L.A.'s will participate ("Assisted Community Homes") and help to finance. The scheme will also include the provision of facilities for physical and mental welfare and means of assessment of the most suitable means of accommodation and treatment in particular cases. The exercise of the functions of a C.H. and an A.C.H. will be through a "management body". The S. o S. will make Regulations for the conduct of such homes and the welfare of juveniles in them (e.g. as to restrictions on liberty, discipline, medical care, appropriate religious instruction, appropriate standards) and can also withdraw approval in respect of any home. Where a voluntary home becomes an A.C.H. the following cease to apply:—

(a) The Children Act 1948, ss. 29, 30, 32 and
(b) The 1933 Act, s. 93.

as to compulsory registration, regulations as to the conduct of voluntary homes and notification of certain particulars to the S. o S.

Inspection.—A person appointed by the S. o S. may enter (on production of his authority), for the purpose of inspection of the premises and/or facilities, and to examine children there, any C.H., any voluntary home (whether A.C.H. or not) and any other premises at which children are accommodated or boarded out by a L.A. or a voluntary organisation, or being cared for by a foster parent. Obstruction of such an inspection is an offence (£5 maximum first offence, £20 subsequently). Refusal to allow entry is evidence that children are being neglected on the premises on which to base an application for a search warrant under 1933, s. 40.

Homes Provided by the Government

Homes providing special facilities to meet special requirements of particular juveniles will be established by the S. o. S. for the accommodation, maintenance and treatment of children accepted there on application of a L.A. in respect of any child in its care.

Discontinuation of Approved Schools, etc.

As soon as adequate community homes have been established in or for any region, the S. o S. will order the cessation of approved schools, remand homes, and probation hostels and homes which have become redundant as a result. No court orders relating to probation of persons under 17, or to approved schools or remand homes could be made after 1st January, 1971, and any accommodation thus becoming vacant can be used by L.A.'s if necessary, for the accommodation of young persons in their care.

Care Proceedings for "Care Orders" (1969 ss. 1–3). (*Applies to persons under* 17 *years of age.*)

(1) Where there are reasonable grounds to believe that grounds exist on which a care order can be made by the court the young person may be brought before a juvenile court by a constable, by a L.A. or by a person authorised by the Home Secretary (the N.S.P.C.C.).

(2) The grounds on which the court can make an order are that the young person is in need of care and control which he is unlikely to get without a court order *and* that one or more of the following applies:—

(a) proper development prevented or neglected, or health impaired or neglected, or ill-treatment;

(b) condition (a) probably applies because a care order based on it was or has been made in respect of another juvenile in the same household;

(c) exposure to moral danger;

(d) beyond control of parent or guardian;

(e) not receiving proper education (proceedings to be taken by Education Authority only);

(f) is guilty of an offence, excluding homicide (called the "offence condition"—see para. (5) below).

Note that (f) makes care proceedings an alternative to prosecution if the need for care or control condition is satisfied.

(3) The court may make one of the following orders:—

(a) *An order requiring the parent or guardian (with consent) to enter recognizances* for the exercise of proper care and control. The recognizance is not to be for more than £50, or more than 3 years or any period beyond the young person's 18th birthday;

(b) *A Supervision Order* (i.e. supervision by local authority or probation officer) which may include certain requirements affecting the supervisor and supervisee;

(c) *A Care Order*—committing the young person to the care of a local authority;

(d) A Hospital Order, or A Guardianship Order } under the Mental Health Act 1959.

No order can be made if the young person is aged 16 years and is or had been married.

(4) *Provisions as to care proceedings generally.*

(a) No proceedings to be taken unless notice has been given to the appropriate L.A. (usually L.A. where juvenile is resident) to enable L.A. to enquire into the case, if necessary, and to the court probation officer as well.

(b) Attendance of juvenile can be achieved by summons or warrant, but a warrant is only issuable on non-appearance (as on p. 133) or if summons cannot be served. If warrant is used the custodian may arrange for the young person to be detained in a place of safety for not more than 72 hours from time of arrest, and within that period must bring him before a justice, who must either make an interim order (in care of L.A.) or direct immediate release.

(c) Attendance of witnesses can be secured as in the hearing of any complaint.

(d) In the case of an infant under 5 years the court can proceed in its absence if the parent or guardian is present or had been notified of hearing in reasonable time beforehand.

(5) *Procedures where "offence condition" exists.*

(a) An offence condition is to be disregarded if it was considered in previous care proceedings or, if a summary offence, the time limit for prosecution expired before care proceedings began, or the defence autrefois convict (or acquit) would prevail in criminal proceedings for the offence;

(b) If an offence condition exists proceedings must be brought by police or L.A. and is not regarded as being satisfied unless, on the evidence, the court would have found the young person guilty of the offence if it had jurisdiction to hear the charge;

(c) If care proceedings are taken on an offence condition the young person cannot be charged with the offence;

(d) If the offence condition is satisfied with regard to an *indictable* offence, the court:—

   (i) can make a compensation order under the Powers of Criminal Courts Act 1973 up to £100.

   (ii) must in the case of a child, and may otherwise, order parent or guardian to pay any sums of money ordered to be paid—subject to certain provisos.

(e) In the case of a young person who consents the court may order his entering a recognizance n/e £25 to keep the peace (or for good behaviour) for period not exceeding one year, instead of making a care order.

(f) *Warrants for Scotland.* If an "offence condition" is alleged a warrant to secure attendance of the young person concerned can be executed in Scotland in same way as a warrant for an offence, if the warrant is endorsed that the proceedings refer to an "offence condition" care proceedings (C.J.A. 1972, s. 51).

(g) *Warrant from Scotland.* A like warrant from Scotland (under the Social Work (Scotland) Act 1968) can be executed in England and Wales in same way as a warrant for an offence (C.J.A. 1972, s. 51).

Care Orders—may result from:—

(a) care proceedings, or

(b) criminal proceedings, or

(c) may be substituted for a supervision order which is being discharged (i.e. withdrawn).

The Order commits to care of L.A. of area in which juvenile is habitually resident—if none, then L.A. of area in which the offence was committed or the circumstances leading to proceedings arose. Terminates on 18th birthday (unless extended) or, if 16 when made, 19th birthday. Gives L.A. same powers and duties as a parent or guardian ordinarily can exercise, including power to restrict liberty.

Accommodation and maintenance—can be boarded with foster parents, or in an L.A. Community Home, or a State provided home, or in a voluntary home, even in an Approved School still being maintained, or in care of parent, guardian, relative or friend.

Review of Order and circumstances to be conducted by L.A. at intervals of six months.

Visitors.—In the case of a child aged 5 or more who:—

(a) is in a C.H. or other place which he does not leave for school or work, and
(b) has very little contact from outside, and
(c) has no parents or guardian (or they do not keep in touch),

a visitor may be appointed, but only with consent of the parents or guardian, if any. Duties are to visit, advise, befriend, i.e. take the place of a parent or guardian.

Extension to 19th birthday—only applied to person in a C.H. or State Home, *and*, if by reason of behaviour or mental condition, this is in own interest and that of public. Application to be made to a juvenile court.

Transfer to Borstal—Consent of Home Secretary required.

Conditions: must be 15 (S. o S. can raise this age first to 16 and then to 17), be accommodated in a C.H. *and* behaviour detrimental to others there. The juvenile court can, for consideration of application, remand for 21 days to Remand Centre (not prison), and this period can be extended by the court to a maximum of 8 weeks. If not sent to Remand Centre, the juvenile has to remain in care.

Supervision order

This Order can be made in care proceedings, criminal proceedings, or to replace a care order. By it a juvenile is placed under the supervision of the L.A. (of the area in which he is or will be habitually resident) or a probation officer. The L.A. and the Petty Sessions area of residence are specified in the Order. A probation officer can be the designated supervisor only if the L.A. so requests *and* the juvenile is 13 years of age or more, or, if under 13 years, if he is already exercising (or has done) statutory duties in relation to another member of the same household. Duties of supervisor are to advise, assist and befriend the supervisee.

Duration—any specified period up to 3 years but not beyond 18th birthday (or 20th birthday in the case of criminal proceedings). Order contains provisions court considers appropriate for facilitating supervision, and may include requirements to be fulfilled by the young person, e.g. a medical requirement, or to reside with a relative, or for a specified period (n/e 90 days) at a specified place.

Discharge, Variation, etc.—Variation can only be made by a juvenile court in the case of a person under 18—on the application of the supervisor (or his parent or guardian on his behalf). The court can vary the order, discharge the order, or make a care order to replace it. In the case of a person above that age (in which case the order would have been made in criminal proceedings) a variation can be made only by an "adult" magistrates' court, no matter where the original order was made. If a requirement of an order is not complied with the court can, on application of the supervisor:—

(a) impose fine n/e £20 or make an attendance centre order;

(b) if it discharges the supervision order, impose any punishment which could have been imposed if the supervisee had just been convicted of the offence leading to the making of the Order (i.e. up to 6 months imprisonment or £400 fine).

Interim Order

This is a "care order" expiring within 28 days or such shorter period as the order may specify. It is made by the court when not in a position to decide what order to make and adjourns proceedings. It cannot be made in the absence of the young person unless he is under 5 or cannot be present through illness or accident. The L.A. has to produce the young person for the next hearing.

Discharge of Orders

Applications may be made for the discharge (i.e. cancellation) of an order made as a result of care proceedings. The general rules are:—

"Care Order"—on application by L.A. or the young person (or his parent or guardian). Court can discharge and make a supervision order instead, though then an appeal would lie to the Crown Court. If dismissed, no further application for three months without consent of court.

"Interim Order"—application by young person (or his parent or guardian). If dismissed, no further application without consent of a juvenile court. Appeal lies to the Crown Court.

"Supervision Order"—application by supervisor or supervisee. If dismissed no further application for three months, except with consent of a juvenile court, though appeal can be made as for an interim order.

Place of Safety

This means a Community Home of a L.A., or Assisted Community Home, or any police station, or any hospital, surgery, or other suitable place the occupier of which is willing temporarily to receive the child (including Remand Homes, until these disappear or are converted into Community Homes).

Venue

The restrictions relating to criminal proceedings do not apply. Proceedings may be begun in *any* juvenile court, but best taken to the court of the area in which the juvenile resides, though it may be necessary otherwise, e.g. where detained and an interim order needed, or the offence is committed far from home, and witnesses are from different areas. In such a case the court will direct transfer to the local court (unless proceedings dismissed), so that home situations and remedial facilities can be considered there, and attendance of parents facilitated. If, however, an offence condition is alleged the first court can determine this allegation, and if it finds the condition satisfied and remits the case, its finding on this is binding on the court to which the case is remitted. If case is remitted the first court may allow the young person to return home and inform the L.A. concerned (who must bring the proceedings within 21 days) or make an interim order putting him in care of L.A. until the hearing at the home court.

Detention Centres

Places in which offenders under 21 years of age serve short periods of detention under suitable discipline as an alternative to imprisonment when no other punishment is suitable (Criminal Justice Act 1961, ss. 4,5). If a more severe measure were needed it would be a question of prison, or Borstal. The normal period of detention is 3 months. If an offender is over 17 and convicted on indictment of an offence punishable by 3 months or more—the period of detention may be 3 to 6 months. Consecutive detention orders may extend the period to a maximum of 9 months. An offender previously sentenced to imprisonment for 6 months or more, to Borstal training, or to a detention centre after he became 17, should not normally be sent to a Detention Centre unless no other method of dealing with him is appropriate. By the 1969 Act the S. o S. can withdraw powers of courts to make detention centre orders in relation to persons under 17. This will be done as and when Community Homes become available for the reception of persons under 17. As to making of an order when offender is not legally represented—see p 174.

Supervision after release

For 12 months from the date of his release from a detention centre, the offender must remain under the supervision of the society or person named in a notice served upon him by the Prison Commissioners on his release and which will prescribe the requirements with which he must comply. If the offender fails to comply with any requirement specified in the notice, he is liable to recall and detention in the detention centre for a period equal to that part of his sentence for which he was excused or for 14 days from the date of his recall, whichever is the longer. If at large after the Prison Commissioners have issued the order for his recall, he is unlawfully at large until the order ceases to have effect, i.e. 12 months from date of his release unless the offender has been retaken and again released under supervision. A person must not be recalled a second time under the same order. See also 'Supervision of short term prisoners after release', p. 210.

Approved Schools (see p. 192)

Attendance Centres (C.J.A. 1948, s. 19 amended)

The 1948 Act authorises Secretary of State to make arrangements with any local authority for the use of suitable premises.

Many such centres have been established by the Home Office in various parts of the country. The object is not only to punish the offender by depriving him of his leisure time, but also to educate him by requiring from him a higher standard of behaviour and by teaching him how to make better use of leisure time.

Persons of or over the age of 17 but less than 21 years convicted of an offence punishable in the case of an adult with imprisonment or for failing to comply with the conditions of probation may be ordered by a *summary court* to attend an Attendance Centre.

The Order requires periodic attendances for supervised instruction or work—not more than once a day for not more than 3 hours. The aggregate hours shall not be less than 12 nor exceed 12 hours unless this is considered inadequate, in which case n/e 24 hours.

Attendance sessions are devoted to physical training, (including games). Instruction on handicraft and personal hygiene.

Courts must be satisfied that available centres are reasonably accessible having regard to the age, etc. of the offender.

If there is failure to comply the court may issue a summons or warrant to bring the offender back before them to be dealt with for the original offence.

Borstal (Criminal Justice Acts 1948, s.20 and 1961, s.1)

An establishment designed to effect the reformation (by detention and training) of persons not less than 15* but under 21 years. A young person may be "sent to Borstal" by:

(a) Sentence of the court of trial, or

(b) Transfer there from a Community Home or a prison.

* This age can be raised by order of the S.o S. first to 16, then to 17.

(1) *Sentence on Conviction*

Requirements:

(a) *Conviction of offence punishable by imprisonment*, either on indictment or by magistrates. Offender has to be committed to a Crown Court for sentence and committal has to be in custody though High Court can later grant bail if appeal is lodged. The Court may, instead of imposing Borstal sentence, deal with case in any way that the magistrates' court could have done.

(b) *Court must have regard to character and antecedents of the prisoner and gravity of offence,* and also *consider the prison report* on his physical and mental condition and suitability for borstal training. May remand for not exceeding three weeks to get this report. Remand may be on bail. (C.J.A. 1972, s. 42).

(c) *Sentence.*—At least 6 months—not longer than 2 years as Home Secretary may decide (No period is specified by the Court).

(d) *Legal representation.*—See p. 174.

(2) *Transfer from Prison*

Transfer from prison to Borstal (and vice versa) may be authorised by the Home Secretary if offender is under 21 years of age and transfer:

(a) to Borstal would be advantageous (the trial judge or Recorder should be consulted);

(b) from Borstal is required by reason of the offender's incorrigibility and bad influence on other inmates.

Discharge.—Until 2 years from the date of his release the offender is under the supervision of a society or person named by the Prison Commissioners. The Secretary of State can modify or cancel requirements in a particular case. On failure to comply he may be recalled to Borstal. Failure to comply with recall makes him unlawfully at large and liable to arrest without warrant and liable to detention until the end of the 2 years or for 6 months after recall, whichever is the longer.

The effect of The Order of Recall ceases after the lapse of 2 years from date of release—the offender is then no longer unlawfully at large.

Return to Borstal.—Persons under supervision or unlawfully at large who are convicted of an offence punishable by imprisonment may be returned to Borstal by the convicting court (including a summary court) instead of being punished in any other way. If under supervision, the court must consider the report of the Prison Commissioners.

> *R.* v. *Fry* (1955)
> In this case the prisoner had been convicted of larceny and conditionally discharged. A few months later he appeared at Quarter Sessions and was convicted of office breaking and sentenced to Borstal Training. No sentence was passed in respect of the earlier offence. On appeal against the sentence Mr. Justice Devlin said—"If no sentence is passed at all in respect of the offence for which

the applicant is conditionally discharged, the conviction does not rank as a conviction and the result of it not ranking as a conviction is that, if thereafter the applicant were to commit further offences and questions were to arise on which it was necessary to prove previous convictions such as questions of sentence, for corrective training, the offence for which he ought to have been sentenced since he had broken his conditional discharge would not rank for that purpose".

N.B. For removal from care to Borstal, see p. 195.

General Limitations

Fines:	A child (under 14) maximum—£10. Young person (14 under 17)—maximum —£50 when tried summarily.
Costs, or Compensation order up to £ 100:	can be imposed, but if *child* must order them to be paid by parent or guardian, unless latter cannot be found or did not conduce to the commission of the offence.
Death Sentence:	not pronounced or recorded if under 18 when the offence was committed (detained during H.M. Pleasure).
Imprisonment:	Not under 21 or for first time unless court considers no other method appropriate. (*Not at all if under* 17).

Final Progress Check

1. What are the legal principles which govern "speeches" to the court or jury?
2. What is the form of oath (a) to be taken in absence of objection, and (b) in the case of a juvenile witness in a juvenile court?
3. What is an "affirmation", and when is it used?
4. In what circumstances may evidence be given by an unsworn witness?
5. What kinds of "examinations" relate to questioning of witnesses in court and explain them?
6. What are "Leading questions", and when are they permitted?
7. What is "rebutting evidence" and in what circumstances is such evidence permitted?
8. In what ways does Crown Court procedure differ from that at a magistrates' court, on a plea of "Not guilty"?
9. What are provisions of law relating to the hearing of a case at a Magistrates' Court in the absence of the defendant?
10. Specify the various ways by which a previous conviction may be proved in court.
11. Specify three cases in which, although the punishment may exceed imprisonment of 3 months, the accused cannot claim trial by jury?

12. What procedure is followed by a magistrates' court acting as "examining justices" under the Magistrates' Courts Act 1952, and what changes have been effected by the Criminal Justice Act 1967?
13. What is an indictment, and what procedure governs its acceptance?
14. What provisions of law relate to witnesses who are (a) unwilling, (b) adverse, (c) hostile, (d) disorderly (e) deaf and dumb, (f) very young, or (g) in prison?
15. What rules of law or practice govern whether witnesses should be in or out of court during proceedings?
16. In what circumstances may a witness be recalled?
17. To what extent might the character of a witness be an important consideration?
18. What is a recognizance? What is the law relating to recognizances to keep the peace, and to be of good behaviour?
19. In what circumstances can a Court discharge an offender either absolutely or conditionally, and what does the sentence invoive in each case?
20. In connection with probation:
    (a) what are the normal conditions of a probation order?
    (b) what other requirements might the court add?
    (c) what is a "supervising court"?
    (d) in what circumstances is consent of offender necessary?
    (e) what is effect of breach of a requirement?
    (f) what is the procedure to be adopted in the case of the commission of a further offence during probation period?
21. What restrictions are there on the imposition of a sentence of imprisonment?
22. In what circumstances may a prisoner be detained in police cells by the order of a court?
23. What special places are provided for the detention of young offenders (a) before trial, or (b) during trial, or (c) for sentence?
24. With regard to extended terms of imprisonment
    (a) what is the purpose of this procedure?
    (b) what conditions apply to the power of the court to impose such a sentence?
25. What do you know about the law relating to suspended sentences?
26. What are the requirements of a Suspended Sentence Supervision Order and when may it be imposed?
27. In what circumstances can a Community Service Order be imposed on conviction and what is its effect?
28. When can a court make a compensation order?
29. What matters cannot be the subject of a compensation order?
30. What is a borstal institution?
31. What are the legal provisions which regulate the imposing of a "borstal" sentence?

32. Explain what is meant by a "place of safety", a detention centre, and an attendance centre under the C. & Y.P. Act 1969.
33. What legal provisions restrict the taking of criminal proceedings against a child or young person?
34. What powers to detain can be exercised by a constable in respect of "care" proceedings?
35. What are the legal provisions which relate to the procedure to be followed immediately after an arrest or detention of a person, under 17, (a) for care proceedings, or (b) for an offence?
36. On what grounds can care proceedings be taken and what is the effect of a care order?
37. What preliminaries are required in connection with proceedings for a care order?
38. What considerations apply in deciding whether the proceedings against a person under 17 should be for a care order or a prosecution for an offence?
39. What restrictions as to length of time apply to the institution of proceedings in the Crown Court after committal for trial by a magistrates' court?
40. In what circumstances can an indictment be preferred against a person who has not been committed for trial?

CHAPTER XI

ADDITIONAL SUBJECTS

1. DOCUMENTARY EVIDENCE

It is often the case that a document becomes important as a means of proving the truth of what it records (as hearsay evidence). Where such a document is admissible it has to be proved to be what it purports to be, i.e. genuine (e.g. made by the person who purports to have made it), and that any legal requirements with respect to its making have been or were complied with. Most of the documents of primary evidential value (depositions, written statements under the C.J. Act 1967, trade or business records, dying declarations, confessions) have been dealt with (see pp. 6–12), but on minor matters statute law has provided opportunities to reduce the need for calling witnesses on matters which are purely formal, or not likely to be disputed. Such are declarations and certificates of service of process, and the statements of facts and form of mitigating circumstances in connection with guilty pleas from absent defendants. In addition to these there are the following statutory provisions.

1. Criminal Justice Act 1948, s. 41.

A plan or drawing duly certified to be correctly drawn to scale is admissible as evidence of the relative positions of things shown. (See Handbook No. 5 on Road Traffic Law, Chapter XIX).

2. Theft Act 1968, s. 27.

In cases of theft of anything in the course of transmission (by post or otherwise) or for handling goods from such theft a Statutory declaration is admissible to prove that the declarant sent, received, or failed to receive the goods or postal packet, or that they were in a particular condition when sent or received.

Conditions:—Copy served on person charged not less than 7 days before hearing (in same way as summons) and he has not served prosecutor with notice requiring attendance of witness not later than 3 days before trial (or further time as court may allow).

R. v. *Marley* (1958)
The declarant must be able to say the goods were handed by him or handed in his presence to some other persons.

3. Proof of Previous Convictions

1. *Prevention of Crimes Act* 1871, *s.* 18

If the accused does not admit a previous conviction, it may be proved in any legal proceedings, by producing:

(i) *If previous conviction on indictment.*—A certificate (record or extract of conviction) signed by the clerk of the court of conviction, or,

(ii) *If previous summary conviction.*—A copy or extract of the court register certified by the clerk of the court by whom kept (and also by M.C. Rules 1968, Rule 56),

but to this must be added:

Oral proof of the identity of the defendant with the person named in the certificate or extract of the court register (i.e. by officer present at the court of conviction who can identify the prisoner as being the same person).

2. *Criminal Justice Act* 1948, *s.* 39 *and* 1967, s. 33. (*By Finger or Palm prints*)

If the accused does not admit a previous conviction it may be proved by producing three certificates, as follows—

(i) From the prison or remand centre to the effect that the copies of the finger or palm prints attached are those taken from the prisoner when in custody on the present charge.

(ii) From the Commissioner of the Metropolitan Police certifying that the copies of the finger or palm prints attached are those of a person when convicted on the previous occasion in question.

(iii) From the Commissioner of Metropolitan Police certifying that both sets of finger or palm prints (above) belong to the same person, i.e. the prisoner.

See also p. 226.

3. *Convictions in Scotland*

A certificate signed by or on behalf of the Lord Advocate that an offence is punishable in Scotland with imprisonment or is punishable on indictment in Scotland with imprisonment for the term of years specified therein is evidence of this fact. (Powers of Criminal Courts Act 1973, s. 52).

4. Proof of Release from Prison, etc.

To prove that a person convicted on indictment is a persistent offender and liable to an extended term of imprisonment, a certificate purporting to be signed by the prison governor that the prisoner was or was not finally released from prison after serving a sentence on a particular date referred to in the certificate, is evidence of those facts.

5. Road Traffic Act 1972—for these see Handbook No. 5.

6. Proof of Private and Public Documents

There remains to be summarised the general law relating to proof of *private* or *public* documents.

1. *Proof of Private Documents*

This arises for example in the case of a lease to property, deeds, wills, receipts, etc.

Secondary evidence of the contents of a private document will not be admissible until good reason for the absence of the original is given. Such documents may be proved as follows:

(i) *If less than* 20 *years old.*—It must be proved that it is signed or written by the person who purports to have signed or written it by proving the handwriting or signature of attestation (if required by law to be attested) in any of the recognised ways of proving handwriting.

(ii) *If* 20 *years old or more.*—The document proves itself if produced from a source whence it might reasonably be expected to come (from the proper though not strictly the legal custody).

Wyne v. *Tynwhitt* (1824)
When a private document 20 years old or more is proved to be produced from the proper custody, no proof is required that it is signed or written by the person purporting to have signed or written it, or that it has been duly executed. In other words it proves itself.

2. *Proof of Public Documents*

Public documents have been made for use or reference by the public, though not necessarily open to their inspection, e.g. public Acts of Parliament, bye-laws, government gazettes, public registers, judicial records and the process of any court of law, corporation and company books, official certificates, etc.

Public documents may be proved by the production of particular kinds of copies, which are admissible as evidence of contents in any court as follows:

(i) *Queen's Printers Copy* of Acts of Parliament, statutory rules, orders, and regulations, etc. need not be proved because the courts are bound to take judicial notice of them.

(ii) *Exemplification.*—a copy of a record set out either under the great seal or under the seal of a court.

(iii) *Certified Copy or Certificate.*—A certified copy of (or certificate by an official) relating to a public document, bye-laws, entries in registers, or extracts therefrom (e.g.—births, deaths and marriages) signed by the officer to whose custody the original is entrusted.

(iv) *Examined Copy.*—I.e. a copy of the contents of any public document which a witness *swears* he has compared with the original and found to be a true copy, e.g.—entries in parish registers, etc.

(v) *Byelaws.*—A certificate endorsed in printed copy of local authority byelaws, signed by clerk to the authority. Certificate must state that the byelaw was made by the authority, that the copy is a true one, that the byelaw was duly confirmed, and give the date on which it came into operation.

(vi) *European Economic Community Documents.*—Judicial notice shall be taken of the treaties, the Official Journal and Decisions of the European Court. An instrument issued by a Community Institution may be proved by:—

(a) Production of copy certified by an official of that institution, or
(b) Production of the Queen's Printer's copy, or,
(c) If the instrument is in the custody of a government department) production of copy certified by an officer of that department so authorised.

2. VENUE

Definition.—Venue, with respect to any offence, means the place or places at which it can be tried. Because, on a question of jurisdiction, the question whether the accused is *lawfully* before the court may be material, the provisions on the issue of process set out below are relevant.

1. Authority of Justice to Issue Summons or Warrant

A justice may issue a summons or warrant in the following circumstances:

(a) where the offence is one which can be tried in any county (or borough) any justice of that county (or borough) can issue the summons or warrant in respect of it (see "Jurisdiction", later).

(b) A justice can issue process in respect of an offence committed outside jurisdiction (as in (a)) *if*, in interests of justice, he considers the accused should be *tried jointly* or *at same time* as another person already charged within his district (e.g. charge of handling to be tried with one of theft).

(c) he can issue process for *indictable offence* wherever committed *if person accused resides* within his jurisdiction. (A similar power exists for a summary offence but is too restricted in range to be of value).

2. Jurisdiction

1. *Magistrates' Courts*

(a) *Summary Offences.*—The general rule is that the court can try any such offence committed within the County (or Borough) for which the justices of the court are appointed. This *territorial limit is extended* to cover an offence:

(i) Committed *on or near boundary*, i.e. on boundary (which may be road, river, harbour, waterway) or within 500 yards of boundary of County (or Borough).

(ii) *Started in one District—finished in another* or vice versa, one of them being within jurisdiction.

(iii) Against person or property *in transit* if on a journey which passed through jurisdiction or along boundary.

(iv) To which 1 (b) above applies and the person has appeared on the summons or been produced on the warrant.

(v) Being a summary offence (including an offence triable either summarily or on indictment which the court agrees to try summarily on application of the prosecutor) *committed anywhere* if, and only if, the court is already trying (not as examining justices) the alleged offender for an offence. (This creates an agreement to be reached whenever practicable between Magistrates' Courts where process has been issued by each court against the same defendant based on the convenience of witnesses, defendant and prosecutor—C.J.A. 1967, s. 28).

NOTE:

This provision enables a magistrates' court to take into consideration summary offences committed outside its jurisdiction.

(vi) *Particular Acts*, e.g. Army Act, Merchant Shipping Act, which give jurisdiction to any Magistrates' Court for offence committed anywhere in England or Wales.

(b) *Indictable Offences.*—The court can normally try indictable offences committed within jurisdiction (as for summary offences). It can also deal with an indictable charge either as examining justices or by summary trial (where it can be so tried) *wherever offence was committed*, if accused appears or is brought before the court on the charge (e.g. as in 1 (b) or 1 (c) above).

(c) *Hybrid Offences.*—(Triable summarily and on indictment). Where hearing is begun as examining justices, court has jurisdiction to try summarily, wherever offence was committed.

(d) *Aiders and Abettors.*—Such persons can be tried where principal is tried or where offence was committed (M.C. Act 1952, s.35).

(e) *Offences on British aircraft*—see para. 3 below.

2. *The Crown Court*

By s. 6 of the Courts Act 1971, a Crown Court can deal with any person charged with an indictable offence, wherever committed, if that person was arrested, or is in custody, or appeared on summons *lawfully* issued for that offence, in the county or place for which the court is held.

3. Committal: To which Court? See p. 37.

NOTE: Any act or omission in a British-controlled aircraft in flight elsewhere than in or over the U.K., which would be an offence if committed in the U.K. constitutes that offence. For the purpose of conferring jurisdiction the offence is deemed to have been committed in any place in the U.K. where the offender may be. Consent of the D.P.P. is necessary, but this does not affect arrest, remand or bail. (Tokyo Convention Act 1967.) As to venue in care proceedings see p. 197.

3. RELEASE FROM PRISON, ETC.

1. Early Release on Remission of Part of Sentence

In the case of any determinate sentence of imprisonment (i.e. for a specified term of months or years) exceeding one month a prisoner can by good conduct earn a remission of part of his sentence. The maximum remission which can be so earned is one-third of the sentence. Release from prison before expiry of full term of imprisonment where remission has been granted is a complete release and not on licence.

2. Release on Licence (C.J.A. 1967, ss. 60, 62)

(a) *After serving one-third of sentence or 12 months.* Secretary of State may, on recommendation of the Parole Board, release on licence after serving one-third of prison sentence (not being life imprisonment) or twelve months, whichever expires later.

(b) *For whole or part of remission period.* Secretary of State may direct the release on licence of any person.

(i) serving an extended sentence, or

(ii) serving 18 months or more who was under 21 when sentence was passed,

instead of remission of sentence, at any time, after the day on which discharge on remission could have been granted. (No recommendation of Parole Board is needed.)

(c) *In cases of life imprisonment,* etc.

The Secretary of State may, on recommendation of Parole Board, release on licence a person serving life imprisonment* or detained (as a young offender) under the C. & Y.P. Act 1933, for a grave crime.

* In this case and that of detention during H.M. pleasure only after consultation with the Lord Chief Justice and the trial judge (if available).

N.B. The person subject to a licence must comply with the conditions, if any, which are specified in the licence. The Secretary of State must consult the Parole Board before including a condition, or subsequently inserting, varying or cancelling a condition in *any* licence.

Duration of licence (unless previously revoked).
Licence in (b) above—until date of expiration of sentence. Licence for young offender detained for grave crime—to the date specified in the licence.

In other cases—until the date on which the prisoner could have been discharged from prison if granted remission, unless he has forfeited remission (by Prison Rules) after release on licence.

3. Revocation of licence (s. 62)

The holder of a licence is liable to have his licence revoked and be recalled to prison—

(a) *By the Home Secretary* on the recommendation of the Parole Board (see later), or, if revocation is necessary in the public interest, without consulting the Board.

(b) *By a Crown Court* on conviction of an offence punishable with imprisonment or on sentence by the Crown Court after conviction at a magistrates' court which committed him for sentence. A magistrates' court can commit to the Crown Court for sentence any person subject to a licence who is convicted before it of an offence punishable on indictment with imprisonment. The licence may be revoked whether or not the court passes any other sentence on him.

A person whose licence is revoked must be detained to serve his sentence and, if at large, is a person unlawfully at large.

NOTES:

(a) A person recalled to prison as in para. (i) above must be informed of the reasons for it and of his right to make written representations. The case of any person recalled by the Home Secretary without consultation with the Parole Board, must be referred for consideration by the Board, as must any written representations made in the case of a person recalled by the Secretary of State.

(b) The Home Secretary must release a prisoner again on licence if the Board so recommends after consideration of the case, and in the case of persons subject to a life sentence no further consultation with the Lord Chief Justice and the trial judge is required.

(c) A person whose licence is revoked by the Crown Court must not be again released on licence until one year or one-third of the period during which the licence was operative, whichever is the longer, has elapsed.

(d) The above provisions apply to young offenders convicted of grave crimes as if the references to "prison" and "imprisonment" were replaced by "detention in any place approved by the Home Secretary".

4. Parole Board (1967 Act, s. 59)

The Parole Board for England and Wales consists of a Chairman and not less than four other members appointed by the Home Secretary. Its main functions are to advise the Home Secretary in relation to—

(a) the selection of prisoners for early release on licence;

(b) the conditions of such licences, as well as variations and cancellation of existing conditions;

(c) matters connected with the grant of licences or the recall of persons whose licences have been revoked.

Local Review Committees are established to review the cases of prisoners who are or will become eligible for release on licence, and to report on them to the Home Secretary, giving their own recommendations and the result of any interview a member of the committee may have had with a prisoner. The constitution and functions of these Committees are governed by rules made by the Home Secretary, who will generally refer their recommendations for consideration by the Parole Board.

5. Supervision after Release from Borstal, etc. (Criminal Justice Act 1961)

Persons released from Borstal, Detention Centres, Approved Schools and in some cases Prison are subject to supervision for a period thereafter, as follows:

(a) *Prison*—person under 21 when sentence was passed after serving sentence of less than 18 months—as for detention centre—(c) below. (C.J.A. 1967, s. 63).

(b) *Borstal* (s.11)—supervision for 2 years by a society or person named by the Prison Commissioners (see p. 199).

(c) *Detention Centre* (s.13 and 1st. Sch.)—supervision for 12 months (as in (b)) (see p. 197).

6. Unlawfully at Large

A prisoner on licence may be recalled for failing to comply with the conditions of his licence or supervision, and if he fails to surrender to his recall, he is deemed to be *unlawfully at large* and may be arrested without warrant by any constable, and required to serve the unexpired term of his sentence. (2 years in the case of Borstal or at least 6 months after his arrest).

Prisoners subject to order of recall are circulated in Police Gazette and arrest is often qualified by the proviso—"If found to be in honest employment, order of recall should not be enforced, but a report to be forwarded for information of the Prison Commissioners".

4. COSTS IN CRIMINAL CASES ACT 1973

Introductory

Criminal proceedings involve the costs of the prosecution (i.e. for solicitor, barrister, witnesses and other incidental costs involved during the investigation of the offence) and similar costs of the defence.

Subject to the provisions of the law regarding the grant of legal aid, the *general principle is that the losing party in any litigation is liable to pay the costs of the opposing side.* This applies in civil more than in criminal proceedings.

Criminal courts are authorised under the Act to allow payment of costs out of "*central funds*", (i.e., money provided by Parliament). The cost of the prosecution is usually authorised to be met out of the central fund but is liable to fall (in whole or in part upon the defence in some criminal cases. Costs against the prosecution in criminal cases are normally authorised to be paid out of the central fund.

The Magistrates' Court

On conviction after summary trial for a *summary offence* (or indictable offence tried summarily) a magistrates' court may order the payment by the accused of the costs (or part) of the prosecution, or on an acquittal the costs (or part) of the defence to be paid by the prosecution. On the discharge of the accused by "examining justices", the court, if of opinion that the charge was not made in good faith, may order the prosecution to pay the costs (or part) of the defence.

On conviction after summary trial of an offence (whether indictable or summary) the court cannot order the offender to pay any costs if the fine, penalty, forfeiture or compensation ordered to be paid for the offence is 25p. or less, and where the offender is under 17 years, the costs must not exceed the amount of the fine imposed (i.e., under 14 years—n/e £10, under 17 years—n/e £50).

By the Magistrates' Courts Act 1952, a magistrates' court may order the payment of costs between parties in proceedings relating to the breach of a recognisance entered into before the court e.g.:—breach of good behaviour, etc. There is a right of appeal if on dismissal of the charge against him the accused is ordered to pay costs exceeding £25.

Where a prosecution is not proceeded with, either by summary trial or by an enquiry by examining magistrates, a magistrates' court may:

(a) in the case of an indictable offence order payment out of central funds of costs to the defence.

(b) in respect of *any* information order costs to be paid by the prosecutor. (Costs in Criminal Cases Act 1973, s. 12)

The Crown Court

Generally speaking the court before which any person is tried on indictment, allows payment of the costs of the prosecution out of local funds, but if the accused is convicted he may be ordered to pay the costs (or part) of the prosecution including the cost of proceedings before the examining justices. If the accused is acquitted the court, where it thinks it right to do so, may order the prosecution to pay the costs or part costs of the defence and the cost of proceedings before the examining justices.

Where the prosecution intends to offer no evidence against a person arraigned on indictment who pleads "not guilty", the Judge may order that he be acquitted without being given in charge of a jury to return that verdict.

The Criminal Justice Act 1967, s. 31, extends the above provisions to apply to proceedings in which an offender is dealt with by a magistrates' court or the Crown Court for the commission of a further offence when subject to a probation order, an order for conditional discharge, when subject to a suspended sentence or for a breach of recognisance to keep the peace or be of good behaviour entered into after conviction on indictment.

The Crown Court may, if a person committed for trail is not tried, order costs to be paid to the defence as if the person had been tried and acquitted. (Costs in Criminal Cases Act 1973, s. 12).

NOTE:

Witnesses' personal expenses are regulated by the Costs in Criminal Cases (Allowances) Regs. 1974 (as amended) and include professional fees, loss of wages, travelling subsistence, and lodging allowances whether the person attending gives evidence or not. The allowances do not apply to police witnesses who are normally reimbursed through police administrative channels.

The amount of costs ordered to be paid by a person under 17 years of age convicted by a Magistrates' Court must not exceed the amount of the fine imposed, i.e. maximum of £10 if under 14 years, or £50 if over 14 years, but the restriction does not apply if the fine is ordered to be paid by the parent or guardian.

5. ATTORNEY-GENERAL

The attorney-general is *ex-officio* the head of the bar, but as a member of Parliament he goes out of office with the ministry from which he received his appointment.

As first law officer and legal adviser of the Crown, he represents the Crown in any suits affecting the royal (by which is really meant the public) interest, and carries on prosecutions in crimes that have a public or great political character. His many other responsibilities include the guarding of the interests of charitable endowments, granting patents and acting on behalf of the Crown in its revenue proceedings.

He ranks above the Solicitor-General who holds a similar position and who may act in his place. In Scotland there is a counterpart of the Attorney-General called the Lord-Advocate.

6. THE DIRECTOR OF PUBLIC PROSECUTIONS

The office of D.P.P. was created by the Prosecution of Offences Act 1879 and the whole of his powers and duties are regulated by this Act, as amended by Acts of 1884 and 1908. The appointment is made by the Home Secretary who can also appoint assistant directors to the number the Treasury sanction. The D.P.P. acts as public prosecutor under the direction of the Attorney-General, and he may engage any solicitor to act as his agent in the conduct of a particular prosecution. His other main duty is to give advice and assistance (orally or in writing) to Chief Constables, clerks to Justices, and other persons, respecting the conduct of criminal proceedings. In addition to the authority given by the 1879 Act for the D.P.P. to take action in *all* cases appearing to him to be of importance or difficulty, or in which he thinks he should intervene, the Prosecution of Offences Regns. 1946 make it a duty for him to institute, undertake or carry on proceedings in the following cases:

(a) offence punishable by *death*.

(b) any referred to him by a *Government Department*, in which he thinks criminal proceedings should be taken.

In addition there are certain cases in which the D.P.P. alone can prosecute, i.e. offences involving public officers or officials, as, for example, in the case of seditious libels on persons holding judicial or public office, corruption of and by public officers, fraudulent conversions by public officials, public mischief and offences under the Official Secrets Acts, as well as prosecutions for conspiracies to defeat justice.

The Prosecution of Offences Regulations 1946

Regulations under the 1879 Act made by the Attorney-General in 1946 place a duty upon chief constables to report to the D.P.P. any arrests made or proceedings taken with respect to:

(1) Any offence punishable by death (i.e. treason; setting fire to H.M. Ship, dockyard, or arsenal; and piracy with violence).

(2) Cases in which the prosecution has (by statute) to be undertaken by or with the consent of the D.P.P., in connection with which note the following:

(a) *Cases where consent of the D.P.P. needed.*—The consent or intervention of the D.P.P. is or may be necessary in respect of certain offences under the Bankruptcy Act 1914, Coinage Offences Act 1936, Gold, Silver (Export Control) Act 1920, Companies Act 1948, Prevention of Fraud (Investments) Act 1958, Incitement to Disaffection Act 1934, Sexual Offences Act 1956 (homosexual acts under s. 1), and other statutes but more commonly to authorise proceedings summarily after the normal time limit of six months, e.g. Firearms Act 1968 (no certificate), or Road Traffic Act 1960 (offences re P.S.Vs.).

(b) *Sanction of Attorney-General needed.*—If the D.P.P. does not institute proceedings, the sanction of the Attorney-General is necessary before proceedings may be taken under the Sexual Offences Act 1956 (Incest—attempted incest) and the Criminal Justice Act 1967, to publish or broadcast in G.B. any report of committal proceedings).

(c) *Sanction of Attorney-General obtained through D.P.P.*—Where the sanction or fiat of the Attorney-General is necessary before criminal proceedings can be instituted it is usual to refer such cases to the D.P.P. who will obtain the fiat, e.g. Explosive Substances Act 1883, Prevention of Corruption Act 1906 and 1916 re Bribery and Corruption including bribes to police officers, Public Order Act 1936 re wearing political uniforms and quasi military organisations, uttering defaced coins, possession of firearm with intent to endanger life. All cases under the Official Secrets Acts, 1911 to 1939. Children and Young Persons (Harmful Publications) Act 1955, Magistrates' Courts Act 1952, re newspaper reports of domestic proceedings, etc.

(3) Cases in which the advice or assistance of the D.P.P. is sought by the Chief Officer of Police.

(4) Cases regarding which the Director has asked for information.

(5) Cases which have been "wholly" withdrawn or abandoned. (This would not include the withdrawal of one or more charges out of the number preferred).

A Chief Constable is also required to report to the D.P.P. the following offences committed in his district:

> Forgery of certain specified and official documents (Forgery Act 1913, ss. 2 and 3), manslaughter, attempted murder, rape, abortion, sexual intercourse with mentally disordered persons, defilement of girls under 13 years, indecent offences upon a number of children or young persons, sexual offences against a child or young person which communicate venereal disease, obscene or indecent libels, exhibitions or publications where proceedings are likely, cases under the Extradition Acts, Fugitive Offenders Acts, etc.

The Criminal Jurisdiction Act 1975, s. 12.

Any statute which requires the authority of the D.P.P. or a "law officer of the Crown" before a prosecution is initiated or carried on is subject to this section, which means that the proviso regarding such consent:—

(a) shall not prevent A.W.W. or execution of a warrant to arrest on, or remand in custody or on bail of, any person charged with an offence, and

(b) shall be subject to any enactment concerning the arrest or detention of juveniles.

NOTES:

"*Law officer of the Crown*".—Includes the Attorney-General and the Solicitor-General.

"Authority".—Includes sanction, fiat, direction or order.

Fiats.—Any document or fiat purporting to be signed by the Attorney-General or the D.P.P. proves itself and may be handed to the Court by the prosecution without further proof (i.e. is judicially noted by the Court).

Appeals.—The D.P.P. must appear for the Crown in every appeal to the Court of Appeal unless this duty is undertaken by the solicitor representing a government department or a private prosecution in which latter case the court may require the Director to undertake the defence of the appeal and be responsible for any further proceedings.

7. WRITS

A "Writ" is the document issued in the Queen's name, by

which action is commenced in the higher or superior courts of law as distinguished from a complaint or summons in a County Court or Summary Court.

1. Certiorari

This is a writ, now replaced by an *Order* from a superior court (i.e. the Queen's Bench Division) to an inferior court directing:

1. *Removal of Proceedings* from that lower court for trial elsewhere because:

(a) a fair and impartial trial cannot be held in the lower court, or is likely to be prejudiced by local feeling, or

(b) a difficult point of law is likely to arise at the trial.

2. *A Re-trial* by requiring a certified record of the proceedings at the lower court to be sent up for review and if necessary quashed because:

(a) there was a defect in the proceedings, or

(b) that it was in excess of jurisdiction.

2. Mandamus

It is a *Writ*, now replaced by an *Order* (as above) directing any person, corporation, or lower court, to do some particular thing relating to their office or duty, e.g. an order requiring a Justice to perform a certain duty.

3. Habeas Corpus

This is a *Writ* or *Order*, of the Queen's Bench Division requiring the production in court of a person detained in custody, for the purpose of either:

(a) remedying his illegal detention or undue detention without trial,

(b) bringing him before another court on another charge or matter (civil or criminal).

8. LIMITATION OF PROCEEDINGS

It is well established that there should be *no delay in proceedings* once the offender is known. In certain cases no proceedings may be taken after the prescribed period has elapsed after the commission of the offence, or in the case of a continuing offence the day on which it ceased to be committed.

1. Indictable Offences

There is no time limit in respect of proceedings for indictable offences at Common Law, but several Acts of Parliament impose a time limit in the case of particular crimes (see later).

2. Summary Offences

The general principle is that proceedings in respect of summary offences shall not be taken unless the *information* was laid or *complaint* was made within *six months* of the date of the offence. This limitation does not apply to any indictable offence which may be dealt with summarily with the consent of the accused no matter how long the period between the offence and the commencement of proceedings. Offences which are punishable both summarily and on indictment (i.e. "hybrid") are triable only on indictment if committed more than six months before proceedings are commenced.

Examples of some offences in which a Time Limit is operative

14 *Days* —*Road Traffic Act* 1972. (Reckless, dangerous or careless riding or driving, exceeding speed limits, failing to conform to traffic signs, and dangerous obstructions).

No proceedings can be taken *unless* warned at the time of the offence of intended prosecution, or the prescribed notice or the summons for the offence has been served within 14 days of the offence.

6 *Months* —Generally all summary offences, but there is an exception in the *Road Traffic Act* 1972.

For offences of forgery, etc., of licences, certificates, plates, marks, etc., if proceedings not commenced within 6 months, the information must be laid within three months of detection of the offence, if also within twelve months after the commission of the offence.

12 *Months*—(a) Proceedings for any corrupt or illegal practice at a Parliamentary or Municipal Election.

(b) Night poaching offences (on indictment).

(c) Sexual intercourse (defilement of girls 13–16 years). Prison Escape.

(d) Gross indecency between men; soliciting by men for homosexual purposes; buggery between males, not amounting to an assault by one on the other, nor an offence upon a boy under 16 years.

(e) False statements with reference to births and deaths and marriages (summarily) but 3 years on indictment in respect of births and deaths and 18 months if for the purpose of procuring any marriage out of the district where either party resides.

3 *Years* —(a) Treason except in cases of attempting to assassinate The Queen or when committed in foreign countries or on the High Seas.

(b) Offences against the Merchandise Marks Acts 1887 to 1953 (but proceedings must be taken within 1 year of discovery of an offence).

4 *Years* —Summary proceedings for an offence against the Firearms Act 1968, may be taken after the expiration of six months and within a period of four years if instituted by or under the direction of the D.P.P.

R. v. *Shellaker* (1914)
Evidence of previous Acts committed outside the limitation of time are not excluded as evidence where otherwise admissible, e.g. to show systematic course of conduct, design or to negative accident or mistake.

9. INTERPRETATION OF STATUTES

General Rule.—The general rule is that words used in Statutes are to be interpreted according to their ordinary (or dictionary) meaning, but where a word, expression or phrase is intended to have a special meaning for the purposes of a particular statute, that statute will contain an "interpretation" section. For this reason, if a statute has to be studied it is essential to start with the preamble and the interpretation section.

Apart from this the Interpretation Act 1889 provides rules of interpretation which apply to all Statutes, and the following examples will illustrate the importance of the Act to law students:

(1) Words importing a masculine gender usually include females unless the contrary intention appears.

(2) Words in the singular usually include the plural, and vice versa, unless the contrary intention appears.

(3) Unless the contrary intention appears when general words follow particular ones, e.g. "or other person", "or other place", they must be construed as relating only to persons or places of the same kind or usage, as those previously referred to (i.e. the *ejusdem generis* rule) and not given their ordinary wide meaning.

Palmer v. *Snow* (1900)
A barber has been held not to be an "other person" ejusdem generis with tradesman, artificer, labourer or other person whatsoever and so not within the scope of s.1 of the Sunday Observance Act 1677.

(4) (a) An Act required by statute to be done within so many days or a notice to be given within so many days "at the

least" means "clear days" i.e. a number of complete intervening days.

(b) If the Act is required to be done within so many days (omitting the words "at the least") the first day should be omitted and the last day included.

(c) Where the statute says nothing about Sunday the days mentioned mean consecutive days, including Sundays, which must therefore be counted.

10. APPEALS

1. Appeals from Summary Court

From summary courts an appeal lies:

(a) On a question of law or jurisdiction to Q.B.D. by way of *case stated,*

(b) Otherwise to *the Crown Court.*

1. *To the Crown Court*

(a) *Against Conviction*—but only if plea was *Not Guilty.*

(b) *Against Sentence or conviction,* if he did not plead guilty—exceptions: Order for costs, probation and conditional discharge.

(c) *Against Dismissal*—(i.e. by complainant or prosecution) no appeal lies except in a few cases relating to Bastardy and Excise.

> *R.* v. *Durham Q.S. Ex Parte Virgo* (1952)
> There is no right of appeal against conviction where the defendant unequivocally pleaded guilty.

NOTE:

Written notice must be given to Clerk of Summary Court and other party within 14 days of conviction.

Extension of time may be granted, for good reason, on application to the Crown Court.

Case is heard anew and the decision is final on all questions of *fact* (as to "law", see "Case stated", below).

> *R.* v. *Surrey Justices* (1892)
> It is not for the appellant to show that the decision of which he complains was wrong, but for the respondent to show that it was right. Hence, if the prosecutor does not appear, the Court will have to quash the conviction (unless the appeal is against sentence only: *R.* v. *Kent Justices* (1935)).

When the appellant has given notice of appeal, the court may release him on bail (with or without sureties) to appear at the Crown Court or to re-appear before them (if by case stated), but not if he has been committed for sentence with a view to Borstal.

Appeal may be abandoned by notice in writing to Clerk of the Summary Court not later than the third day before hearing—may have to pay costs.

> *R.* v. *East Riding Q.S.* (1967)
> There is a right of appeal against a refusal to grant, renew or transfer a music and dancing licence (as an action by a "Magistrates' Court") even though there is no such right in the Licensing Act. 1964

2. *To Queen's Bench Division (by Case Stated)*

Either party (i.e. prosecutor or accused) or person aggrieved by the conviction, order, determination or other proceedings of the court may question the proceedings on the ground that it is (a) wrong in law, or (b) in excess of jurisdiction, by applying to the magistrates to state a case for the opinion of the High Court.

> *R.* v. *Nottingham Quarter Sessions, Ex. p. Harlow* (1952)
> "A person aggrieved" is one who, by the decision of the Justices, has had cast on him a legal burden.

NOTE:

Written application to clerk within 14 days (as above). Enter into recognisance to prosecute appeal without delay, submit to judgment of High Court and pay any costs awarded.

Justices: have 3 months in which to state a case.
may refuse if application is considered frivolous (High Court may issue mandamus), but shall not refuse if made by/on behalf of Attorney-General.

Case is stated giving facts as found, decisions and reasons. Applicant to lodge case within 10 days at Crown Office *and* serve copy on other party, together with notice of appeal, within 14 days.

Abandonment of Appeal.—The court against whose decision the appeal was brought, may, on the abandonment of the appeal, issue process for enforcing its decision and, on application by the other party, order appellant to pay that party such costs as appear reasonable. (M.C.A. 1952, s. 85).

2. From the Crown Court

1. *To Queen's Bench Division (By Case Stated)*

Either party to an appeal to the Crown Court (i.e. from a Magistrates' Court) can apply to the court to state a case for the opinion of the High Court, but only on a point of law, or that the court has acted in excess of jurisdiction.

Application must be made within 7 days and similar conditions regarding bail and recognisance apply as with appeal from a Magistrates' Court.

Either party has the right of appeal from the decision of the Q.B.D. direct to the House of Lords (see p. 34).

NOTE: The above does not apply to any appeal on which, by law, the decision of the Crown Court is final, namely appeals under the Betting, Gaming and Lotteries Act 1963, the Licensing Act 1964, and the Gaming Act 1968.

2. *To the Court of Appeal after conviction on indictment*

The Criminal Appeal Acts 1964, 1966 and 1968).

There is no appeal (by the prosecution) against acquittal. A person convicted on indictment at a Crown Court may appeal—

(a) *against the conviction*

(i) on a question of law alone,

(ii) on a question of fact alone or mixed law and fact,

(iii) on grounds which appear to the court to be sufficient,

(b) *against the sentence* (except one fixed by law).

Except in the case of (a) (i) above, a certificate of the trial Judge is required and if refused, leave must be sought of the C.A. The application for leave to appeal must be made within 28 days of conviction and in most cases, the Director of Public Prosecutions will defend the appeal.

The C.A. can quash the conviction, confirm it, vary the sentence or by virtue of the Criminal Appeals Act 1964, order a re-trial.

3. *To the Court of Appeal—otherwise than on conviction on indictment*

Where a person is dealt with by a Crown Court otherwise than after conviction on indictment (see below) he may appeal *against the sentence* imposed by that court (provided he obtains the consent of the C.A.) in any of the following cases:

(a) where the sentence is for six months or more (for one or more offences).

(b) Where the sentence is one which the court convicting (i.e· the magistrates' court) could not legally impose.

(c) Where there is made a recommendation for deportation, or a driving licence disqualification, or an order relating to a suspended sentence order previously imposed.

The proceedings to which the above right of appeal applies are those in which there has been a conviction by a magistrates' court and the offender:—

(i) is committed to be dealt with by the Crown Court, or

(ii) being subject to a probation order, or suspended sentence. is brought before the Crown Court to be dealt with.

On appeal against sentence the C.A. may quash any sentence or order which is the subject of the appeal, or confirm it, or substitute for it any sentence or order which the court below could have passed or made, but it cannot impose a sentence which would be more severe than the sentence appealed against.

Any sentence passed by the C.A. will commence from the time it would have begun to start if imposed by the lower court.

Appeal Against Verdict of "Insanity".—By the Criminal Appeal Act 1968, an appeal lies to the C.A. against a "special verdict" of "Not Guilty by reason of insanity" which, by this Act, replaces the one of "Guilty but insane". The same rules apply as to certificate and leave to appeal.

Unfitness to Plead.—By the Criminal Procedure (Insanity) Act 1964, when the question of accused being fit or otherwise to plead (or be tried) is raised the court should deal with this issue as soon as it arises, but an exception applies in the case where the court thinks it expedient (and in interest of accused) to postpone determination of this issue until any time up to the opening of the case for the defence. If at or before this stage a verdict of acquittal is given the question ceases to exist.

The question of "fitness" is one for a jury, and

(a) when it is determined at opening (i.e. arraignment), then if trial proceeds it must be before another jury, and
(b) if later in proceedings, by the same jury or a separate jury as the court directs.

Appeal lies to C.A. against finding of "unfit to plead", as it does against the special verdict "Not Guilty by reason of insanity".

Evidence of Appeal.—The general rule is that appeals to the House of Lords, Court of Appeal and the Queen's Bench Division are dealt with by reference to a transcript of the shorthand notes, and notes of the trial judge, etc., recorded at the trial court. However, appeals from Magistrates' Courts to a Crown Court (except an appeal against sentence only) are by way of a complete hearing, even new witnesses who were not heard at the Magistrates' Court being permitted to testify.

For appeals to the House of Lords, see p. 34.

11. EXTRADITION

Introductory

Extradition is the legal means by which a person in one country can be brought from that country to face trial in another country (or for punishment if already convicted there) for a crime committed therein. The "traffic" is "two-way" and so far as this country is concerned relates to:

(a) The bringing back for trial persons who have gone abroad and

(b) The surrender to another country for trial or to undergo sentence there of a person who is in this country

The law with regard to extradition to or from *Foreign Countries* is mainly provided by the *Extradition Acts* 1870 *and* 1873. The Acts apply (and extradition is possible) only:

(i) Where an Extradition Treaty exists between this country and the foreign country concerned, and
(ii) In relation to the crimes specified in the treaty.

NOTE: Eire is a notable omission from the long list of countries with which treaties have been made. With regard to the return from this country to any of the Dominions or U.K. Dependencies of persons "wanted" therein, the procedure, similar to that under the Extradition Acts, is provided by the Fugitive Offenders Act 1967.

1. Extradition from any country outside U.K.

Procedure.—To trace a person who has gone abroad enquiries should be directed to the British National Central Bureau of the International Police Organisation (Interpol) at New Scotland Yard. The return of a fugitive can be properly obtained only by extradition, and no attempt should be made to secure this end by other means. When the whereabouts of the wanted person is known, an extradition treaty exists, and the crime is within that treaty, the Director of Public Prosecutions will undertake arrangements (if extradition proceedings are approved) to secure the return of the wanted person.

2. Extradition to a Country outside the U.K.

(a) To a Country not being a Dominion or U.K. Dependency

Initial procedure is to get the wanted person before a *Police Magistrate*, i.e. a chief magistrate of the Metropolitan District or *any* magistrate of *Bow Street*, as follows:

(i) *Where application is made by the foreign government*

Has to be made to the Home Secretary who can issue his order directing a *Police Magistrate* to issue a warrant for the arrest, but will not do so if he considers the offence a "political" one.

NOTE: The Warrant can be executed anywhere in U.K. and directs arrest and conveyance before a police magistrate, usually at *Bow Street.*

(ii) *Not on application of foreign government*

In this case action can be taken *without* the order of the Home Secretary. Would apply to a case where information comes to hand that a person wanted in a foreign country is within local jurisdiction.

Any Justice can issue warrant for arrest but must forthwith inform Home Secretary and send information and evidence (or copies).

Procedure: (a) Home Secretary can cancel warrant and proceedings.

(b) If he does not, prisoner is to be brought before a justice and, if evidence suffices, sent on warrant to appear before a *Police Magistrate* (i.e. at Bow Street).

(c) The Bow Street magistrate must discharge prisoner unless within the time he fixes as suitable he gets from the Home Secretary an order signifying that a request has been received from the foreign government for extradition.

(iii) *Hearing case elsewhere than at Bow Street*

(a) By the 1895 Act the Home Secretary on proof that removal of prisoner would be prejudicial to his life or health, can direct case to be heard by magistrate (named in the Order) at the place where prisoner was apprehended, or is for the time being.

(b) In such a case the magistrate can order committal to any place not likely to endanger life or health to await extradition.

(b) To a Designated Dominion or a U.K. Dependency

Fugitive Offenders Act 1967

The Act makes provisions for the return from the U.K. to other Commonwealth countries and U.K. dependencies of persons accused or convicted of offences in those countries. The procedures are almost identical with those which apply to other countries under the Extradition Act, see p. 223, though under this Act an additional ground on which the Home Secretary can refuse extradition is the absence of any satisfactory guarantee from the country concerned that the trial or punishment will not be prejudiced by the race, religion, or nationality of the person concerned. "U.K." includes the Channel Islands and the Isle of Man.

12. EVIDENCE (PROCEEDINGS IN OTHER JURISDICTIONS) ACT 1975

This Act authorises the taking of evidence by certain courts in the U.K. (High Court of Justice in England and Wales and in N. Ireland, and Court of Session in Scotland) on behalf of each other and, also, for foreign courts, but in the later case the evidence must be related only to criminal proceedings which have already been instituted. Political offences are excluded, and the Perjury Act 1911 has been amended to include evidence under the Act.

13. FINGER AND PALM PRINTS

1. Main Uses

1. *Identification of prisoners.*—This is carried out primarily on the national collections at the Central Criminal Registry at New Scotland Yard, which receives impressions from all Police Forces and H.M. Prisons. A copy of any previous record is sent to the arresting Force. If a prisoner has given a wrong name to obviate the consequences of a bad record the fingerprints will reveal his true identity because searching is made on fingerprint formulae if nothing is found on name search. Moreover, once identity is established, the criminal records may reveal that the prisoner is wanted elsewhere, perhaps for more serious crimes than that for which he has been arrested. Females are often found to have previous convictions under a maiden name.

H.O. Circular 212/67.—Attention is drawn to the greater need for a fingerprint check on all persons coming before a court for a "fingerprintable" offence. This applies particularly where the prisoner is subject of a suspended sentence because the knowledge that it is likely to become operative if discovered may tempt him to give a false name.

2. *To serve as a reliable foundation for Criminal Records.*—Prisoners should be fingerprinted on each occasion of arrest, so that there is a set of fingerprints for each occasion of conviction. Each set of prints will be identical if taken from the one person. This is the most positive way of differentiating between criminals with very common names and having the same age group.

3. *Identification of marks found at scenes of crime.*—

(1) From search made on one or other of the collections maintained in the Fingerprint Bureaux.

(2) By comparison with the impressions of a criminal quoted to the Bureaux, or with impressions obtained from an unrecorded suspect.

N.B.—A series of crimes is often linked as being the work of one criminal when the same mark is found at each crime.

4. *Proving previous convictions by certificates.*—See "Documentary Evidence", p. 203.

5. *Identification of dead bodies.*—For immediate success, the deceased would have had to be fingerprinted for a criminal offence and placed on record, but in the case of persons reported missing from home, identifications have been made sometimes between impressions taken from the body and marks found at the normal place of residence.

N.B.—Some sections of the civil population have their fingerprints on record, e.g. regular Merchant Navy Seamen, serving Police Officers.

6. *Identification of persons suffering from loss of memory.*—Same applies as for para. 5, above.

7. *Identification of Property.*—Marks developed on property which is not identifiable by serial numbers, etc., can be checked with the impressions of a person who is possibly the true owner or lawful custodian.

2. Powers of the Police to take Finger and Palm Prints

The impressions of any person can be taken at any time or place *provided that the person consents.* The H.O. advises (1968) that the consent of his parents or guardian, whenever practicable, should be obtained for taking the prints or a photograph of a person under 17 years of age. Where a prisoner refuses, application should be made to a Magistrates' Court for an Order granting the authority for the police to take them. The conditions of granting the Order are laid down in s. 40, of the Magistrates' Courts Act 1952 and the Criminal Justice Act 1967, s. 33. The main points are:

1. Person not to be less than 14 years of age.
2. Arrested or summoned for an offence and charged before Court.
3. Application by officer not below rank of Inspector who gives reasons (e.g. to establish identity, believed engaged in commission of crime, prints required for evidence purposes, etc.).
4. Finger and palm prints can be taken at the court or any place to which remanded.
5. Constable may use any necessary force to take them.
6. Impressions (and any copies) to be destroyed if person is acquitted or discharged.

N.B. When it is necessary to obtain impressions for court exhibits from a prisoner already serving a prison sentence, provision is made in the Prison Regulations under s. 16 of the Prison Act 1952, for them to be taken in prison and forwarded to a specified police force (i.e. with a fingerprint expert) but the application to the prison governor must be made by a Superintendent (or above) on the ground that the prisoner is suspected of having been previously convicted or has been engaged in crime.

If the impressions of a prisoner in custody on remand are required for comparison or to prove previous convictions by certificate (see below) and he refuses to allow this, or is likely to refuse (as he is entitled to do), the applications from a Superintendent (or above) must be endorsed by a Justice of the Peace (H.O. Letter and Prison Regulations).

3. Proving Previous Convictions by Means of Finger or Palm Print Certificates (Criminal Justice Acts 1948, s. 39 and 1967, s. 33).

This is often required when a prisoner committed for trial is liable by virtue of previous convictions to be sentenced to an extended term sentence, and he denies such previous convictions.

The procedure involves the production at the Court of Trial of *three* Certificates:

1. One on the back of a special fingerprint (or palm print) form, signed by the Governor of the Prison to where the prisoner has been remanded, certifying that the impressions on the form are those of the prisoner committed from a specified Magistrates' Court for the offence charged.

2. A form bearing photographic copies of the impressions on record at New Scotland Yard for a particular conviction, and certified on the back by or on behalf of the Commissioner of Police of the Metropolis with details of the conviction. (A separate form and certificate is required for each conviction.)

3. A third certificate, signed by or on behalf of the Commissioner of Police of the Metropolis, certifying that the impressions on Certificate No. 1. are identical with those on Certificate(s) No. 2. This third certificate is recorded on the back of the special fingerprint (or palm print) form used with Certificate No. 1.

N.B.—The prosecution produces the certificates at the end of the trial if necessary, and no oral evidence is required. This method of proving previous convictions can be used instead of or in conjunction with other methods.

Where certificate No. 1 is unavailable (i.e. offender not in custody) and other methods of proving previous convictions are not practicable (e.g. no oral evidence of identity) then *as a last resort* an officer from the Fingerprint Branch of New Scotland Yard will attend court with Certificates Nos. 2 and 3 and give evidence that the fingerprints are identical with those taken by the police in connection with the offence for which he now appears before the court. It will, of course, be necessary for the police officer concerned to prove the taking of the fingerprints and forwarding them to New Scotland Yard.

4. Examination of Scenes of Crime and Packing of Exhibits

One of the best clues that can be found at a scene of crime is a finger or palm mark. It can lead to an early detection and even without any other evidence is sufficient to secure a conviction, even for murder (*R.* v. *Cummings* (1941); *R.* v. *Robinson* (1955)).

It is imperative that such marks are searched for by properly trained personnel, because the majority of marks are derived from perspiration transferred from the ridges on the inner part of the hand. They are very fragile and careless or inexperienced powdering can easily ruin them.

The first officer at the scene of a crime should be responsible for safeguarding it as far as possible pending the arrival of trained staff. Occupiers should be warned not to touch anything. Some initiative is also required, e.g. placing broken glass in a dry safe place; protecting points of entry from adverse weather, etc.

Any article which has to be moved should be handled on narrow edges or rims, bottles with one finger on top and one underneath, i.e. not handled in the same way as an ordinary person would. *On no account should anything be wrapped up in cloth or paper.*

Reference should be made to the H.O. Scientific Aids to Criminal Investigation Pamphlet, 1961, Paras. 8–18, 30 and 33 for further notes and illustrations on the correct methods of handling and packing exhibits.

It should be remembered that finger or palm marks are not the only clues that should be searched for at scenes of crime.

14. LATIN LEGAL TERMS IN GENERAL USE

A fortiori	so much the more so; with greater reason.
Ab initio	from the beginning.
Aliunde	from elsewhere; from another person, place or quarter.
Animus furandi	intent to steal.
Ante	before.
Bona fide	in good faith.
Certiorari	(literally) to be more fully informed of; an order which issues from the High Court of Justice removing causes from inferior courts of record to the High Court for review.
Contra	against.
Contra pacem	against the peace.
Corpus delicti	the body of essential fact constituting a criminal offence.
Dictum, dicta (pl.)	a saying, sayings.
Doli incapax	incapable of crime.
Ejusdem generis	of the same kind or nature.
Et seq. (*Et sequentes*)	and the following.
Ex hypothesi	following from this assumption.
Ex officio	by virtue of office.
Ex parte	on behalf of.
Flagrante delicto	in the commission of the offence.
Habeas corpus	(literally) you must have the body; a prerogative writ to a person detaining another in custody commanding him to produce that person before the court.

Ibid. (*ibidem*)	in the same place, in the same book, chapter, passage, etc.
In camera	the public excluded from court or heard in the judge's private room.
Infra	below.
Intra vires	(literally) within the powers; valid
Inter alia	among other things.
Ipso facto	by the very fact.
Mandamus	(literally) we command; an Order which issues from the High Court of Justice to compel the performance of a public duty.
Mens rea	guilty mind.
Modus operandi	the way in which anything is done; mode or manner of operation.
Obiter dictum, *Obiter dicta* (pl.)	a mere saying by the way; a chance remark, which is not binding upon future courts, though it may be respected according to the reputation of the judge, the eminence of the court and the circumstances in which made.
Onus probandi	the onus (or burden) of proof.
Per	by
Per se	by or in itself.
Post	after.
Prima facie	at first sight, on the face of it.
Quaere	query.
Sic	so, thus.
Simpliciter	absolutely, without qualification.
Sine die	without naming a day, indefinitely.
Sub judice	under judicial consideration.
Subpoena duces tecum	a writ commanding a person to attend in court under a penalty and to bring with him certain documents in his possession.
Supra	above.
Ultra vires	(literally) beyond the powers; an act in excess of the authority conferred by law and therefore invalid.
Viva voce	orally.
Viz. (*videlicet*)	that is to say; (in other words); namely.

APPENDICES

APPENDIX 1

ARRESTABLE OFFENCES (CRIMINAL LAW ACT 1967)

Definition

An arrestable offence is one for which the sentence is fixed by law (i.e. capital or life imprisonment) or for which an adult (not previously convicted) is liable by statute to be sentenced to imprisonment for at least 5 years and an attempt to commit such an offence.

The following is a summary of the main arrestable offences.

Abandoning Child under 2 years

Abduction.

Abortion.

Arson.

Assaults—causing bodily harm.

Blackmail.

Buggery (unlawful), or assault with intent to commit.

Burglary.

Child Destruction.

Choking, attempt to commit indictable offence by.

Coinage—coining, possession of instruments, defacing gold or silver coins, uttering or possession counterfeit coin (gold or silver) with intent to utter.

Criminal possession, of article made or adapted for use for burglary, theft, criminal deception.

Death by Dangerous driving.

Deception—obtain property or pecuniary advantage credit by.

Electricity—dishonestly abstracting.

Endangering life—by explosive or poison.

Endangering railway passengers.

Explosive—offences against the person with.

False accounting.

False statements by company directors etc.

Firearms—criminal use and possession.

Forgery—of authority for payment of money, or transfer of goods, of receipts, uttering such forged documents, demanding by forged document.

Indecent assault on female under 13 years.

Infanticide.

Malicious damage—firing crops, maiming cattle, letters threatening to burn or destroy, destroying sea walls, docks or harbours, river banks, etc.

Manslaughter.

Murder, including accessory after, and acts with intent to murder.

Perjury.

Poisons, endanger or cause harm by, administer to annoy or injure.

Prostitution, live on earnings of.

Rape.

Riot—after proclamation, demolish or damage buildings, etc., prevent proclamation being read.

Robbery.

Sexual offences—intercourse with girl under 13; permitting offence with girl under 13.

Stolen goods—handling.

Suicide, aiding and abetting.

Taking conveyance without authority*.

Theft.

Woundings.

Valuable securities—dishonestly destroy, deface, conceal, etc.

* Though the maximum imprisonment for this offence is 3 years, the Theft Act 1968, s. 12 (3) makes it an A.O.

Remember—"Arrestable offence" includes any *attempt* to commit an arrestable offence.

APPENDIX 2

STATEMENT OF WITNESS

(*C. J. Act* 1967, *ss.* 2, 9; *M.C. Rules* 1968, *r.* 58.)

STATEMENT OF (name of witness)

Age of witness (if over 21 enter "over 21")

Occupation of witness

Address

BODY OF STATEMENT

This statement[, consisting of pages each signed by me,] is true to the best of my knowledge and belief and I make it knowing that, if it is tendered in evidence, I shall be liable to prosecution if I have wilfully stated in it anything which I know to be false or do not believe to be true.

Dated the day of , 19 . A.B.

[A.B. being unable to read the above statement I,
C.D. of
read it to him before he signed it.

Dated the day of , 19 . C.D.]

NOTE:

Wherever possible statements taken in the above form should be on foolscap size paper. If typed, double spacing should be used. Use one side only of the paper and leave a space at the top of the first page for headings to be entered by the Clerk of the Court, as well as a wide margin on the left of each page. It has been recommended that after any reference to a document (or other exhibit) in a statement the words "Committal Document No." (in the case of a document) followed by the words, "Exhibit No." should be inserted in brackets, leaving space for the actual number(s) to be filled in at a later stage.

APPENDIX 3

ENFORCEMENT OF PAYMENT OF FINES, ETC.

A. Penalties Imposed by Magistrates' Courts

(C.J. Act 1967, ss. 44–47)

When a sum of money is ordered to be paid on conviction by a magistrates' court the question arises of the enforcement of payment if it is not made immediately. In such cases the following principles apply:—

1. At time of conviction

(1) There is no power to commit immediately to prison (or detention centre) in default of payment unless one of the following conditions apply—

(a) the offence is punishable with imprisonment and the offender appears to the court to have the means to pay the sum forthwith, or

(b) it appears to the court that the offender is not likely to remain in a place of abode in the U.K. long enough to permit payment to be enforced by other means, or

(c) the court has sentenced him to imprisonment (or to a detention centre) for the offence, or another offence, or he is already serving a sentence in prison or a detention centre.

NOTE
The warrant must state the reason for committal.

(2) Wherever (1) above applies (but not otherwise) the court can, instead of committing in default immediately, grant time to pay *and* fix the term of imprisonment which is to be served in the event of default, which means that the issue of the warrant of commitment is suspended for the period in which payment has to be made.

2. Subsequent procedure—Means enquiry or special hearing

(1) In all other cases where time to pay has been granted the commitment warrant cannot be issued for default nor the term of imprisonment for it fixed unless the court has:

(a) *at least once* since the conviction enquired into the defaulter's means *in his presence*, and also.

(b) has considered or tried all other means of enforcement which appear to it to be inappropriate or unsuccessful.

Condition (b) does not apply if the offence is punishable by imprisonment and offender appears to have sufficient means to pay, forthwith.

(2) Except where the term has been fixed at the time of conviction (see (2) above), the court cannot fix the term or issue the warrant of commitment except at a means enquiry or special hearing at

which the defaulter is present to either of which his presence can be secured by summons or warrant (if necessary). The offender may be required by the court or a justice (under penalty of £50 fine) to furnish a statement of means. Knowingly failing to disclose a material fact or making a false statement is an offence. (4 months and/or £100).

NOTE:

If a warrant of commitment in default is issued it must state reasons for committal. The court can make a Community Service Order instead of issuing the warrant (C.J.A. 1972, s. 49).

(3) The means enquiry or hearing may remit the whole or part of the original fine (not including any damages, costs or compensation awarded) and the corresponding term of imprisonment fixed by the court if the circumstances of the offender have changed since his conviction.

3. Enforcement of payment by civil proceedings or attachment

After consideration of the information at the means enquiry or hearing, the court may—

(1) instruct the clerk of the court to *enforce payment as for a civil debt* by proceedings in the High Court or a county court, or

(2) *make an attachment of earnings order*, for enforcement of payment by his employers as in the case of payments on a court maintenance order or legal aid contributions.

B. Fines Imposed and Recognisances Forfeited at Higher Courts (s. 47)

(Powers of Criminal Courts Act 1973, s. 31 and s. 32)

(1) Crown Courts as well as the Court of Appeal and House of Lords on appeal from the latter are required—

(a) *to fix the term of imprisonment* to be served (not to exceed 12 months) if the fine imposed or recognisance ordered to be forfeited is not duly paid, and

(b) *not to commit an offender to prison* at the time of imposing a fine or forfeiting a recognisance instead of granting time to pay, unless the same conditions apply as are prescribed for magistrates' court, see p. 233.

(2) Fines imposed or recognisances forfeited by higher courts are treated for the purpose of collection and enforcement subsequent to conviction in the same manner as having been imposed or forfeited by—

(a) the magistrates' court which committed the offender to the higher court, or

(b) any magistrates' court specified by order of the higher court because of convenience, e.g.:— where the offender lives.

The clerk of the higher court notifies the Home Secretary and the clerk of the magistrates' court responsible for enforcement, and supplies particulars of the fines and recognisances concerned.

The subsequent procedure (the holding of a means enquiry or special hearing prior to committal in default of payment) by the magistrates' court responsible for dealing with the case will be the same as if the court had imposed the fine, etc., with the following exemptions:—

(a) if ultimately committed in default, the offender must serve the term of imprisonment fixed by the higher court subject to any reduction for part payment or remission allowed by the court, irrespective of the term it could itself have imposed.

(b) before it can remit (in whole or in part) a higher court fine or recognisance, the magistrates' court must obtain the consent of the judge or recorder of the crown court who dealt with the case.

APPENDIX 4

INDICTABLE OFFENCES BY ADULTS WHICH CAN BE DEALT WITH SUMMARILY WITH CONSENT OF ACCUSED

(*Magistrates' Courts Act*, 1952. *First Schedule*)

1. Offences under Theft Act 1968

All offences under the Act except—

(a) robbery, aggravated burglary and blackmail;

(b) burglary involving committing (or intention to commit) an offence *not* in this Schedule;

(c) burglary in dwelling, if entry obtained by force, deception, or using any tool or appliance, or if any person in dwelling was subjected to violence or threat of violence;

(d) handling stolen goods from offence *not* committed in the U.K.

2. Forgery, etc

False statements in statutory declarations; forgery with intent to defraud; demanding money on forged documents; uttering forged documents where value of goods or chattels involved does not exceed £100.

3. Criminal Damage Act 1971

Every offence except that under s. 1 (2) (that of destroying or damaging property and being reckless as to (or intending) the endangering the life of another person.

4. Offences against person

Wounding, grievous bodily harm, actual bodily harm; indecent assaults; abandoning or exposing child; concealment of birth; indictable common assault.

5. Aiding, abetting, etc. Any of the above.

6. Attempts

Attempts to commit any of the above offences or to commit any "hybrid" offence, i.e. one punishable both on indictment and summarily.

7. Incitement

To commit any of the offences in paras. (1) to (4) above, or to commit any summary offence.

8. Offences added by later statutes

And to which paras. (5) to (7) do not apply:

(a) *Coinage Offences Act 1936.* Defacing and uttering defaced coins; uttering and possession w/i to utter; import or export counterfeit coin, making, possessing or selling medals resembling gold or silver.

(b) *Criminal Law Act 1967*

(i) assist an offender guilty of an AO or inciting a person to commit such an offence (if that offence is in this Schedule).

(ii) concealing an AO or not disclosing information concerning it if that offence is in this Schedule.

(c) *Sexual Offences Act 1967.* Offences of procuring another man to commit with a third man an act of buggery which is not an offence, and gross indecency between men.

(d) *Forgery Offences.* Forgery of receipts or release or discharge of debt, and forgery of documents in general, or uttering any forged document the forgery of which is triable summarily with the consent of the accused. (All under the Act of 1913. Added to the Schedule by the C.J.A. 1967).

Note.—The above list is not complete but includes the most important from the police point of view.

APPENDIX 5

THE REHABILITATION OF OFFENDERS ACT 1974

and the Exceptions Order of 1975

NOTE: In this summary "R.P." means "Rehabilitation Period".

(1) *The general principle.*—The Act gives effect to the general principle that a conviction for an offence, subject to exceptions, should be capable of being wiped out (or become "spent") through the passage of time, so that the person concerned can become rehabilitated in respect of that conviction so far as the law is concerned.

(2) *Rehabilitated persons.*—A "rehabilitated person" is to be treated for all purposes of law as if he had never committed, or been charged with, or prosecuted for, or convicted of, of sentenced for, the offence concerned. S. 4 of the Act, however, provides that the law relating to certain disclosures of convictions during criminal proceedings is not affected (see para. (5) below).

(3) *Exceptions*

(a) *On account of the nature of the conviction*—there can be no rehabilitation from a conviction for which the sentence was:

(i) imprisonment for life, or

(ii) imprisonment (or corrective training) exceeding 30 months, or

(iii) preventive detention, or

(iv) detention during H.M. Pleasure, or for life, or under C. & Y.P. Act 1933 s. 53 (grave crimes by young persons) for a term exceeding 30 months.

(b) *Necessary disclosures.* "Spent" convictions must continue to be disclosed by:

(i) applicants for appointment as police constables, cadets, special constables, traffic wardens, or any other post connected with police duties, or applicants join naval, military or air force police.

(ii) applicants for certificates under the Gaming Act 1968.

(iii) applicants for licences as dealers in securities.

(iv) persons connected with children going abroad to perform.

(v) persons involved in police disciplinary enquiries.

(vi) applicants for firearm and shotfun certificates or for registration as a firearm dealer.

NOTE: "Spent" convictions may also be used as grounds for revocation, etc., of a firearms dealer's certificate.

(4) *Rehabilitation Periods* (*R.P.*).—These range, for adults, from six months for an absolute discharge to 10 years for an imprisonment or

detention n/e 30 months. The R.P. begins on date of conviction and continues for the period specified by the Act in relation to the sentence, but the R.P. for the offence may become extended in certain circumstances, as follows:

(a) *By an order for disqualification, etc.* Where the sentence for the offence includes an order for a disqualification, a disability, or a prohibition, for a period longer than the R.P. for the other part of the sentence, the R.P. in respect of that other part does not end until the disqualification, etc., ceases to have effect.

(b) *By a plural sentence.* Where there are two parts to a sentence and the R.P. for one part is for a longer period than that for the other, the longer period applies to the conviction.

(c) *By conviction of an INDICTABLE offence during R.P.*

(i) If the sentence for this conviction *is subject to a R.P.* which will expire later than the existing one—*both* periods run until *both* have been completed.

Example: Fined £100 1.1.75 (R.P. = 5 years, normally to 31.12.79.
1.1.78 imprisonment for theft—3 months (R.P. = 7 years, until 31.12.84.
Result: R.P. for both sentences run to 31.12.84.

NOTE: Another conviction for an *indictable* offence before 31.12.84 could extend the expiry of all three to still later date, and so on.

(ii) *If the sentence is NOT subject to a R.P.*, then neither conviction becomes "spent".

Example: If the person in the example in (i) above is, before 31.12.84, sent to prison for an I.O. for more than 30 months, this sentence is not subject to a R.P. and none of the three convictions could ever become "spent".

NOTE: The following qualification of the above applies. Where the subsequent conviction takes place during a R.P. extended by virtue of an order of disqualification, disability or prohibition, the extension is ignored and reference is made only to the R.P. (if any) which would have applied if the order for disqualification, etc., had not been made.

Example: 1.1.71. Six months imprisonment (R.P. = 7 years) and disqualified (for driving licence) for life. This conviction can never become "spent" (see para. (4) (a) above). 6.1.78. Fined £50 for an indictable offence (R.P. = 5 years). By the above rule the disqualification period is discounted, and as this conviction takes place after the expiry of the R.P. for the other part of the previous sentence, the previous conviction has no effect and the 5 years R.P. applies.

NOTE: If the second conviction had occurred more than 5 years before the expiry of the 1971 imprisonment R.P. (say, on 1.2.72) the 5 years R.P.

would have been extended to expire on 31.12.77, the date on which the R.P. for the 1971 imprisonment expires, instead of after 5 years.

(d) *By breach of probation or discharge.* Where a person has been conditionally discharged or placed on probation and after rehabilitation in respect of this is dealt with for a breach of the discharge or the probation, he is not to be regarded as rehabilitated if a further sentence is imposed which attracts a longer R.P. than the one already expired. In such a case the R.P. for the conviction becomes that relating to the sentence imposed for the breach.

Example: 1.1.76. Placed on probation for one year (R.P. = 1 year).
1.2.77. Convicted of theft committed during probation period (now expired) and given imprisonment for 3 months (R.P. = 7 years to run from 1.2.77) and also 3 months for the original offence, to run concurrently.
Result. The original conviction is now deemed not to have become "spent" and attracts a R.P. of 7 years (to run from 1.1.76) in place of the original 12 months.

(5) *Disclosure of Convictions etc.*—By s. 4 of the Act a person who has become rehabilitated is to be treated as if he had never committed, been charged with, prosecuted for, convicted of, or sentenced for offences which have become spent. It also provides that:

(a) No evidence shall be admissible in any judicial proceedings to prove that any such person has committed, or been charged with, etc., any offence which was the subject of a spent conviction, and

(b) A person shall not in any such proceedings be asked, and, if asked, shall not be required to answer, any question relating to a spent conviction or circumstances connected with it.

Criminal Proceedings. S. 4, however, does not apply to evidence given in criminal cases, though in a Practice Direction the Lord Chief Justice has recommended that courts and counsel should give effect to the general intention of Parliament by never referring to a spent conviction when such a reference can reasonably be avoided.

NOTE: As to the use of convictions, e.g. to prove system or rebut allegations as to character, see pages 28–30.

(6) *Offences*

(a) Unauthorised disclosure of a "spent" conviction by any person having custody of or access to records during the course of official duties—except to or on behalf of a rehabilitated person or a person reasonably believed to be so.

(b) Obtaining specified information by fraud, dishonesty or bribe. *NOTE:* Proceedings for these offences cannot be instituted except by or on behalf of the D.P.P.

(7) *Sentences and appropriate rehabilitation periods*

Table A.

Sentence	*R.P.*
Imprisonment or corrective training for more than 6 but n/e 30 months.	10 years.
Cashiered from (or discharged with ignominy from) H.M. Forces.	10 years.
Imprisonment n/e 6 months	7 years.
Dismissal from H.M. Forces	7 years.
Sentence of detention in H.M. Forces disciplinary proceedings	5 years.
A fine or other sentence not connected with a sentence in Table B nor with one under the heading of "Others" (below)	5 years.

Young Persons. In the case of a person under 17 years the period is reduced by half.

Table B. (*Offences committed by young offenders—under* 17).

Sentence.	*R.P.*
Borstal.	7 years.
Detention for more than 6 months but n/e 30 months under C. & Y.P. Act 1933, s. 53.	5 years.
Detention n/e 6 months under the same section	3 years.
Detention Centre Order under C.J. Act 1961, s. 4.	3 years.

Table C. *Others.* (*Subsections* (3) *to* (8) *of s.* 5.

Nature of Order	*R.P.*
Absolute discharge.	6 months.
Conditional discharge, a binding over, or probation.	12 months or when order ceases, whichever longer.
To care of fit person, supervision order under C. & Y.P. Acts or care order under 1969 Act.	12 months or when order ceases, whichever longer.
Order committing to custody to remand home, approved school order, attendance centre order.	Period beginning on date of order and ending one year after order ceases.
Hospital orders under Pt. V of the Mental Health Act 1959.	5 years from date of conviction or continuing for 2 years after order ceases, whichever is the longer.

APPENDIX 6

THE POLICE (PROPERTY) ACT 1897

and the Police (Disposal of Property) Regulations 1975.

(1) *Property subject to the Act.* The Regulations relate to the ways and means by which property subject to the Act of 1897 can be disposed of by the police. "Property subject to the 1897 Act" means property which has come into the possession of the police:

(a) in connection with the investigation of a suspected offence, or

(b) under the Acts relating to powers of the Metropolitan (and City of London) police, or

(c) under the Pawnbrokers Act 1872, s. 34 (offences by pawners), and to these have been added property in police possession

(d) by virtue of seizure under a search warrant on the ground that it has been used or was intended for use to destroy or damage property (Criminal Damage Act, 1971, s. 6)*, and

(e) by order of a court as having been used or intended for use to commit crime (Powers of Criminal Courts Act 1973, s. 43).

* In most cases property thus seized will become possessed by the police by virtue of a court order under (e).

NOTE: By reason of its closeness to this subject attention should be paid to the provisions of the Magistrates' Courts Act 1952, s. 39 (property taken from a prisoner of defendant—see page 106).

(2) *Time Factors.* Such property must not be disposed of by the police until the expiry of:

(a) in the case of money (including proceeds of sales) and any property not received under a court order—12 months.

(b) in the case of property received under a court order (1973 Act) —6 months from the date of the order, but if a person makes a claim for it under s. 1 of the 1897 Act (see para. (5) below) within 6 months, not until the application has been dealt with by the court (including appeal).

Exceptions for perishables. If the property is perishable or its retention would involve unreasonable expense or inconvenience it can be sold at any time, but proceeds of such sale must remain in police possession for 12 months.

(3) *Property to which Regulations apply.* The Regulations (as to disposal of property subject to the 1897 Act) apply where:

(a) *property possessed by a court order*

(i) has not been claimed within 6 months, or

(ii) if claimed, the application for it did not succeed, or

(b) *in the case of other property*

(i) the owner has not been ascertained, and

(ii) no order of a competent court is in force respecting it.

Exception. All money (including proceeds of sales) has to be placed in the Police (Property) Act Fund, the income from which may be used to defray expenses, pay reasonable compensation, make payments to charity, or may be invested.

(4) *Means of disposal.* Property, when available for disposal, may be disposed of by the police by:

(a) sale, as directed by the chief officer of police, or

(b) where the police consider it not to be in the public interest to sell particular property—its destruction or by application to a particular purpose, dependant on the nature of the particular property, e.g. by donation where the article would be of value to a charity, or by retention for a police purpose (e.g. for police training).

NOTE: Where the property is possessed by reason of a court order under the 1973 Act, that Act extinguishes the right of any claimant who has not within 6 months made a successful application for it under s. 1 of the 1897 Act. In any other case, where doubt exists as to whether it is safe legally to dispose of property, advantage should be taken of s. 1 of the 1897 Act by seeking an order from the magistrates' court.

(5) *Power of a summary court to make an order.* (1897, *s.* 1). On an application by the police or by a claimant of any property subject to the Act a magistrates' court may make an order for the delivery of the property to the person appearing to be the owner of it, or, if the owner cannot be ascertained, make such order relating to the property as the court may consider most appropriate.

NOTE: Any person may within 6 months of the date of an order under this section (but not later) take legal proceedings against the possessor under the order for its recovery.

APPENDIX 7

EVIDENCE OF IDENTIFICATION

The question as to the acceptability and weight which should be given to evidence of identification has been under consideration for a long time and was one of the subjects reported on in 1972 by the Criminal Law Revision Committee on "Evidence". Now the Court of Appeal (in *R.* v. *Turnbull and others* (1976)) has provided guide lines for judges, and the Attorney-General has given guidelines for prosecutors on this matter, the importance of which has been very much emphasised during recent years, in particular by the number of convictions based solely on evidence of identification which have been quashed.

Guidelines given to Judges by the Court of Appeal.

(1) When a case depends wholly or substantially on identification of the accused alleged by the defence to be mistaken, the judge must warn the jury of the special need for caution before convicting on such evidence.

(2) The judge should direct the jury to consider that the reason for the warning for caution lies in the fact that a mistaken witness can still appear convincing, and that a number of witnesses could all be mistaken.

(3) The judge should direct the jury to examine all the circumstances prevailing when the accused was witnessed, and the following seven questions should be considered:*

(a) How long did witness have accused under observation?
(b) How far away was he?
(c) What were the lighting conditions at the time?
(d) Was the observation impeded in any way, e.g. by passers-by or by traffic?
(e) Had the witness ever seen the accused before and, if so, how often?
(f) How long was the time between sighting and subsequent identification?
(g) Was there any material discrepancy between the description given to the police and the accused's actual appearance?

* and these appear to be most useful to be borne in mind when statements are being taken from identification witnesses.

(4) As to item (g) above the Court advised that where the prosecution has reasonable cause to believe a material discrepancy exists they should, at the request of the defence, forward particulars of any such description to the defence, in both summary and indictable cases.

Proviso to the above. When the evidence of identification is corroborated by other evidence and the circumstances illustrated by the seven questions in (3) above favour identification it will be sufficient for the judge to warn the jury to consider with caution the evidence of identification.

Guidance given to prosecutors by the Attorney-General.

(a) Where evidence of identification is likely to be a material factor in a trial on indictment, full committal proceedings should be held, with the opportunity for the defence to bring alibis or challenge otherwise the evidence at that stage.

(b) Unless exceptional circumstances prevail witnesses who have not identified the defendant at an identification parade will not be asked to make a dock identification.

(c) All identification cases referred to the D.P.P. would be given his personal consideration, or that of his deputy, and, where necessary, the law officers would be consulted.

(d) Failure to comply with present or future Home Office guidance on the manner of holding identification parades, or of showing photographs to potential witnesses, would continue to be regarded as an important factor in considering whether to institute or continue proceedings.

(e) The D.P.P. will continue the practice of making material available to the defence where it will assist them. In particular, defence solicitors would be supplied on request with names and addresses of witnesses who state that they have seen accused persons in the circumstances of a crime, together with a copy of any description of the criminal given by such a witness.

INDEX

D

F

H

I

J

L

M

Q

R

T

V

Printed in Great Britain by
Butler & Tanner Ltd, Frome and London